LITURGICS FOR ORTHODOX

LITURGICAL SINGING

VOLUME 1

In Memory of
my grandfather,
Anthony Lukashevich
( + 1967 ),

and

Dedicated to
Christopher Holwey.

# Liturgics for Orthodox Liturgical Singing Volume 1

BY

David Barrett

Foreward by
Father Sergei Glagolev

Orthodox Liturgical Press
Southbury, Connecticut
July 2015

**Library of Congress Cataloging-in-Publication Data**

Barrett, David
1956 –

Liturgics for Orthodox Liturgical Singing • Volume 1

Library of Congress Control Number: 2015932310

## LITURGICS FOR ORTHODOX LITURGICAL SINGING • VOLUME 1

Copyright © 2015 by
David Barrett

Orthodox Liturgical Press
Southbury, CT 06488

All Rights Reserved.

ISBN 978-0-9915905-1-3

Printed in the United States of America by
Lightning Source Inc.
1246 Heil Quaker Boulevard
La Vergne, TN 37086 – 3515

# CONTENTS

FOREWORD — xi
PREFACE — xiii

1. VESPERS — 1
   - A. RESURRECTIONAL VESPERS — 1
   - B. GREAT VESPERS — 24
   - C. DAILY VESPERS — 46
   - D. DAILY LENTEN VESPERS — 61

2. MATINS — 77
   - A. RESURRECTIONAL MATINS — 77
   - B. FESTAL MATINS — 108
   - C. DAILY MATINS — 138
   - D. DAILY LENTEN MATINS — 163

3. THE DIVINE LITURGY  185
   A. THE DIVINE LITURGY  185
   B. VESPERAL LITURGY  245
   C. BAPTISMAL DIVINE LITURGY  253
   D. MATRIMONIAL DIVINE LITURGY  259
   E. FUNERAL DIVINE LITURGY  264
   F. CONSECRATION OF A CHURCH  272

4. SACRAMENTAL SERVICES  283
   A. HOLY BAPTISM  283
   B. HOLY CHRISMATION  289
   C. HOLY MATRIMONY  299
   D. HOLY UNCTION  317

5. NON – SACRAMENTAL SERVICES   347
- A. THE HOURS   347
- B. THE LENTEN HOURS   358
- C. THE ROYAL HOURS   363
- D. GRAND COMPLINE   383
- E. THANKSGIVING   397
- F. CHURCHING OF WOMEN   409
- G. NEW HOUSE BLESSING   412
- H. HOUSE BLESSING   422

BIBLIOGRAPHY   427

[ For the liturgics for Funeral, Interment, and Memorial; Lenten Services; and, Holy Week, Pascha, and Bright Week; please see Volume 2! ]

# FOREWARD

Most assuredly, this first Volume of David Barrett's ***Liturgics for Orthodox Liturgical Singing*** is a labor of love, not simply a respect for the injunction that is in Orthodox worship: "Let all things be done decently (properly) and in order" (1 Cor 14:40). It is understood that, when two or three are gathered together in Christ's Name (Mt 18:20) and enter into the holiness that is "Church," we offer what is appointed for the service of God's glory: "Therefore, brethren, stand fast and hold the traditions which you were taught, whether by word or epistle" (2 Thess 2:15). It is not just what we pray, but when we pray, how we pray, and why. We "enter into" prayer as sacred song in worship.

Liturgical singing is the norm of faith – the witness to the belief of the praying Church (***lex orandi lex est credendi***). The rule of prayer is the rule of belief. We sing our prayer. What we sing is what we believe as offering in the Presence of God.

The worship of the Holy Church has **structure**, sanctifying time and place, saints and holy events we celebrate as our Salvation History. The Paschal cycle and Pentecost, and the Sundays and weeks that follow; the festal cycle, the fasts and feasts, anticipation, preparation, celebration, and leave-taking of feasts: the rhythm of worship by hours, days, weeks, seasons, and years – all celebrating "in the Now" of Church Time – "the Eternal Now of Today" of our Salvation History. "The time is fulfilled and the Kingdom of Heaven is at hand!" (Mk 1:14). "Blessed is the Kingdom of the Father, and of the Son, and of the Holy Spirit, now and ever!"

The structure of this divine action of the people who come together as the worshipping community in Christ is called "liturgy." Liturgics, or the "**ordo**," is the shape of the liturgical worship. Liturgy is the norm of faith – the witness to the belief of the praying Church. Liturgics give continuity – the living links to the past; the past is always present in the here and now, now and ever. What is past, present, and future in reality is celebrated in liturgy as "Today!"

Ritual and rites give us the sense of identity and community in Christ by the grace of the Holy Spirit. We remember, we belong, we celebrate, we anticipate, we give thanks for what is given – for what we ourselves both offer and receive.

Indeed, in Liturgical Singing we "enter into" worship – that which is given through Holy Tradition.

We thank David Barrett for this "how to" volume that helps us understand and "organize" within its shape and structure. In Orthodox worship, we "enter in" in order to "reach out."

> Fr Sergei Glagolev
> *East Meadow, NY*
> March 2015

# PREFACE

This book is intended as an outline or a guide for choir directors in the Orthodox Church who wish to understand the structure and *liturgics* (rules regarding the celebration of the divine services). The basic book that is followed for this is the *Typikon*, which is the liturgical book that contains instructions about the order of the various Church services, in the form of a perpetual calendar. The Typikon arose within the monastic movements of the early Christian era as a way to regulate the life of a monastery. Two monastic centers have influenced the services of the Orthodox Church more than any other: the Holy Lavra of Saint Savvas (or, Sabbas) the Sanctified near Jerusalem, and the Monastery of Saint John (Studium) in Constantinople.[1] The development of these two forms of the Typikon is as follows.

The Orthodox Church recognizes ***The Typikon of Saint Savvas - formally The Typikon of the Church Service of the Holy Lavra at Jerusalem of our God-Bearing Father St. Sabbas*** - as the standard of monastic usage. The original Typikon of Saint Savvas

---

[1] The Internet site, "Wikipedia," under "Typikon."

was developed to organize the lavra (monastic community) that St Sabbas the Sanctified founded in Jerusalem in the year 484 AD. It incorporated the practices and customs of existing Christian monastic communities in Palestine, Egypt, and Asia Minor, and was influenced by the Cathedral Office (services) in Jerusalem. The Typikon of Saint Sabbas was expanded in the 7th and 8th centuries to include large amounts of ecclesiastical poetry. It is also sometimes called the **Sabbaite** or **Jerusalem Typikon**.

Another Typikon, the Palestinian Typikon, was brought to the monasteries of Constantinople during the iconoclastic controversies of the 8th century, and was adopted and expanded for use in the Monastery of Stoudios. The Monastery's synthesis incorporated additional poetry and elements of the Cathedral Office of Constantinople. In the 11th century, the Studite usage was revised and updated. From this effort, a new version of the Typikon of Saint Savvas was created.

The newly revised Typikon of Saint Savvas became adopted widely, and by the 15th century had displaced both the Cathedral Office of Constantinople and the prior synthesis of the Studite Monastery, and had become the standard Typikon for all the Orthodox world. Its usage was further solidified when it was published in 1545, the first printed Typikon.  It is still in widespread use among most Orthodox monastic communities, and in large areas of the Orthodox world, including Russia.

By the 19th century, the Ecumenical Patriarchate in Constantinople, headquartered at one time at Hagia Sophia, **The Great Church of Christ**, recognized that the monastic strictures of the Typikon of Saint Savvas, while eminently useful in a monastic or cathedral setting, were not suitable for typical parish life as experienced by most Orthodox Christians.  It published a new Typikon with the goal of creating an order of services that could be celebrated in a typical parish.  Thus, ***The Ecclesiastical Typikon According to the Style of the Great Church of Christ*** (*Τύπικον της εκκλησιάστικον κατα το Ήφος της του Χριστού Μεγάλης Εκκλήσιας* ***[Typikon Ekklisiastikon kata to ifos tis tou Christou Megalis Ekklisias])*** (Konstantinos Protopsaltis, Constantinople, 1839) was created.  Subsequent corrections and revisions were published with the new title, ***The Typikon of the Great Church of Christ*** *(Τύπικον της του Χριστού Μεγάλης Εκκλήσιας **[Typikon tis tou Christou Megalis Ekklisias])*** (George Violakis, Constantinople, 1888).[2]  This Typikon was

---

[2] Bogdanos, Theodore, *The Byzantine Liturgy: Hymnology and Order*, Greek Orthodox Diocese of Denver Choir Federation, 1993, p. xviii.

soon adopted by the Ecumenical Patriarchate, and is now in use by all churches under the direct jurisdiction of the Ecumenical Patriarchate (for example, the Greek Orthodox Archdiocese of North America) and most Greek-speaking churches (including the Church of Greece and the Church of Cyprus), as well as in some other Orthodox jurisdictions.[3]

For clarity of thought and presentation, in the remainder of this book, the liturgics will be presented according to the "Slavic" or "Russian" tradition as followed in the Orthodox Church in America. Whenever the liturgics from the other traditions are according to **both** the Greek **and** the Antiochian practices, they will be referred to as the "Byzantine tradition" or the "Byzantine practice". Whenever the Greek and Antiochian practices differ from each other (that is, they stand alone), then they will be referred to by their own designation ("Greek tradition [or practice]" and "Antiochian tradition [or practice]").

This author frequently gets frustrated when, perusing specifics in a reference volume on the appropriate page and section, the book says, "See

---

[3] Mother Mary and Ware, Kallistos (Timothy), *The Festal Menaion* (3rd printing), 1969, St. Tikhon's Seminary Press, p. 543.

such-and-such back on page so-and-so." Therefore, each separate service presented here will give the essential details completely, even if they have been presented in another section for another service. So, for example, the details regarding the Augmented Litany for a Great Vespers does **not** say, "Refer to the discussion on the Augmented Litany in the section on Resurrectional Vespers," but gives, **_again_ in the section on Great Vespers**, the full details necessary for the celebration of the Augmented Litany in that particular service. In fact, the **only** times I made reference to previous pages was when I presented the sections on Baptismal and Matrimonial Divine Liturgies, where, calling for the celebration of two prokeimena, I footnoted the reader to the section above on the celebration of two prokeimena in the Divine Liturgy section proper. The other occasion was, when concluding the discussion of the Funeral Divine Liturgy, I referenced that the rubrics for Interment at the cemetery were to be found in the chapter on Funerals (as separate from the Divine Liturgy) and Interments. Again, since this is a totally separate service (and at a totally different location [the cemetery, instead of the church]), this again is not a violation of the policy. Everywhere else, the rubrical information is re-presented in full for each and every liturgical service.

Another point to keep in mind regarding this book is the following.  In addition to presenting the basic outline and shape (or, "***ordo***") of the various services, as well as the liturgics concerning them, mention will be made of various popular or widely practiced liturgical customs.  To cite an example: when Resurrectional or Great Vespers is served with a Vigil, "Rejoice, O Virgin!" is often used as the concluding troparion of Vespers.  When either of these forms of Vespers is served alone, a dismissal is celebrated at the end of the service, and, therefore, the ***dismissal*** troparion will either be the Resurrectional or festal troparion.  However, in popular practice, many parishes that serve Resurrectional or Great Vespers alone will sing "Rejoice, O Virgin!" twice, and then either the Resurrectional or festal troparion.  The essential point to remember is this:  liturgical practices are ***not*** "written in stone," so to speak, but are flexible and varied from parish to parish.  In the Orthodox Church, the main celebrant (whether it be the parish priest, a "substitute" priest filling in, a diocesan bishop, or the Metropolitan) makes all final decisions regarding the pattern of elements taken or deleted from the customary parish practice.  It behooves the choir director to sit down with the main celebrant and discuss the order of the liturgical services, to determine what liturgical elements will be celebrated and what elements will be omitted. As with everything in our life in Christ, all things must be done, as St Paul reminds us, "decently and in order" (1 Corinthians 14:40), with the love, compassion, and cooperation that come from God.

Another item of note: Despite the increasingly-common use of reading prayers, hymns, and Scripture readings in the style of using a regularly spoken voice (as though reading aloud an article or editorial from a newspaper) borrowed from the Western churches, it has consistently been the official practice in the Orthodox Church throughout the centuries to use a chanting voice (usually on one note that may go up or down for emphasis, **not** being sung on a melody, however) for celebrating these prayers, hymns, and Scripture readings. Therefore, throughout this work, the word "chanting" will refer to the proper reading by a celebrant or reader on one note, and the word "singing" will refer to the celebration of hymns sung to melodies by a choir and the people. Whatever the local practice is within a given parish or jurisdictional tradition can be reinterpreted or adjusted accordingly.

This work is in two volumes. Volume 1 covers Vespers; Matins; the Divine Liturgy; Sacramental Services (Holy Baptism, Holy Chrismation, Holy Matrimony, and Holy Unction); and, in the last chapter, Non-Sacramental Services (the Hours, the Lenten Hours, the Royal Hours, Grand Compline, Thanksgiving, Churching of Women, New House Blessing, and House Blessing). Volume 2 covers Funerals, Interments, and Memorials; Lenten Services; and, in the last chapter, Holy Week, Pascha, and Bright Week.

I want to thank Christopher Holwey of the Antiochian Archdiocese, Fr Peter DeFonce of the Greek Archdiocese, and Dr Paul Meyendorff of St Vladimir's Orthodox Theological Seminary, for their wonderful assistance, comments, and feedback, especially regarding the Byzantine tradition practices.

May you find this liturgical guide to be of help to you and make the understanding of our liturgical services clear and easy as you serve Christ in this wonderful and rewarding ministry of singing praises, worship, and thanksgiving to God, for the salvation of the world and to the glory of His eternal Kingdom.

# 1
# VESPERS

## A.  RESURRECTIONAL VESPERS

*Doxology*

The doxology for Resurrectional Vespers, as well as for ***all*** Vespers when served alone, is "Blessed is our God, always now and ever and unto ages of ages!"  The response (singing) on the part of the people is "Amen."  The only exceptions to this are Vesperal Liturgies and the Liturgy of the Presanctified Gifts, where the doxology is "Blessed is the Kingdom of the Father, and of the Son, and of the Holy Spirit, now and ever and unto ages of ages!"  Here, again, the response is "Amen."  Also, if, per the Slavic (Russian) practice, both Vespers and Matins are to be celebrated together as a Vigil, the doxology **at the beginning of <u>Vespers</u>** is, "Glory to the Holy, consubstantial, life-creating and undivided Trinity, always now and ever and unto ages of ages!"  Again, the response by the people is to sing, "Amen."

## "Come, Let Us Worship"

After the doxology, "Come, Let Us Worship" is sung by the people, except during the forty days between Pascha and Ascension.  On Pascha and during Bright Week, the clergy sing "Christ is Risen!" **three** times, followed by the people also singing "Christ is Risen!" **three** times.  The celebrant then sings the Paschal verses (such as, "Let God Arise!"), one at a time.  After each one, the people sing a fast "Christ is Risen!"  Then, the celebrant chants, "Christ is Risen!" once more, stopping during the third time with "trampling down death by death."  The people then take up the final half of the third singing, with the words, "and, upon those in the tombs, bestowing life."  For the remainder of the forty days, the clergy sing "Christ is Risen!" **two-and-a-half** times, stopping during the third time with "trampling down death by death."  The people then take up the **final half** of the third singing, with the words, "and, upon those in the tombs, bestowing life."  In the Greek practice, the clergy and people sing "Christ is Risen!" **together** three times, with the priest coming out of the sanctuary to bless the people with the paschal candle during the third singing.

## Psalm 103

During the censing of the entire church by the clergy, the people sing Psalm 103, "Bless the Lord, O my soul!"[4] Depending on the size of the church building needing to be censed during this great censing (the sanctuary, the iconostasis, the icons, the perimeter of the church, and the people [modern practice has the people censed before the perimeter of the church]), the tempo of the singing of this psalm may be sped up or slowed down. In the Greek practice, there is *no* censing done during this Psalm, and is always chanted by a reader.

The exception to this is at Vespers on Pascha and during Bright Week. At those Vespers, Ps. 103 is not chanted. Rather, the Paschal verses, along with "Glory,… Now and ever…" and the Paschal troparion are chanted (as at Paschal Matins and Liturgies).

---

[4] Here, and throughout this book, the Psalm numbering is rendered according to the officially accepted version of the Orthodox Church, namely, the number rendering according to the Septuagint.

## The Great Litany

As with **all** forms of Vespers, the Great Litany is then chanted by the clergy, with responses sung by the people. There are eleven petitions, with the people singing, "Lord, have mercy" after each one. However, in some Greek parishes, there are twelve petitions of the Great Litany: Between what is usually the fourth petition ("For this holy house,…!") and the fifth petition ("For His Beatitude, our Metropolitan…!"), there is a petition that states, "For pious and Orthodox Christians, let us pray to the Lord!". When the priest or deacon chants the petition that begins, "Commemorating our most holy, most pure, most blessed and glorious Lady,…," the people respond to that petition with, "To You, O Lord!" The priest then chants the exclamation, to which the people respond by singing, "Amen."

## Kathisma 1: "Blessed is the Man"

The 1$^{st}$ Kathisma of the Psalter, Psalms 1-8, beginning with "Blessed is the Man," is then sung on **all** Saturdays of the year **except** for the Vesperal Liturgy of Holy Saturday. Since this 1$^{st}$ Kathisma is **only** prescribed for Saturday evening Vespers, it is *not* appropriate to sing it at any other Great Vespers during the week, although it is sometimes prescribed (not always) for the Vespers of feast days that occur on other weekdays. In most Greek parishes, this Kathisma 1 is **omitted**.

## *"Lord, I Call Upon You" and Resurrectional Stikhera*

After the singing of "Lord, I Call Upon You" and "Let My Prayer Arise (in the tone of the first stikheron)," there is a refrain verse by a reader, and then there are usually seven Resurrectional **stikhera** (sets of sung verses), with refrain verses in between that are chanted by the reader. In the Antiochian tradition, however, before any of the ten refrain verses are intoned, the reader chants the prayer that begins, "Set a guard over my mouth, O Lord,…!" Then, the reader chants the "Glory…now and ever…" and the people sing the **Dogmatikon**, a stikheron about the Incarnation of Christ from the Theotokos (Virgin Mary). With feasts of saints coinciding with the particular Sunday (of which Saturday evening Vespers is the preparation), there will be extra stikhera for the feast after a particular number of the usual Resurrectional stikhera. Therefore, there may be up to ten stikhera sung before the "Glory."

The ten possible verses of the reader that are chanted in between the stikhera are as follows:

10) Bring my soul out of prison that I may give thanks to Your Name!
9) The righteous will surround me until You deal bountifully with me!
8) Out of the depths, I cry to You, O Lord! Lord, hear my voice!
7) Let Your ears be attentive to the voice of my supplications!
6) If You, O Lord, should mark iniquities, Lord, who could stand? But, there is forgiveness with You!
5) For Your Name's sake, I wait for You, O Lord! My soul waits for Your Word! My soul has hoped in the Lord!
4) From the morning watch until night, from the morning watch, let Israel hope in the Lord!
3) For, with the Lord there is mercy, and with Him is plenteous redemption! And He will deliver Israel from all his iniquities!

2) Praise the Lord, all nations! Praise Him, all peoples!
1) For, His mercy is confirmed on us, and the truth of the Lord endures forever!

Theoretically, the entire Psalms are chanted. These verses are numbered backwards to match the number of stikhera sung. Therefore, if there are seven stikhera to be sung, the reader will start (after "Let My Prayer Arise" is sung) with #7, "Let Your ears be attentive to the voice of my supplications!"; if there are nine stikhera to be sung, the reader will start with #9, "The righteous will surround me until You deal bountifully with me!"; and so forth.

There are certainly exceptions here: The Great Vespers that precede the Liturgy of Chrysostom for Annunciation (designated in the Typikon for March 26 - the service is the "end" of the 25th, a full lenten day of fasting) specifies that eleven stikhera be sung on "Lord, I call." The verse preceding the "extra" 11th stikheron is "added in" (after the usual 10) and is: "He makes His angels spirits, and His ministers a flame of fire!" After this stikheron comes the "Glory,...now and ever..." and the stikheron designated for the Feast. Vespers prior to the last singing of the Kanon of St. Andrew (Thursday of the 5$^{th}$ week of Lent) requires 29!

Also, if there is a "Glory" stikheron for the particular feast, the reader will chant what is called a "split Glory," that is, they will chant "Glory" up to the point of saying "the Holy Spirit," and then stop. The people will then sing the "Glory" stikheron for the particular feast. The reader will then chant the "now and ever," and the people will sing the Dogmatikon.

### *"Gladsome Light"*

During the singing of the Dogmatikon, the clergy and servers process from the sanctuary out into the nave, for the Vesperal Entrance. After the Dogmatikon is concluded, the priest or deacon then raises the censer and says, "Wisdom! Let us be attentive!" The people then sing the Vesperal Entrance hymn, "Gladsome Light," which is the central hymn of Vespers, acknowledging Christ as the Light of the world! The clergy and servers then process back into the sanctuary.

## *The Evening Prokeimenon:   "The Lord is King"*

The clergy go to the high place at the back of the altar (except in the Greek practice, where they go and stand around the altar), and then the Evening Prokeimenon, which, on Saturday evenings, is always taken from Psalm 93, "The Lord is King!," is chanted. The clergy begin by chanting, "Wisdom! Let us be attentive! Peace be with you all!," and then continue, "The Prokeimenon is in the 6$^{th}$ tone: The Lord is King! He is robed in majesty!" The people respond by singing "The Lord is King! He is robed in majesty!" in Tone 6. This is sung by the people after each verse is chanted by the clergy. After the last verse is chanted, the priest or deacon then chants the first half of the verse, "The Lord is King!" The people then respond with the second half of the verse, "He is robed in majesty!," to conclude the Prokeimenon. In the Greek practice, at the beginning of the Prokeimenon, the deacon will intone, "Evening! Prokeimenon!", and the singers will intone and sing the entire Prokeimenon themselves. Also, in the Greek practice, only two verses from the Psalm are intoned.

Each of the other days of the week has its own Vesperal Prokeimenon.

## [Old (New) Testament Readings]

If it is a feast that contains Old (or, sometimes, New) Testament readings, these are read at this point. If so, there will usually be three readings, though there can be more. The format for introducing these readings is as follows:

*Deacon:* Wisdom!

*Reader:* The Reading is from [name of the Biblical Book from which the reading comes]!

*Priest :* Let us be attentive!

*Reader:* [begins the Reading with no special introduction (like, "Brethren").]

## [Resurrectional Matins Gospel]

Although not called for in the Typikon, many parishes that do not celebrate Resurrectional Matins will, at this point in the service, chant the Resurrectional Matins Gospel prescribed for that week.  There are eleven different Resurrectional Matins Gospel readings, which begin on Saint Thomas Sunday and continue until the 5th Sunday of Great Lent the following year (there is a special Matins Gospel reading for Palm Sunday).  The clergy chant, "And that we may be accounted worthy to listen to the Holy Gospel, let us pray to the Lord our God!"  The people then sing a "***triple*** 'Lord, have mercy'," that is, "Lord, have mercy" sung ***three*** times.  The clergy then chant, "Wisdom!  Let us be attentive!  Let us listen to the Holy Gospel!," then the priest turns and faces the people and, while blessing them, says, "Peace be with you all!"  The people then respond by singing, "And with your spirit!"  The priest then says, "The Reading is from the Holy Gospel according to Saint [Matthew, Mark, Luke, ***or*** John the Theologian]!"  The people then respond by singing, "Glory to You, O Lord!  Glory to You!"  The priest then reads the prescribed Reading for the Resurrectional Matins Gospel.  At the conclusion of the Reading, the people then again sing, "Glory to You, O Lord!  Glory to You!"

Again, this is ***not*** prescribed in the Typikon, and is not practiced in all parishes.  In those parishes that do ***not*** read the Resurrectional Matins Gospel, the practice is to go from the Evening Prokeimenon directly into the Augmented Litany that follows.  In parishes that ***do*** read the Resurrectional Matins

Gospel, the practice is to go from the Evening Prokeimenon to the Resurrectional Matins Gospel, and then to the Augmented Litany that follows.

### The Augmented Litany

The correct practice for the Augmented Litany at Resurrectional and Great Vespers is as follows: Following each of the first two petitions ("Let us say…!" and "O Lord Almighty,…!"), there is a *single* "Lord, have mercy." Then, beginning with the third petition ("Have mercy on us, O God,…!") and for the subsequent petitions, the people respond with a *triple* "Lord, have mercy." In the Greek practice, however, the people sing a *triple* "Lord, have mercy." starting with the ***first*** petition. As with the Great Litany, when the priest or deacon gets to the petition that begins, "Commemorating our most holy…," the people respond with, "To You, O Lord." After the exclamation chanted by the priest, the people respond with, "Amen."

Some parishes, however, follow the practice of celebrating the Augmented Litany as is done at Daily Vespers and Daily Lenten Vespers, that is, to eliminate the first two "single" petitions and begin with "Have mercy on us, O Lord,…," which is responded to by the "***triple*** 'Lord, have mercy'." The choir director and singers should observe whatever practice is in place by the bishop and the parish priest.

## *"Vouchsafe, O Lord"*

This prayer is supposed to be chanted, not sung, except during Bright Week (this is really a monastic prayer, ***not*** a hymn). However, most of the time, the people ***then*** sing the hymn, "Vouchsafe, O Lord," in its entirety. In the Greek practice, if a bishop is present, he will chant "Vouchsafe, O Lord". If there is no bishop, a reader will chant it, but it is ***never*** sung by the singers in the Greek tradition.

## *Litany of Supplication*

The Litany of Supplication is chanted. The first two petitions of the Litany are responded to by the people with the singing of "Lord, have mercy." When the priest or deacon chants the petition, "That the whole evening may be perfect, holy, peaceful, and sinless, let us ask of the Lord," the people respond with singing, "Grant it, O Lord." This is done for the remaining petitions until, again, the petition that begins, "Commemorating our most holy,…," with the people responding, "To You, O Lord." After an exclamation by the priest and the "Amen" by the people, the priest faces the people and, blessing them, says, "Peace be with you all!" The people then respond by singing, "And with your spirit!" The priest or deacon then says, "Bow your heads unto the Lord." The people sing, "To You, O Lord." The priest reads a prayer, ending with an exclamation, to which the people respond with, "Amen."

### [Litya Verses and Petition Responses]

If there is a feast coinciding with this Sunday that calls for a Litya (the blessing of wheat, wine, loaves, and oil), the people sing the prescribed Litya verses as the clergy and servers exit the sanctuary and go to the back of the church, at the entrance of the narthex into the nave (while staying in the nave). **However**, in the Antiochian tradition, the practice is to have a table in the middle of the solea, so the clergy and servers do **not** go to the back of the church. Technically, a Litya is supposed to be done **only** at a Vigil.

When the clergy are at the back of the nave and the singing of the Litya verses is concluded, the priest or deacon chants five special petitions. After the first **three** petitions, the people respond with "Lord, have mercy" sung **twelve** times. After the next **two** petitions, the people respond with "Lord, have mercy" sung **three** times. Then, there is the conclusion of these petitions, which is similar to the conclusion of the Litany of Supplication: After an exclamation by the priest and the "Amen" by the people, the priest faces the people and, blessing them, says, "Peace be with you all!" The people then respond by singing, "And with your spirit!" The priest or deacon then says, "Bow your heads unto the Lord." The people sing, "To You, O Lord." The priest reads a prayer, ending with an exclamation, to which the people respond with, "Amen."

In the Greek tradition for the celebration of the Litya, an analogion is put in the center of the solea. For the Litany, there are **six** sets of petitions celebrated. **Each** is accompanied by a threefold "Lord, have mercy.". Near the conclusion of the Great Prayer of Intercession, the priest dialogues with the faithful, meaning that his final six petitions are punctuated by the people shouting "Amen!" at the end of each petition (the first of these begins "Make our prayer acceptable...!" and the last begins "O Lord, have mercy upon us and upon Your world, and save our souls...!" although, of course, the final public "Amen" is chanted, as usual). After this prayer, he censes the gifts on the table, while chanting "Rejoice O Virgin..." **three** times (or the Paschal Troparion during Bright Week), and then reads the official Prayer of Blessing, kisses the main loaf of bread. and returns to the sanctuary, chanting one time the Psalm verse, in Tone 7: "Those who were wealthy have become poor and hungry. but they who eagerly seek the Lord will never be in want of any good thing!". After he sings this hymn, the people sing it **twice**.

If there *is* a Litya, the people then sing the Resurrectional Apostikha stikhera as the clergy move to the center of the church. If there is **not** a Litya, the people go directly from the Litany of Supplication to the Resurrectional Apostikha stikhera. The blessing of the wheat, wine, and oil is done at this point. In the Antiochian tradition, this is followed by the singing of, "Rejoice, O Virgin!"

### *Resurrectional Apostikha Stikhera*

The Resurrectional Apostikha stikhera are sung. After each stikheron, a refrain verse is chanted by a reader. These refrain verses for

Saturday evening Vespers are fixed, and are as follows:

- The Lord is King!  He is robed in majesty!
- For, He has established the world, so that it will never be moved!
- Holiness befits Your house, O Lord, forevermore!

There is no need to number these refrain verses, since they do not vary.  In other words, there are **always** four Resurrectional Apostikha stikhera to be sung.  Therefore, the people sing the first stikheron, and the reader chants, "The Lord is King!…"; the people sing the second stikheron, and the reader chants, "For, He has established the world,…"; the people sing the third stikheron, and the reader chants, "Holiness befits Your house,…"; the people sing the fourth stikheron.

For most Sundays, the reader chants the "Glory,…now and ever…" verse after the last stikheron, with the people responding with the Theotokion, a stikheron concerning the Mother of God.  If there is a feast that calls for a "Glory" stikheron, the reader will chant "Glory" up to the point of saying "the Holy Spirit," and then stop. The people will then sing the "Glory" stikheron for the particular feast. The reader will then chant the "now and ever," and the people will sing the Theotokion *in the **same** **tone** as the "Glory" stikheron for the feast!* Therefore, if the tone of the week is tone 3 and the festal "Glory" stikheron is in tone 5, the people will sing the Resurrectional Apostikha stikhera in tone 3, the festal "Glory" stikheron in tone 5, and the Theotokion *in **tone** 5*.

Other refrains are prescribed for other feasts and daily usage.

### St. Symeon's Prayer

The people then sing St. Symeon's Prayer, "Lord, Now Let Your Servant," in tone 6. In the Greek practice, the priest chants this prayer.

### Trisagion Prayers

A reader then reads the Trisagion Prayers, which consist of the following: "Holy God! Holy Mighty! Holy Immortal! Have mercy on us!"

chanted **three** times; "Glory to the Father, and to the Son, and to the Holy Spirit, now and ever and unto ages of ages. Amen."; "Most Holy Trinity, have mercy on us! Lord, cleanse us from our sins! Master, pardon our transgressions! Holy One, visit and heal our infirmities, for Your Name's sake!"; "Lord, have mercy" **three** times; another "Glory...now and ever..."; then, the Lord's Prayer. In some parish communities, the Lord's Prayer is said by the entire congregation. After the exclamation by the priest, the people respond with, "Amen."

## Concluding Tropraria

The concluding troparia are then sung by the people. For most Sundays, this will consist of one of two practices called for:

1) If Resurrectional Vespers is served along with Resurrectional Matins together, as a Vigil, the people sing, "Rejoice, O Virgin Theotokos!" **twice**, followed by the Resurrectional troparion sung **once**. For a feast day with**out** a Litya, the people sing "Rejoice, O Virgin Theotokos!" **once**, the Resurrectional troparion **once**, and the troparion for the feast **once**.

2) If Resurrectional Vespers is served alone, there will be a Dismissal at the end of the service. Therefore, as the *dismissal* troparion, the people sing according to the rubrics for "God is the Lord" at Resurrectional Matins: if there is no other feast coinciding with the Sunday, the Resurrectional troparion is sung, followed by "Glory, now and ever," and then the Theotokion in the tone of the week. If another feast *does* coincide with the Sunday, then the Resurrectional troparion is sung, followed by "Glory...Spirit," followed by the troparion for the feast, then "now and ever," and then the Theotokion *in the tone of the festal troparion that immediately preceded the Theotokion*.

This practice may differ from parish to parish. For example, in many parishes, even when Resurrectional Vespers is served alone, the people sing as per 1) above: "Rejoice, O Virgin!" *twice*, followed by the Resurrectional troparion sung *once*. For a feast day with*out* a Litya, the people sing "Rejoice, O Virgin Theotokos!" *once*, the Resurrectional troparion *once*, and the troparion for the feast *once*. As always, check with the main celebrant (usually the pastor of the parish) for the practice celebrated in your particular parish.

In the Greek practice, prior to the Dismissal, after the Resurrectional troparia, the priest chants, "Let us pray to the Lord.", and the people sing, "Lord, have mercy.". The priest then chants, "May the blessing of the Lord and His mercy come upon you through His divine grace and love for mankind, always, now and ever, and to the ages of ages.". The people then sing "Amen." in a fashion somewhat similar to the "Blessed be the Name of the Lord..." Antiochian practice.

## ["Blessed be the Name of the Lord"]

For a feast day **with** a Litya, after the triple singing of the festal troparion, the people sing "Blessed be the Name of the Lord!" **three** times, and then go to the Dismissal. At all other times, the people go directly from the concluding troparia to the Dismissal. The singing of "Blessed be the Name of the Lord!" is **omitted** in the Antiochian practice.

## Dismissal

If Matins follows Vespers, there is **no** Dismissal. Otherwise, the Dismissal begins with the priest or deacon chanting, "Wisdom!" Then, the people respond with "Father, bless!" (or, if a bishop is present, "Master, bless!" If the Metropolitan is present, the people will sing, "Most blessed Master, bless!") The priest says, "Christ, the One Who Is, is blessed always, now and ever and unto ages of ages!" The people respond with "Amen. Preserve, O God, the Holy Orthodox Faith and Orthodox Christians, now and ever and unto ages of ages."

The priest then chants, "Most Holy Theotokos, save us!" The people respond with, "More honorable than the Cherubim and more glorious beyond compare than the Seraphim! Without defilement, you gave Birth to God the Word! True Theotokos, we magnify you!"

During most of the year, the priest then chants, "Glory to You, Christ our God and our Hope, glory to You!" The people then respond with "Glory...now and ever...Amen. Lord, have mercy (**three** times). Father, bless!" (or, if a bishop is present, "Master, bless!" If the Metropolitan is present, the people will sing, "Most blessed Master, bless!") If it is Pascha or Bright Week, the priest will sing "Christ is Risen!" **three** times, and the people will respond also by singing "Christ is Risen!" **three** times. If it is between Bright Week and Ascension, the priest will chant the usual, "Glory to You, Christ our God and our Hope, glory to You!", and the people respond by singing, "Christ is Risen!" **three** times.  (Though it is not called for, in some parishes, the practice for the period between Bright Week and Ascension is for the priest to chant "Christ is Risen!" **two-and-a-half** times, with the people responding with the **final half**, "and, upon those in the tombs, bestowing life!"  Again, this is purely a local practice in some places, and is **not** called for in the rubrics of the Typikon.)  In the Greek practice, the clergy and people sing "Christ is Risen!" **together three** times, with the priest coming out of the sanctuary to bless the people with the paschal candle during the third singing.

In any case, the priest will then chant the Dismissal.  The people respond with "Amen," sung either once or twice, according to the parish practice.  If it is during the time between Pascha and Ascension, the people then sing, "And, unto us, He has given eternal life!  Let us worship His Resurrection on the third day!"

As the people come forward to venerate the Holy Cross (which is **not** prescribed, but **is** practiced) and the icons, the Resurrectional and/or festal troparia may be sung, according to the parish practice.  Then, before closing the Royal Doors, the priest chants, "Through the prayers of our holy fathers, O Lord, Jesus Christ, have mercy on us and save us!".  The people then sing "Amen." and, usually, a **triple** "Lord, have mercy.". If it is during the Pascha season, after the "Amen.", the people will sing the Paschal troparion ("Christ is Risen from the dead!").

## B. GREAT VESPERS

*Doxology*

The doxology for Resurrectional Vespers, as well as for **all** Vespers when served alone, is "Blessed is our God, always now and ever and unto ages of ages!" The response (singing) on the part of the people is "Amen." The only exceptions to this are Vesperal Liturgies and the Liturgy of the Presanctified Gifts, where the doxology is "Blessed is the Kingdom of the Father, and of the Son, and of the Holy Spirit, now and ever and unto ages of ages!" Here, again, the response is "Amen." Also, if, per the Slavic (Russian) practice, both Vespers and Matins are to be celebrated together as a Vigil, the doxology **at the beginning of <u>Great Vespers</u>** is, "Glory to the Holy, consubstantial, life-creating and undivided Trinity, always now and ever and unto ages of ages!" Again, the response by the people is to sing, "Amen."

## *"Come, Let Us Worship"*

After the doxology, "Come, Let Us Worship" is sung by the people, except during the forty days between Pascha and Ascension.  On Pascha and during Bright Week, the clergy sing "Christ is Risen!" ***three*** times, followed by the people also singing "Christ is Risen!" ***three*** times.  The celebrant then sings the Paschal verses (such as, "Let God Arise!"), one at a time.  After each one, the people sing a fast "Christ is Risen!"  Then, the celebrant chants, "Christ is Risen!" once more, stopping during the third time with "trampling down death by death."  The people then take up the final half of the third singing, with the words, "and, upon those in the tombs, bestowing life."  For the remainder of the forty days, the clergy sing "Christ is Risen!" ***two-and-a-half*** times, stopping during the third time with "trampling down death by death."  The people then take up the ***final half*** of the third singing, with the words, "and, upon those in the tombs, bestowing life."  In the Greek practice, the clergy and people sing "Christ is Risen!" ***<u>together</u> three*** times, with the priest coming out of the sanctuary to bless the people with the paschal candle during the third singing.

## Psalm 103

During the censing of the entire church by the clergy, the people sing Psalm 103, "Bless the Lord, O my soul!" Depending on the size of the church building needing to be censed during this great censing (the sanctuary, the iconostasis, the icons, the perimeter of the church, and the people [modern practice has the people censed before the perimeter of the church]), the tempo of the singing of this psalm may be sped up or slowed down. In the Greek practice, there is **no** censing done during this Psalm, and is always chanted by a reader.

The exception to this is at Vespers on Pascha and during Bright Week. At those Vespers, Ps. 103 is not chanted. Rather, the Paschal verses, along with "Glory,... Now and ever..." and the Paschal troparion are chanted (as at Paschal Matins and Liturgies).

## The Great Litany

As with **all** forms of Vespers, the Great Litany is then chanted by the clergy, with responses sung by the people. There are eleven petitions, with the people singing, "Lord, have mercy" after each one.

However, in some Greek parishes, there are twelve petitions of the Great Litany:  Between what is usually the fourth petition ("For this holy house,…!") and the fifth petition ("For His Beatitude, our Metropolitan…!"), there is a petition that states, "For pious and Orthodox Christians, let us pray to the Lord!".  When the priest or deacon chants the petition that begins, "Commemorating our most holy, most pure, most blessed and glorious Lady,…," the people respond to that petition with, "To You, O Lord!"  The priest then chants the exclamation, to which the people respond by singing, "Amen."

### [*NO* Kathisma 1:  "Blessed is the Man"]

Because Kathisma 1 from the Psalter (Psalms 1-3), beginning with "Blessed is the Man," is prescribed **_only_** for Saturday evening Resurrectional Vespers, when there is a Great Vespers for any other evening of the week (Sunday through Friday evenings), "Blessed is the Man" is **_not_** sung (although "Blessed is the Man" is sometimes prescribed [not always] for the Vespers of feast days that occur on other weekdays)!  If the prescribed Kathisma for the Great Vespers for the particular evening of the week is available (as is the case in most monasteries), that may be sung at this point.  Otherwise, the people go directly from the Great Litany to the singing of "Lord, I Call Upon You."

### "Lord, I Call Upon You" and Festal Stikhera

After the singing of "Lord, I Call Upon You" and "Let My Prayer Arise," there is a refrain verse by a reader, and then there are festal **stikhera** (sets of sung verses), with refrain verses in between that are chanted by the reader. In the Antiochian tradition, however, before any of the ten refrain verses are intoned, the reader chants from the Psalms, beginning, "Set a guard over my mouth, O Lord,…!" Then, the reader chants the "Glory…now and ever…" and the people sing the stikheron relating to the feast and Christ. There may be up to ten stikhera sung before the "Glory."

The ten possible verses of the reader that are chanted in between the stikhera are as follows:

10) Bring my soul out of prison that I may give thanks to Your Name!
9) The righteous will surround me until You deal bountifully with me!

8) Out of the depths, I cry to You, O Lord! Lord, hear my voice!

7) Let Your ears be attentive to the voice of my supplications!

6) If You, O Lord, should mark iniquities, Lord, who could stand? But, there is forgiveness with You!

5) For Your Name's sake, I wait for You, Lord! My soul waits for Your Word! My soul has hoped in the Lord!

4) From the morning watch until night, from the morning watch, let Israel hope in the Lord!

3) For, with the Lord there is mercy, and with Him is plenteous redemption! And He will deliver Israel from all his iniquities!

2) Praise the Lord, all nations! Praise Him, all peoples!

1) For, His mercy is confirmed on us, and the truth of the Lord endures forever!

These verses are numbered backwards to match the number of stikhera sung. Therefore, if there are seven stikhera to be sung, the reader will start (after "Let My Prayer Arise" is sung) with #7, "Let Your ears be attentive to the voice of my supplications!"; if there are nine stikhera to be sung, the reader will start with #9, "The righteous will surround me until You deal bountifully with me!"; and so forth.

There are certainly exceptions here: The Great Vespers that precede the Liturgy of Chrysostom for Annunciation (designated in the Typikon for March 26 - the service is the "end" of the 25th, a full lenten day of fasting) specifies that eleven stikhera be sung on "Lord, I call." The verse preceding the "extra" 11th stikheron is "added in" (after the usual 10) and is: "He makes His angels spirits, and His ministers a flame of fire!" After this stikheron comes the "Glory,...now and ever..." and the stikheron designated for the Feast. Vespers prior to the last singing of the Kanon of St. Andrew (Thursday of the 5$^{th}$ week of Lent) requires 29 stikhera!

In any case, before the final stikheron, the reader chants the "Glory,...now and ever...".

## "Gladsome Light"

During the singing of the "Glory..., now and ever..." stikheron, the clergy and servers process from the sanctuary out into the nave, for the Vesperal Entrance. The priest or deacon then raises the censer and says, "Wisdom! Let us be attentive!" The people then sing the Vesperal Entrance hymn, "Gladsome Light," which is the central hymn of Vespers, acknowledging Christ as the Light of the world! In the Antiochian tradition, however, the practice is for a reader to chant "Gladsome Light" at Daily Vespers. The clergy and servers then process back into the sanctuary.

## The Evening Prokeimenon

The clergy go to the high place at the back of the altar (*except* in the Greek practice, where they go and stand around the altar), and then the Evening Prokeimenon is chanted. The clergy begin by chanting, "Wisdom! Let us be attentive! Peace be with you all!," and then continue, "The Prokeimenon is in the [1$^{st}$ through 8$^{th}$] tone." The main verse of the Prokeimenon is then chanted. The people respond by singing the main verse of the

Prokeimenon in the prescribed tone. This is sung by the people after each verse is chanted by the clergy. After the last verse is chanted, the priest or deacon then chants the first half of the verse. The people then respond with the second half of the verse to conclude the Prokeimenon. In the Greek practice, at the beginning of the Prokeimenon, the deacon will intone, "Evening! Prokeimenon!", and the singers will intone and sing the entire Prokeimenon themselves. Also, in the Greek practice, only two verses from the Psalm are intoned.

The various Prokeimena for Great Vespers, Sunday through Friday evenings, are as follows. The virgule (or slash, "/") within these Prokeimena designates the first and second halves of the Prokeimena for the final rendition by both the clergy and the people.

Sunday evening:  **Tone 8 (Psalm 133)**

"Come, bless the Lord, / all you servants of the Lord!"*

---

*In the Antiochian tradition, this Prokeimenon is, "You who stand in the temple of the Lord, / in the courts of the house of our God!"

Monday evening: **Tone 4 (Psalm 4)**

"The Lord hears / when I call to Him!"

Tuesday evening: **Tone 1 (Psalm 22)**

"Your mercy, O Lord, / will follow me all the days of my life!"

Wednesday evening: **Tone 5 (Psalm 53)**

"Save me, O God by Your Name, / and judge me by Your strength!"

Thursday evening: **Tone 6 (Psalm 120)**

"My help comes from the Lord, / Who made Heaven and Earth!"

Friday evening: **Tone 7** (**Psalm 58**)

"You, O God, are my Helper, / and Your steadfast love will go before me!"

## *Old (New) Testament Readings*

After the Evening Prokeimenon, three Old (or, sometimes, New) Testament readings are read at this point. If so, there will usually be three readings, though there can be more.  The format for introducing these readings is as follows:

> ***Deacon:*** Wisdom!
>
> ***Reader:*** The Reading is from [name of the Biblical Book from which the reading comes]!
>
> ***Priest :*** Let us be attentive!
>
> ***Reader:*** [begins the Reading with ***no*** special introduction (like, "Brethren").]

## *[Festal Matins Gospel]*

Although not called for in the Typikon, many parishes that do not celebrate Festal Matins will, at this point in the service, read the Festal Matins Gospel prescribed for this feast.  The clergy chant, "And that we may be accounted worthy to listen to the Holy Gospel, let us pray to the Lord our God!"  The people then sing a "***triple*** 'Lord, have mercy'," that is, "Lord, have mercy" sung ***three*** times.  The clergy then chant, "Wisdom!  Let us be attentive!

Let us listen to the Holy Gospel!," then the priest turns and faces the people and, while blessing them, says, "Peace be with you all!" The people then respond by singing, "And with your spirit!" The priest then says, "The Reading is from the Holy Gospel according to Saint [Matthew, Mark, Luke, *or* John the Theologian]!" The people then respond by singing, "Glory to You, O Lord! Glory to You!" The priest then reads the prescribed Reading for the Festal Matins Gospel. At the conclusion of the Reading, the people then again sing, "Glory to You, O Lord! Glory to You!"

Again, this is **not** prescribed in the Typikon, and is not practiced in all parishes. In those parishes that do **not** read the Festal Matins Gospel, the practice is to go from the Old (or New) Testament Readings directly into the Augmented Litany that follows. In parishes that **do** read the Festal Matins Gospel, the practice is to go from the Old (or New) Testament Readings to the Festal Matins Gospel, and then to the Augmented Litany that follows.

### The Augmented Litany

The correct practice for the Augmented Litany at Resurrectional and Great Vespers is as follows:

Following each of the first two petitions ("Let us say...!" and "O Lord Almighty,...!"), there is a ***single*** "Lord, have mercy."  Then, beginning with the third petition ("Have mercy on us, O God,...!") and for the subsequent petitions, the people respond with a ***triple*** "Lord, have mercy.".  In the Greek practice, however, the people sing a ***triple*** "Lord, have mercy." starting with the ***first*** petition.  As with the Great Litany, when the priest or deacon gets to the petition that begins, "Commemorating our most holy...," the people respond with, "To You, O Lord." After the exclamation chanted by the priest, the people respond with, "Amen."

Some parishes, however, follow the practice of celebrating the Augmented Litany as is done at Daily Vespers and Daily Lenten Vespers, that is, to eliminate the first two "single" petitions and begin with "Have mercy on us, O Lord,...," which is responded to by the "***triple*** 'Lord, have mercy'." The choir director and singers should observe whatever practice is in place by the bishop and the parish priest.

*"Vouchsafe, O Lord"*

This prayer is supposed to be chanted, not sung, except during Bright Week (this is really a monastic prayer, **not** a hymn). However, most of the time, the people **then** sing the hymn, "Vouchsafe, O Lord," in its entirety. In the Greek practice, if a bishop is present, he will chant "Vouchsafe, O Lord". If there is no bishop, a reader will chant it, but it is **never** sung by the singers in the Greek tradition.

### Litany of Supplication

The Litany of Supplication is chanted. The first two petitions of the Litany are responded to by the people with the singing of "Lord, have mercy." When the priest or deacon chants the petition, "That the whole evening may be perfect, holy, peaceful, and sinless, let us ask of the Lord," the people respond with singing, "Grant it, O Lord." This is done for the remaining petitions until, again, the petition that begins, "Commemorating our most holy,...," with the people responding, "To You, O Lord." After an exclamation by the priest and the "Amen" by the people, the priest faces the people and, blessing them, says, "Peace be with you all!" The people then respond by singing, "And with your spirit!" The priest or deacon then says, "Bow your heads unto the Lord." The people sing, "To You, O Lord." The priest reads a prayer, ending with an exclamation, to which the people respond with, "Amen."

### [Litya Verses and Petition Responses]

If there is a feast coinciding with this Sunday that calls for a Litya (the blessing of wheat, wine, loaves, and oil), the people sing the prescribed Litya verses as the clergy and servers exit the sanctuary and go to the back of the church, at the entrance of the narthex into the nave (while staying in the nave). **However**, in the Antiochian tradition, the practice is to have a table in the middle of the solea, so the clergy and servers do **not** go to the back of the church. Technically, a Litya is supposed to be done **only** at a Vigil.

When the clergy are at the back of the nave and the singing of the Litya verses is concluded, the priest or deacon chants five special petitions. After the first **three** petitions, the people respond with "Lord, have mercy" sung **twelve** times. After the next **two** petitions, the people respond with "Lord, have mercy" sung **three** times. Then, there is the conclusion of these petitions, which is similar to the conclusion of the Litany of Supplication: After an exclamation by the priest and the "Amen" by the people, the priest faces the people and, blessing them, says, "Peace be with you all!" The people then respond by singing, "And with your spirit!" The priest or deacon then says, "Bow your heads unto the Lord." The people sing, "To You, O Lord." The priest reads a prayer, ending with an exclamation, to which the people respond with, "Amen."

In the Greek tradition for the celebration of the Litya, analogion is put in the center of the solea. For the Litany, there are *six* sets of petitions celebrated. **Each** is accompanied by a threefold "Lord, have mercy.". Near the conclusion of the Great Prayer of Intercession, the priest dialogues with the faithful, meaning that his final six petitions are punctuated by the people shouting "Amen!" at the end of each petition (the first of these begins "Make our prayer acceptable...!" and the last begins "O Lord, have mercy upon us and upon Your world, and save our souls...!" although, of course, the final public "Amen" is chanted, as usual). After this prayer, he censes the gifts on the table, while chanting "Rejoice O Virgin..." three times (or the Paschal Troparion during Bright Week), and then reads the official Prayer of Blessing, kisses the main loaf of bread. and returns to the sanctuary, chanting one time the Psalm verse, in Tone 7: "Those who were wealthy have become poor and hungry. but they who eagerly seek the Lord will never be in want of any good thing!".  After he sings this hymn, the people sing it **twice**.

If there **is** a Litya, the people then sing the Festal Apostikha stikhera as the clergy move to the center of the church.  If there is **not** a Litya, the people go directly from the Litany of Supplication to the Festal Apostikha stikhera.

### *Festal Apostikha Stikhera*

The Festal Apostikha stikhera are sung.  After each stikheron, a refrain verse is chanted by a reader.  There is no need to number these refrain verses, since there are fixed refrain verses for each particular feast.  Before the final stikheron, the reader chants the "Glory…, now and ever…" as the refrain verse.

## St. Symeon's Prayer

The people then sing St. Symeon's Prayer, "Lord, Now Let Your Servant," in tone 6. In the Greek practice, the priest chants this prayer.

## Trisagion Prayers

A reader then reads the Trisagion Prayers, which consist of the following: "Holy God! Holy Mighty! Holy Immortal! Have mercy on us!" chanted **three** times; "Glory to the Father, and to the Son, and to the Holy Spirit, now and ever and unto ages of ages. Amen."; "Most Holy Trinity, have mercy on us! Lord, cleanse us from our sins! Master, pardon our transgressions! Holy One, visit and heal our infirmities, for Your Name's sake!"; "Lord, have mercy" **three** times; another "Glory…now and ever…"; then, the Lord's Prayer. In some parish communities, the Lord's Prayer is said by the entire congregation. After the exclamation by the priest, the people respond with, "Amen."

## Concluding Troparion

The concluding troparion is then sung by the people. For most feasts, this will consist of one of two practices called for:

1) If Great Vespers is served along with Festal Matins together, as a Vigil, the people sing, "Rejoice, O Virgin Theotokos!" **twice**, followed by the festal troparion sung **once**.

2) If Great Vespers is served alone, there will be a Dismissal at the end of the service. Therefore, as the **dismissal** troparion, the people sing according to the rubrics for "God is the Lord" at Festal Matins: the festal troparion is sung, followed by "Glory, now and ever," and then the Theotokion **in the tone of the festal troparion**.

This practice may differ from parish to parish. For example, in many parishes, even when Great Vespers is served alone, the people sing as per 1) above: "Rejoice, O Virgin!" **twice**, followed by the festal troparion sung **once**. As always, check with the main celebrant (usually the pastor of the parish) for the practice celebrated in your particular parish.

## ["Blessed be the Name of the Lord"]

For a feast day **with** a Litya, after the triple singing of the festal troparion, the people sing "Blessed be the Name of the Lord!" **three** times, and then go to the Dismissal.  At all other times, the people go directly from the concluding troparia to the Dismissal.  The singing of "Blessed be the Name of the Lord!" is **omitted** in the Antiochian practice.

## Dismissal

If Matins follows Vespers, there is **no** Dismissal.  Otherwise, the Dismissal begins with the priest or deacon chanting, "Wisdom!"  Then, the people respond with "Father, bless!" (or, if a bishop is present, "Master, bless!"  If the Metropolitan is present, the people will sing, "Most blessed Master, bless!")  The priest says, "Christ, the One Who Is, is blessed always, now and ever and unto ages of ages!"  The people respond with "Amen.  Preserve, O God, the Holy Orthodox Faith and Orthodox Christians, now and ever and unto ages of ages."

The priest then chants, "Most Holy Theotokos, save us!"  The people respond with, "More honorable than the Cherubim and more glorious beyond compare than the Seraphim!  Without defilement, you gave Birth to God the Word!  True Theotokos, we magnify you!"

During most of the year, the priest then chants, "Glory to You, Christ our God and our Hope, glory to You!"  The people then respond with "Glory...now and ever...Amen.  Lord, have mercy (**three** times).  Father, bless!" (or, if a bishop is present, "Master, bless!"  If the Metropolitan is present, the people will sing, "Most blessed Master, bless!")  If it is Pascha or Bright Week, the priest will sing "Christ is Risen!" **three** times, and the people will respond also by singing "Christ is Risen!" **three** times.  If it is between Bright Week and Ascension, the priest will chant the usual, "Glory to You, Christ our God and our Hope, glory to You!", and the people respond by singing, "Christ is Risen!" **three** times.  (Though it is not called for, in some parishes, the practice for the period between Bright Week and Ascension is for the priest to chant "Christ is Risen!" **two-and-a-half** times, with the people responding with the **final half**, "and, upon those in the tombs, bestowing life!"  Again, this is purely a local practice in some places, and is **not** called for in the rubrics of the Typikon.)  In the Greek practice, the clergy and people sing "Christ is Risen!" **_together_ three** times, with the priest coming out of the sanctuary to bless the people with the paschal candle during the third singing.

In any case, the priest will then chant the Dismissal.  The people respond with "Amen," sung either once or twice, according to the parish practice.  If it is during the time between Pascha and Ascension, the people then sing, "And, unto us, He has given eternal life!  Let us worship His Resurrection on the third day!"

As the people come forward to venerate the Holy Cross (which is not prescribed, but is practiced) and the icons, the Resurrectional and/or festal troparia may be sung, according to the parish practice.  Then, before closing the Royal Doors, the priest chants, "Through the prayers of our holy fathers, O Lord, Jesus Christ, have mercy on us and save us!".  The people then sing "Amen." and, usually, a *triple* "Lord, have mercy.".  If it is during the Pascha season, after the "Amen.", the people will sing the Paschal troparion ("Christ is Risen from the dead!").

## C. DAILY VESPERS

*Doxology*

The doxology for Daily Vespers is "Blessed is our God, always now and ever and unto ages of ages!" The response (singing) on the part of the people is "Amen." For Pascha and Bright Week, the celebrant chants, "Christ is Risen!" **three** times, followed by the people singing it **three** times. This is then followed by the Paschal verses ("Let God Arise!", etc.), each one followed by the singing of "Christ is Risen!" Then, the celebrant sings half of "Christ is Risen!", with the people finishing the last half, at the point of "And, upon those in the tombs,...!" From Thomas Sunday to the Leavetaking of Pascha right before Ascension, the celebrant sings "Christ is Risen!" **two-and-a-half** times, with the people finishing the **final half**, at the point of "And, upon those in the tombs,...!" The rest of the year, a reader chants, "O Heavenly King!".

## Psalm 103

The reader then chants the Trisagion Prayers, the Lord's Prayer, "Come, Let Us Worship God, our King!" and Psalm 103, "Bless the Lord, O my soul!". At the conclusion of the Psalm, the reader chants a "Glory…, now and ever…," and then chants "Alleluia! Alleluia! Alleluia! Glory to You, O God!" **three** times.

## The Great Litany

As with **all** forms of Vespers, the Great Litany is then chanted by the clergy, with responses sung by the people. There are eleven petitions, with the people singing, "Lord, have mercy" after each one. However, in some Greek parishes, there are twelve petitions of the Great Litany: Between what is usually the fourth petition ("For this holy house,…!") and the fifth petition ("For His Beatitude, our Metropolitan…!"), there is a petition that states, "For pious and Orthodox Christians, let us pray to the Lord!". When the priest or deacon chants the petition that begins, "Commemorating our most holy, most pure, most blessed and glorious Lady,…," the people respond to that petition with, "To You, O

Lord!" The priest then chants the exclamation, to which the people respond by singing, "Amen."

## [Kathisma Reading from the Psalter]

Most of the time in Daily Vespers, the people go directly from the Great Litany to the singing of "Lord, I Call Upon You." In some parishes (as well as in most monasteries), there may be a Kathisma reading from the Psalter, especially during Great Lent. In those cases, the people sing the Great Litany, the reader chants a Kathisma reading from the Psalter, and the people then sing, "Lord, I Call Upon You.".

## "Lord, I Call Upon You" and Stikhera

After the singing of "Lord, I Call Upon You" and "Let My Prayer Arise" in the tone of the week, there are **stikhera** (sets of sung verses), with refrain verses in between that are chanted by the reader. Then, the reader chants the "Glory…now and ever…" and the people sing the final stikheron. There are usually three daily stikhera (followed by stikhera from the Menaion) sung before the "Glory." In the

Greek tradition, "Lord, I Call Upon You", "Let My Prayer Arise", and the stikhera are ***not*** sung, but chanted by readers.

With Daily Vespers, after the singing of "Let My Prayer Arise," the reader begins chanting with the longer set of verses from the Psalms that begins with "Set a guard over my mouth, O Lord! Keep watch over the door of my lips!" These verses then go directly into the ten refrain verses that precede the singing of the stikhera. These ten refrain verses are as follows:

10) Bring my soul out of prison that I may give thanks to Your Name!

9) The righteous will surround me until You deal bountifully with me!

8) Out of the depths, I cry to You, O Lord! Lord, hear my voice!

7) Let Your ears be attentive to the voice of my supplications!

6) If You, O Lord, should mark iniquities, Lord, who could stand? But, there is forgiveness with You!

5) For Your Name's sake, I wait for You, Lord! My soul waits for Your Word! My soul has hoped in the Lord!

4) From the morning watch until night, from the morning watch, let Israel hope in the Lord!

3) For, with the Lord there is mercy, and with Him is plenteous redemption! And He will deliver Israel from all his iniquities!

2) Praise the Lord, all nations! Praise Him, all peoples!

1) For, His mercy is confirmed on us, and the truth of the Lord endures forever!

If there are three stikhera sung after "Let My Prayer Arise" and before the "Glory…, now and ever" stikheron, the reader will chant the longer Psalm verses (beginning with "Set a guard over my mouth, O Lord!"), and then continue, uninterrupted, into the ten refrain verses, stopping at the end of refrain verse # 3, "For, with the Lord there is mercy, and with Him is plenteous redemption! And He will deliver Israel from all his iniquities!" The people then sing the first stikheron. The reader then chants refrain verse # 2, "Praise the Lord, all nations! Praise Him, all peoples!" The people then sing the second stikheron. The reader then chants refrain verse # 1, "For, His mercy is confirmed on us, and the truth of the Lord endures forever!" The people then sing the third stikheron. The reader then chants the "Glory…, now and ever…," and the people conclude by singing the final stikheron.

## "Gladsome Light"

There is **_no_** Vesperal Entrance at Daily Vespers. Therefore, the people *immediately* follow the singing of the "Glory…, now and ever…" stikheron by singing the Vesperal Entrance hymn, "Gladsome Light," which is the central hymn of Vespers, acknowledging Christ as the Light of the world!

## The Evening Prokeimenon

The Evening Prokeimenon is then chanted. The clergy begin by chanting, "Wisdom! Let us be attentive! Peace be with you all!," and then continue, "The Prokeimenon is in the [1st through

8ᵗʰ] tone."  The main verse of the Prokeimenon is then chanted.  The people respond by singing the main verse of the Prokeimenon in the prescribed tone.  This is sung by the people after each verse is chanted by the clergy.  After the last verse is chanted, the priest or deacon then chants the first half of the verse.  The people then respond with the second half of the verse to conclude the Prokeimenon.  In the Greek practice, at the beginning of the Prokeimenon, the deacon will intone, "Evening!  Prokeimenon!", and the singers will intone and sing the entire Prokeimenon themselves.  Also, in the Greek practice, only two verses from the Psalm are intoned.

      The various Prokeimena for Great Vespers, Sunday through Friday evenings, are as follows.  The virgule (or slash, "/") within these Prokeimena designates the first and second halves of the Prokeimena for the final rendition by both the clergy and the people.

Sunday evening: **Tone 8  (Psalm 133)**

> "Come, bless the Lord, / all you servants of the Lord!"*

Monday evening: **Tone 4  (Psalm 4)**

> "The Lord hears / when I call to Him!"

Tuesday evening: **Tone 1  (Psalm 22)**

> "Your mercy, O Lord, / will follow me all the days of my life!"

Wednesday evening: **Tone 5  (Psalm 53)**

> "Save me, O God by Your Name, / and judge me by Your strength!"

Thursday evening: **Tone 6  (Psalm 120)**

> "My help comes from the Lord, / Who made Heaven and Earth!"

Friday evening: **Tone 7  (Psalm 58)**

> "You, O God, are my Helper, / and Your steadfast love will go before me!"

---

*In the Antiochian tradition, this Prokeimenon is, "You who stand in the temple of the Lord, / in the courts of the house of our God!"

## "Vouchsafe, O Lord"

Unlike Resurrectional and Great Vespers, which has the Augmented Litany at this point, Daily Vespers places the Augmented Litany at the **_end_** of the service.  Therefore, in Daily Vespers, the Evening Prokeimenon is **_immediately_** following by "Vouchsafe, O Lord" being chanted by a reader.

## Litany of Supplication

The Litany of Supplication is chanted.  The first two petitions of the Litany are responded to by the people with the singing of  "Lord, have mercy."  When the priest or deacon chants the petition, "That the whole evening may be perfect, holy, peaceful, and sinless, let us ask of the Lord," the people respond with singing, "Grant it, O Lord."  This is done for the remaining petitions until, again, the petition that begins, "Commemorating our most holy,…," with the people responding, "To You, O Lord."  After an exclamation by the priest and the "Amen" by the people, the priest faces the people and, blessing them, says, "Peace be with you all!"  The people then respond by singing, "And with your spirit!"  The priest or deacon then says, "Bow your heads unto the Lord." The people sing, "To You, O Lord." The priest reads a prayer, ending with an exclamation, to which the people respond with, "Amen."

## Daily Apostikha Stikhera

The Daily Apostikha stikhera are sung. After each stikheron, a refrain verse is chanted by a reader. There is no need to number these refrain verses, since there are fixed refrain verses for the day. There are two sets of refrain verses: one for Sunday through Thursday evenings, and one for Friday evenings. These two sets of refrain verses are as follows:

### Sunday through Thursday evenings:

- To You, I lift up my eyes, You Who are enthroned in the Heavens. Behold, as the eyes of servants look to the hand of their master, as the eyes of a maiden to the hand of her mistress; so, our eyes look to the Lord our God, until He has mercy on us.

- Have mercy on us, O Lord; have mercy on us! For, we have had more than enough of contempt. Too long our soul has been sated with the scorn of those who are at ease, the contempt of the proud.

### Friday evenings:

- Blessed are those whom You have chosen and taken, O Lord!

- Their memory is from generation to generation! Their souls will dwell with the blessed!

Before the final stikheron, the reader chants the "Glory…, now and ever…" as the refrain verse.

## St. Symeon's Prayer

A reader then chants St. Symeon's Prayer, "Lord, Now Let Your Servant". In the Greek practice, the priest chants this prayer.

## Trisagion Prayers

The reader then ***immediately***, at the conclusion of St. Symeon's Prayer, reads the Trisagion Prayers, which consist of the following: "Holy God! Holy Mighty! Holy Immortal! Have mercy on us!" chanted **three** times; "Glory to the Father, and to the Son, and to the Holy Spirit, now and ever and unto ages of ages. Amen."; "Most Holy Trinity, have mercy on us! Lord, cleanse us from our sins! Master, pardon our transgressions! Holy One, visit and heal our infirmities, for Your Name's sake!"; "Lord, have mercy" **three** times; another "Glory…now and ever…"; then, the Lord's Prayer. In some parish communities, the Lord's Prayer is said by the entire congregation. After the exclamation by the priest, the people respond with, "Amen."

## Concluding Troparia

The people then sing the concluding troparia of the day. If there is only one troparion, for the tone of the week, the people will sing this troparion, then "Glory..., now and ever...," and then the Theotokion in the tone of the week. If there is more than one troparion, the people will sing a "split Glory," that is, "Glory" until the words, "the Holy Spirit" before the final troparion, then the final troparion, then the remainder of the "Glory" from "now and ever," and then the Theotokion **that is in the _same_ _tone_ as the _final_ troparion!**

## The Augmented Litany

As mentioned before, unlike Resurrectional and Great Vespers, where the Augmented Litany precedes "Vouchsafe, O Lord," at Daily Vespers, the Augmented Litany comes at the end, following the concluding troparia. However, during Great Lent, the Augmented Litany is eliminated from Daily Vespers.

Also, unlike Resurrectional and Great Vespers, the first two "single" petitions ("Let us say with all our soul and with all our mind, let us say..." and "O Lord Almighty, God of our fathers...") are **omitted**. The first petition is "Have mercy on us, O God...", to which the people respond with a "***triple*** 'Lord, have mercy'," that is, "Lord, have mercy" sung **three** times. Each subsequent petition is responded to by singing a ***triple*** "Lord, have mercy." As with the Great Litany, when the priest or deacon gets to the petition that begins, "Commemorating our most holy...," the people respond with, "To You, O Lord." After the exclamation chanted by the priest, the people respond with, "Amen."

## *Dismissal*

The Dismissal begins with the priest or deacon chanting, "Wisdom!" Then, the people respond with "Father, bless!" (or, if a bishop is present, "Master, bless!" If the Metropolitan is present, the people will sing, "Most blessed Master, bless!") The priest says, "Christ, the One Who Is, is blessed always, now and ever and unto ages of ages!" The people respond with "Amen. Preserve, O God, the Holy Orthodox Faith and Orthodox Christians, now and ever and unto ages of ages."

The priest then chants, "Most Holy Theotokos, save us!" The people respond with, "More honorable than the Cherubim and more glorious beyond compare than the Seraphim! Without defilement, you gave Birth to God the Word! True Theotokos, we magnify you!"

During most of the year, the priest then chants, "Glory to You, Christ our God and our Hope, glory to You!" The people then respond with "Glory...now and ever...Amen. Lord, have mercy (*three* times). Father, bless!" (or, if a bishop is present, "Master, bless!" If the Metropolitan is present, the people will sing, "Most blessed Master, bless!") If it is Pascha or Bright Week, the priest will sing "Christ is Risen!" *three* times, and the people will respond also by singing "Christ is Risen!" *three* times. If it is between Bright Week and Ascension, the priest will chant the usual, "Glory to You, Christ our God and our Hope, glory to You!", and the people respond by singing, "Christ is Risen!" *three* times. (Though it is not called for, in some parishes, the practice for the period between Bright Week and Ascension is for the priest to chant "Christ is Risen!" *two-and-a-half* times, with the people responding with the *final half*, "and, upon those in the tombs, bestowing life!" Again, this is purely a local practice in some places, and is *not* called for in the rubrics of the Typikon.) In the Greek practice, the clergy and people sing "Christ is Risen!" **_together_ _three_** times, with the priest coming out of the sanctuary to bless the people with the paschal candle during the third singing.

In any case, the priest will then chant the Dismissal. The people respond with "Amen," sung either once or twice, according to the parish practice. If it is during the time between Pascha and Ascension, the people then sing, "And, unto us, He has given eternal life! Let us worship His Resurrection on the third day!"

## D.  DAILY LENTEN VESPERS

*Doxology*

The doxology for Daily Lenten Vespers is "Blessed is our God, always now and ever and unto ages of ages!" The response (chanted) on the part of a reader is "Amen."

## Psalm 103

The reader then chants the Trisagion Prayers, the Lord's Prayer, "Come, Let Us Worship God, our King!" and Psalm 103, "Bless the Lord, O my soul!". At the conclusion of the Psalm, the reader chants a "Glory…, now and ever…," and then chants "Alleluia! Alleluia! Alleluia! Glory to You, O God!" **three** times.

## The Great Litany

As with **all** forms of Vespers, the Great Litany is then chanted by the clergy, with responses sung by the people. There are eleven petitions, with the people singing, "Lord, have mercy" after each one. However, in some Greek parishes, there are twelve petitions of the Great Litany: Between what is usually the fourth petition ("For this holy house,…!") and the fifth petition ("For His Beatitude, our Metropolitan…!"), there is a petition that states, "For pious and Orthodox Christians, let us pray to the Lord!". When the priest or deacon chants the petition that begins, "Commemorating our most holy, most pure, most blessed and glorious Lady,…," the people respond to that petition with, "To You, O

Lord!" The priest then chants the exclamation, to which the people respond by singing, "Amen."

## Kathisma Reading from the Psalter

Most of the time in Daily Lenten Vespers, the people go directly from the Great Litany to the singing of "Lord, I Call Upon You." In some parishes (as well as in most monasteries), there may be a Kathisma reading from the Psalter. In those cases, the people sing the Great Litany, the reader chants a Kathisma reading from the Psalter, and the people then sing, "Lord, I Call Upon You." In the Greek practice, there is **no** Kathisma reading from the Psalter.

## "Lord, I Call Upon You" and Stikhera

After the singing of "Lord, I Call Upon You" and "Let My Prayer Arise" in the tone of the week, there are **stikhera** (sets of sung verses), with refrain verses in between that are chanted by the reader. Then, the reader chants the "Glory…now and ever…" and the people sing the final stikheron. In the Greek tradition, "Lord, I Call Upon You", "Let My Prayer

Arise", and the stikhera are *not* sung, but chanted by readers.  There are usually three daily stikhera (followed by stikhera from the Menaion) sung before the "Glory."  In the Greek tradition, "Lord, I Call Upon You", "Let My Prayer Arise", and the stikhera are *not* sung, but chanted by readers.

With Daily Lenten Vespers, after the singing of "Let My Prayer Arise," the reader begins chanting with the longer set of verses from the Psalms that begins with "Set a guard over my mouth, O Lord! Keep watch over the door of my lips!"  These verses then go directly into the ten refrain verses that precede the singing of the stikhera.  These ten refrain verses are as follows:

10) Bring my soul out of prison that I may give thanks to Your Name!
9) The righteous will surround me until You deal bountifully with me!
8) Out of the depths, I cry to You, O Lord! Lord, hear my voice!
7) Let Your ears be attentive to the voice of my supplications!
6) If You, O Lord, should mark iniquities, Lord, who could stand?  But, there is forgiveness with You!

Vespers

5) For Your Name's sake, I wait for You, Lord! My soul waits for Your Word! My soul has hoped in the Lord!

4) From the morning watch until night, from the morning watch, let Israel hope in the Lord!

3) For, with the Lord there is mercy, and with Him is plenteous redemption! And He will deliver Israel from all his iniquities!

2) Praise the Lord, all nations! Praise Him, all peoples!

1) For, His mercy is confirmed on us, and the truth of the Lord endures forever!

If there are three stikhera sung after "Let My Prayer Arise" and before the "Glory..., now and ever" stikheron, the reader will chant the longer Psalm verses (beginning with "Set a guard over my mouth, O Lord!"), and then continue, uninterrupted, into the ten refrain verses, stopping at the end of refrain verse # 3, "For, with the Lord there is mercy, and with Him is plenteous redemption! And He will deliver Israel from all his iniquities!" The people then sing the first stikheron. The reader then chants refrain verse # 2, "Praise the Lord, all nations! Praise Him, all peoples!" The people then sing the second stikheron. The reader then chants refrain verse # 1, "For, His mercy is confirmed on us, and the truth of the Lord endures forever!" The people then sing the third stikheron. The reader then chants the "Glory…, now and ever…," and the people conclude by singing the final stikheron.

## "Gladsome Light"

There is **no** Vesperal Entrance at Daily Lenten Vespers. Therefore, the reader *immediately* follows the singing of the "Glory…, now and ever…" stikheron by chanting the Vesperal Entrance hymn, "Gladsome Light," which is the central hymn of Vespers, acknowledging Christ as the Light of the world!

## The Evening Prokeimenon

The Evening Prokeimenon is then chanted. The clergy begin by chanting, "Wisdom! Let us be attentive!  Peace be with you all!," and then continue, "The Prokeimenon is in the [1$^{st}$ through 8$^{th}$] tone."  The main verse of the Prokeimenon is then chanted.  The people respond by singing the main verse of the Prokeimenon in the prescribed tone.  This is sung by the people after each verse is chanted by the clergy.  After the last verse is chanted, the priest or deacon then chants the first half of the verse.  The people then respond with the second half of the verse to conclude the Prokeimenon.  In the Greek practice, at the beginning of the Prokeimenon, the deacon will intone, "Evening!  Prokeimenon!", and the singers will intone and sing the entire Prokeimenon themselves.  Also, in the Greek practice, only two verses from the Psalm are intoned.

The various Prokeimena for Daily Lenten Vespers, Sunday through Friday evenings, are as follows.  The virgule (or slash, "/") within these Prokeimena designates the first and second halves of the Prokeimena for the final rendition by both the clergy and the people.

Sunday evening: **Tone 8 (Psalm 133)**
"Come, bless the Lord, / all you servants of the Lord!"*

Monday evening: **Tone 4 (Psalm 4)**
"The Lord hears / when I call to Him!"

Tuesday evening: **Tone 1 (Psalm 22)**
"Your mercy, O Lord, / will follow me all the days of my life!"

Wednesday evening: **Tone 5 (Psalm 53)**
"Save me, O God by Your Name, / and judge me by Your strength!"

Thursday evening: **Tone 6 (Psalm 120)**
"My help comes from the Lord, / Who made Heaven and Earth!"

Friday evening: **Tone 7 (Psalm 58)**
"You, O God, are my Helper, / and Your steadfast love will go before me!"

---

*In the Antiochian tradition, this Prokeimenon is, "You who stand in the temple of the Lord, / in the courts of the house of our God!"

## Old Testament Readings

During Great Lent, **two** Old Testament readings are chanted by a reader or readers at this point in Daily Vespers, the first reading from Genesis and the second reading from Proverbs.

## "Vouchsafe, O Lord"

Unlike Resurrectional and Great Vespers, which has the Augmented Litany at this point, Daily Lenten Vespers places the Augmented Litany at the **end** of the service. Therefore, in Daily Lenten Vespers, the Evening Prokeimenon is **immediately** following by "Vouchsafe, O Lord" being chanted by a reader.

## Litany of Supplication

The Litany of Supplication is chanted. The first two petitions of the Litany are responded to by the people with the singing of "Lord, have mercy." When the priest or deacon chants the petition, "That the whole evening may be perfect, holy, peaceful, and sinless, let us ask of the Lord," the people respond with singing, "Grant it, O Lord." This is done for the remaining petitions until, again, the petition that begins, "Commemorating our most holy,...," with the people responding, "To You, O Lord." After an exclamation by the priest and the "Amen" by the people, the priest faces the people and, blessing them, says, "Peace be with you all!" The people then respond by singing, "And with your spirit!" The priest or deacon then says, "Bow your heads unto the Lord." The people sing, "To You, O Lord." The priest reads a prayer, ending with an exclamation, to which the people respond with, "Amen."

### *Daily Apostikha Stikhera*

The Daily Apostikha stikhera are sung. After each stikheron, a refrain verse is chanted by a reader. There is no need to number these refrain verses, since there are fixed refrain verses for the day. There are two sets of refrain verses: one for Sunday through Thursday evenings, and one for Friday evenings. These two sets of refrain verses are as follows:

### *Sunday through Thursday evenings:*

- To You, I lift up my eyes, You Who are enthroned in the Heavens. Behold, as the eyes of servants look to the hand of their master, as the eyes of a maiden to the hand of her mistress; so, our eyes look to the Lord our God, until He has mercy on us.

- Have mercy on us, O Lord; have mercy on us! For, we have had more than enough of contempt. Too long our soul has been sated with the scorn of those who are at ease, the contempt of the proud.

### *Friday evenings:*

- Blessed are those whom You have chosen and taken, O Lord!

- Their memory is from generation to generation! Their souls will dwell with the blessed!

Before the final stikheron, the reader chants the "Glory..., now and ever..." as the refrain verse.

**St. Symeon's Prayer**

A reader then chants St. Symeon's Prayer, "Lord, Now Let Your Servant". In the Greek practice, the priest chants this prayer.

**Trisagion Prayers**

The reader then ***immediately***, at the conclusion of St. Symeon's Prayer, reads the Trisagion Prayers, which consist of the following: "Holy God! Holy Mighty! Holy Immortal! Have mercy on us!" chanted **three** times; "Glory to the Father, and to the Son, and to the Holy Spirit, now and ever and unto ages of ages. Amen."; "Most Holy Trinity, have mercy on us! Lord, cleanse us from our sins! Master, pardon our transgressions! Holy One, visit and heal our infirmities, for Your Name's sake!"; "Lord, have mercy" **three** times; another "Glory...now and ever..."; then, the Lord's Prayer. In some parish communities, the Lord's Prayer is said by the entire congregation. After the exclamation by the priest, the people respond with, "Amen."

### Concluding Lenten Troparia

Then, there are special Lenten troparia that are sung at this point, in tone 5: "Rejoice, O Virgin!", then a ***prostration*** is done; then, the singing of "Glory…Spirit!" and "O baptizer of Christ, remember us all!", and then a ***prostration***; then, the singing of "Now and ever…Amen." and "Intercede, O holy Apostles!", and then a ***prostration***; and then, the singing of "Beneath your compassion!", followed by a ***metania*** (bow).

### Concluding Readings and Prayer of St. Ephraim

During Great Lent, there are concluding readings chanted by a reader, which are then followed by the Prayer of St. Ephraim. At the end of the singing of the concluding troparia, the reader chants the following: "Lord, have mercy." (***three*** times); "Glory…, now and ever…"; "More honorable than the Cherubim…"; "In the Name of the Lord, Father (or, Master) bless." The priest or bishop then gives the exclamation that begins, "May Christ our true God." (In the Antiochian tradition, the exclamation begins, "Christ, the One Who Is!".) The reader then chants the following: "Amen. O Heavenly King, establish the Orthodox Christians! Confirm the Faith! Quiet the heathen! Give peace to the world! Place our departed fathers and brethren in the tabernacles of the righteous, and accept us sorrowers and penitents! For, You are good and the Lover of mankind!"

The Prayer of St. Ephraim, with interspersed prostrations and metania, is then chanted. Since the Augmented Litany is eliminated from Daily Vespers during Great Lent, the Dismissal immediately follows the conclusion of the Prayer of St. Ephraim.

At this point, in the Antiochian tradition, the reader chants the Trisagion Prayers and the Lord's Prayer, with the exclamation and the "Amen." Then, the reader chants, "Lord, have mercy." **twelve** times. The celebrant then intones a prayer that begins, "O All-Holy Trinity,…!" The people then sing, "Blessed Be the Name of the Lord!" **three** times, with a prostration after each time. The reader then chants Psalm 33 ("I will bless the Lord at all times!"). When the celebrant intones, "Wisdom!", the reader chants, "It is Truly Meet!" The celebrant intones, "Most holy Theotokos, save us!" The reader chants, "More honorable than the Cherubim!…" The celebrant intones, "Glory to You, O Christ our God and our Hope, glory to You!" The reader chants a full "Glory,...now and ever...!", a ***triple*** "Lord, have mercy.", and then, "Father (or, if a bishop is present, "Master, bless!" If the Metropolitan is present, the people will sing, "Most blessed Master"), bless! The Dismissal Prayer is then intoned.

As mentioned before, at Daily Lenten Vespers, the Augmented Litany is eliminated.

## *Dismissal*

The Dismissal begins with the priest or deacon chanting, "Wisdom!" Then, the people respond with "Father, bless!" (or, if a bishop is present, "Master, bless!" If the Metropolitan is present, the people will sing, "Most blessed Master, bless!") The priest says, "Christ, the One Who Is, is blessed always, now and ever and unto ages of ages!" The people respond with "Amen. Preserve, O God, the Holy Orthodox Faith and Orthodox Christians, now and ever and unto ages of ages."

The priest then chants, "Most Holy Theotokos, save us!" The people respond with, "More honorable than the Cherubim and more glorious beyond compare than the Seraphim! Without defilement, you gave Birth to God the Word! True Theotokos, we magnify you!"

The priest will then chant the Dismissal. The people respond with "Amen," sung either once or twice, according to the parish practice.

# 2
# MATINS


## A.  RESURRECTIONAL MATINS

When it comes to Matins, there is a difference in practice between the Byzantine (Greek) and Slavic (Russian) styles.  When both Vespers **_and_** Matins are to be celebrated (either for a Sunday or for a feast), they are usually celebrated **_separately_** in the Byzantine practice, but usually celebrated **_together_** (as a **_Vigil_** service) in the Slavic practice.[5]

**_Doxology_**

If a Vigil (both Resurrectional Vespers and Resurrectional Matins together) is to be celebrated according to the Slavic practice, there is **_no_** Doxology at the beginning of Resurrectional Matins.  The

---

[5] Cf. Mother Mary and Ware, Archimandrite Kallistos, *The Festal Menaion*, Faber and Faber, London, 1977, p. 70, footnote 1.

Doxology for the Vigil is exclaimed **at the beginning of Resurrectional <u>Vespers</u>**.[6]  In this case, the reader will begin the Matins at the beginning of the Six Psalms, with no introductory exclamation by the clergy.

If, however, Resurrectional Matins is to be celebrated separately from Resurrectional Vespers (as per the Byzantine practice), then the Matins will begin with the exclamation by the priest (or bishop), "Blessed is our God, always now and ever and unto ages of ages!"  The reader then chants, "Amen," followed by Psalms 19 and 20 (these Psalms are **not** done at this point in the Byzantine practice, but only during Daily Lenten Matins).  After this, the reader chants "Glory to You, our God, glory to You!", "O Heavenly King!", the Trisagion Prayers ("Holy God!..." **three** times; "Glory,...now and ever...;" "Most Holy Trinity, have mercy on us!...;" "Lord, have mercy" **three** times; "Glory,...now and ever...;" "Our Father,...!").  This is followed by special troparia (the same troparia that the clergy use in their Entrance Prayers before the Divine Liturgy) that, in the Slavic tradition, are:  "O Lord, save Your

---

[6] Cf. "Doxology" in chapter 1, "Vespers", p. 1.

people,…;" "Glory… Spirit!"; "We venerate Your most pure image,…!"; "now and ever…"; "Blessed Theotokos, open the doors of compassion to us…!". In the Byzantine tradition, after "O Lord, save Your people,…!" and "Glory… Spirit!", the troparion is "Do You, Who, of Your own good will,…!", then "Now and ever…Amen.", then "O dread champion, who cannot be put to confusion,…!". Then, there is an abbreviated Augmented Litany, consisting of the first three petitions, the response for each being "Lord, have mercy" sung **three** times, then an exclamation, and an "Amen." After this, the reader chants, "In the Name of the Lord, Father (or, if it be a bishop, "Master"; or, if it be the Metropolitan, "Most blessed Master"), bless!", and then the priest (or bishop) exclaims, "Glory to the Holy, consubstantial, life-creating and undivided Trinity, always now and ever and unto ages of ages!" The reader responds with "Amen." The reader then continues by chanting "Glory to God in the highest and, on Earth, peace, good will towards men!" **three** times, and "Lord, open my lips, and my mouth will show forth Your praise!" **two** times. The reader then proceeds to chant the Six Psalms. (This entire elaborate opening is a remnant of an imperial office, originating in monasteries founded by the Byzantine emperor.)

    In many parishes, there is an abbreviated version of the above. When following this celebration of Matins separate from Vespers, these parishes will begin with "Blessed is our God…," followed by the "Amen", "Glory to You, our God, glory to You!", "O Heavenly King!", the Trisagion Prayers, and the Lord's Prayer, with the "Amen" following the Lord's Prayer, the "Amen." and "In the Name of the Lord, Father (or, if it be a bishop, "Master"; or, if it be the Metropolitan, "Most blessed Master"), bless!"; then, the exclamation, "Glory to the Holy, consubstantial, life-creating and undivided Trinity, always now and ever and unto ages of ages!" The reader responds with "Amen." The reader then continues by chanting "Glory to God in the highest and, on Earth, peace, good will towards men!" **three** times, and "Lord, open my lips, and my mouth will show forth Your praise!" **two** times. The reader then proceeds to chant the Six Psalms.

### The Six Psalms

The reader chants the Six Psalms of Matins, Psalms 3, 37, 62, 87, 102, and 143. After the third Psalm (62) is chanted, it is customary to chant, "Glory,...now and ever...," "Alleluia! Alleluia! Alleluia! Glory to You, O God!" **three** times, "Lord, have mercy" **three** times, and then, once again, "Glory,...now and ever."

Also, it is customary in many parishes to have **two** readers chant the Six Psalms. In that case, the practice is for the **first** reader to chant the **first** three Psalms (through Psalm 62), then the "Glory,...now and ever," the "Alleluia!" and "Lord, have mercy" elements, each **three** times, then a "**split** 'Glory'," with the first reader chanting the final "Glory" through the words, "the Holy Spirit." The **second** reader then takes up the **second** half of this final "Glory" with the words, "now and ever and unto ages of ages. Amen." The **second** reader then proceeds with chanting the **second** three of the Six Psalms, beginning with Psalm 87. In the Greek practice there is **no** "split 'Glory'": The first reader would chant the full "Glory,... now and ever...!", and the second reader would begin chanting Psalm 87.

## The Great Litany

As with **all** forms of Matins, the Great Litany is then chanted by the clergy, with responses sung by the people. There are eleven petitions, with the people singing, "Lord, have mercy" after each one. However, in some Greek parishes, there are twelve petitions of the Great Litany: Between what is usually the fourth petition ("For this holy house,…!") and the fifth petition ("For His Beatitude, our Metropolitan…!"), there is a petition that states, "For pious and Orthodox Christians, let us pray to the Lord!". When the priest or deacon chants the petition that begins, "Commemorating our most holy, most pure, most blessed and glorious Lady,…," the people respond to that petition with, "To You, O Lord!" The priest then chants the exclamation, to which the people respond by singing, "Amen."

## "God is the Lord" and Troparia

The singing of "God is the Lord" and the troparion or troparia for the day is then sung. "God is the Lord" is chanted in the tone *of **the first***

***troparion* to be sung**.  The singing of "God is the Lord" is interspersed with verses Psalm 117, chanted by the deacon (or priest, if there is no deacon serving).  Once the Six Psalms are concluded, the chanting between the deacon and the people is as follows (in the Byzantine tradition, the deacon does **not** start the "God is the Lord".  Rather, a reader chants, "O give thanks to the Lord, for He is good! For, His steadfast love endures forever!", and the rest proceeds as presented below, with a reader being substituted for the deacon):

**Deacon:** God is the Lord, and has revealed Himself to us.  Blessed is He Who comes in the Name of the Lord!  O give thanks to the Lord, for He is good!  For, His steadfast love endures forever!

**People:** God is the Lord, and has revealed Himself to us.  Blessed is He Who comes in the Name of the Lord!

**Deacon:** All nations surrounded me!  But, in the Name of the Lord, I destroyed them!

***People:*** God is the Lord, and has revealed Himself to us. Blessed is He Who comes in the Name of the Lord!

***Deacon:*** I will not die, but live, and recount the deeds of the Lord!

***People:*** God is the Lord, and has revealed Himself to us. Blessed is He Who comes in the Name of the Lord!

***Deacon:*** The stone that the builders has become the head of the corner! This is the Lord's doing, and it is marvelous in our eyes!

***People:*** God is the Lord, and has revealed Himself to us. Blessed is He Who comes in the Name of the Lord!

In the Greek tradition, instead of four interspersed verses from Psalm 117, **some** parishes celebrate ***only*** **three**! The one that is **omitted** is, "I will not die, but live, and recount the deeds of the Lord!".

## Kathisma, Kathisma Hymns, Polyeleos, Evlogitaria, Hypakoe, and Hymns of Degrees

For Resurrectional Matins, Kathisma 2 (Psalms 9-16) and Kathisma 3 (Psalms 17-23 ) are called for, but are **almost always omitted** in parish practice. (During Great Lent, Kathisma 17 [Psalm 118] is also called for, but this is usually omitted in parish practice.)  These are interspersed with Kathisma Hymns in the tone of the week, along with the Polyeleos (meaning, "many praises," verses taken from Psalms 134 and 135), the Evlogitaria (beginning with the words, "Blessed are You, O Lord!  Teach me Your statutes!"), and the Hypakoe, a troparion (in the tone of the week) in preparation for the Resurrectional Matins Gospel, emphasizing the discovery of the empty tomb by the myrrh-bearing women.  Kathisma Hymns are also known as "Sedalen" or "Sessional Hymns."

The Polyeleos is prescribed to be sung on all Sundays from the Leavetaking of the Exaltation of the Holy Cross (22 September) through Forgiveness (Cheesefare) Sunday.  However, in parish practice, the Polyeleos is **usually** sung all year round.

Furthermore, in the Byzantine tradition, the Polyeleos is sung **only** for certain feasts.

After the Hypakoe, the First Antiphon of the Hymn of Degrees (beginning with the words, "From My Youth") is called for to be sung in the $4^{th}$ tone in the Slavic tradition, but is usually done only at Festal Matins for major feasts. In the Byzantine tradition, instead of "From My Youth", the Antiphons for the tone of the week are sung.

Little Litanies are also interspersed here. The content of a Little Litany is as follows:

*Deacon:* Again and again, in peace, let us pray to the Lord.

*People:* Lord, have mercy.

*Deacon:* Help us, save us, have mercy on us, and keep us, O God, by Your grace.

*People:* Lord, have mercy.

***Deacon:*** Commemorating our most holy, most pure, most blest and glorious Lady, the Theotokos and ever-Virgin Mary, with all the saints, let us commend ourselves and each other and all our life unto Christ our God.

***People:*** To You, O Lord.

***Priest:*** For, to You are due all glory, honor, and worship: to the Father, and to the Son, and to the Holy Spirit, now and ever and unto ages of ages.

***People:*** Amen.

The order, then, for this entire "block" of liturgical elements is as follows:

- 1st Kathisma reading from the Psalter
- Little Litany
- Kathisma Hymn
- 2nd Kathisma reading from the Psalter

- Little Litany
- Kathisma Hymn
- Polyeleos
- Evlogitaria
- Little Litany
- Hypakoe
- Hymn of Degrees: First Antiphon in Tone 4

In the Greek practice, however, the order for this entire "block" of liturgical elements is as follows:

- 1$^{st}$ Kathisma Hymns (3 per set)
- "Glory,… now and ever…!"
- 2$^{nd}$ Kathisma Hymns (3 per set)
- Evlogitaria
- Little Litany
- Hypakoe
- Hymn of Degrees: First Antiphon in Tone 4

## Prokeimena and Resurrectional Matins Gospel

At this point, the Prokeimenon in the tone of the week is chanted.  This is followed by a litany petition and exclamation, and then by a fixed Prokeimenon.  After this, one of the eleven prescribed Resurrectional Matins Gospels is chanted, **except** in the Greek practice, whereby the chanting of the Resurrectional Matins Gospel is moved, being celebrated after the 3$^{rd}$ ode of the Kanon.  The order for these elements is as follows (in the Byzantine tradition, the deacon is replaced with a reader doing the chanting):

> ***Deacon:***     Wisdom!  Let us be attentive!
>
> ***Priest:***     Peace be with you all!
>
> ***Deacon:***     And with your spirit!
>
> ***Priest:***     Wisdom!
>
> ***Deacon:***     The Prokeimenon is in the [1$^{st}$ – 8$^{th}$] tone:  [chants ***first*** Prokeimenon verse].
>
> ***People:***     [sing ***first*** Prokeimenon verse].

| | |
|---|---|
| ***Deacon:*** | [chants ***second*** Prokeimenon verse]. |
| ***People:*** | [sing ***<u>first</u>*** Prokeimenon verse]. |
| ***Deacon:*** | [chants ***<u>first half</u>*** of ***<u>first</u>*** Prokeimenon verse]. |
| ***People:*** | [sing ***<u>second half</u>*** of ***<u>first</u>*** Prokeimenon verse]. |
| ***Deacon:*** | Let us pray to the Lord. |
| ***People:*** | Lord, have mercy. |
| ***Priest:*** | For, You are holy, our God, Who rest in the saints, and unto You do we ascribe glory: to the Father, and to the Son, and to the Holy Spirit, now and ever and unto ages of ages. |
| ***People:*** | Amen. |
| ***Deacon:*** | Let every breath praise the Lord! |
| ***People:*** | Let every breath praise the Lord! [sung in the tone of the week] |
| ***Deacon:*** | Praise God in His sanctuary! Praise Him in His mighty firmament! |
| ***People:*** | Let every breath praise the Lord! |

*Matins*

***Deacon****:* Let every breath!

***People:*** Praise the Lord!

***Deacon:*** And that we may be made worthy to listen to the Holy Gospel, let us pray to the Lord our God!

***People:*** Lord, have mercy. **(3)** [meaning, sung **three** times]

***Deacon:*** Wisdom! Let us be attentive! Let us listen to the Holy Gospel!

***Priest:*** Peace be with you all!

***People:*** And with your spirit!

***Priest:*** The Reading is from the Holy Gospel according to Saint [Matthew, Mark, Luke, **or** John the Theologian]!

***People:*** Glory to You, our God, glory to You!

***Deacon:*** Let us be attentive!

***Priest:*** [reads the prescribed Resurrectional Matins Gospel.]

***People:*** Glory to You, our God, glory to You!

In the Greek practice, at the beginning of the Prokeimenon, the deacon will intone, "Evening! Prokeimenon!", and the singers will intone and sing the entire Prokeimenon themselves. Also, in the Greek practice, **only two** verses from the Psalm are intoned.

### "Having Beheld the Resurrection of Christ", Psalm 50, and Troparion

After the Resurrectional Matins Gospel, the hymn, "Having Beheld the Resurrection of Christ!" is celebrated (in the Slavic tradition, the people sing it; in the Byzantine tradition, a reader chants it). This is followed, in the Slavic tradition, by a reader chanting Psalm 50, concluding with, "Glory, ...now and ever...!," and then, "Alleluia! Alleluia! Alleluia! Glory to You, O God!" **three** times. The people then sing the Resurrectional troparion. In the Byzantine tradition, Psalm 50 is chanted antiphonally, in tone 6, with**out** concluding with the "Glory,... now and ever...!" or "Alleluia!" elements. Also, in the Greek practice, the priest comes out with the Gospel Book towards the end of the chanting of Psalm 50, and the people come forward to venerate it.

Furthermore, in the Byzantine tradition, there are stikhera sung at this point, in tone 2: "Glory…Spirit!", "Through the intercessions of the Apostles,…!", "Now and ever…Amen.", and "Through the intercessions of the Theotokos,…!". Then, "Have mercy on me, O God,…!" and "Jesus has Risen from the tomb,…!".

## Litany of Intercession

The Litany of Intercession is now chanted, with the deacon chanting the petition that begins, "O God, save Your people and bless Your inheritance." This long petition, asking for the prayers of numerous saints, is responded to by the people singing "Lord, have mercy" **twelve** times. The priest then gives an exclamation that begins, "Through the mercy and compassion…," to which the people respond by singing "Amen."

## The Kanon

The Kanon is a structured hymn, consisting of nine **odes**, sometimes called **canticles** or **songs** depending on the translation, based on the Biblical canticles. Most of these are found in the Old Testament, but the final ode is taken from the Magnificat and the Song of Zechariah in the New Testament. For clarity, we will use the term "canticle" to refer to the original biblical text, and "ode" to refer to the composed liturgical hymns. An ode is also referred to as an "heirmos" or "irmos" (pronounced, "EAR-mose"). After each heirmos, troparia and refrains are chanted, usually by two different readers. In this case, the troparia are verses that expound the theme of the heirmos being sung. After the heirmos, a reader will chant a refrain appropriate for the day, such as, "Glory to You, our God, glory to You!" or "Glory to Your Holy Resurrection, O Lord!" The other reader will then chant a troparion. The first reader will then alternately chant the same refrain between the remaining troparia. However, before the final troparion, the "refrain" reader will chant a "Glory,...now and ever....". In the Antiochian practice, the troparia for Resurrectional Matins are **not** celebrated, but **only** the heirmos and the

Katavasia.  Furthermore, in the Greek tradition, the troparia and Katavasia are *not* celebrated, and the heirmos is chanted by a reader, *not* sung by the people.

The Kanon dates from the 7th century and was either devised or introduced into the Greek language by St. Andrew of Crete, whose penitential Great Kanon is still used in Grand Compline during Great Lent.  It was further developed in the 8th century by Ss. John of Damascus and Cosmas of Jerusalem, and in the 9th century by Ss. Joseph the Hymnographer and Theophanes the Branded.

Over time the Kanon (coming from Palestinian monastic usage) came to replace the Kontakion (which grew out of the cathedral practice of Constantinople), a form of which is still used on several occasions and that has been incorporated into the performance of the Kanon (after the $6^{th}$ ode).  Each Kanon develops a specific theme, such as repentance or honouring a particular saint.  Sometimes more than one Kanon can be chanted together, as frequently happens at Matins.  However, in parish practice, usually just one Kanon is celebrated, and, on Sundays, this is the Kanon of the Resurrection.

The nine biblical canticles are:

1. The Song of Moses in Exodus (Exodus 15: 1-19)
2. The Song of Moses in Deuteronomy (Deuteronomy 32: 1-43)
3. The Prayer of Anna the mother of Samuel the Prophet (1 Samuel 2: 1-10)
4. The Prayer of Habakkuk the Prophet (Habakkuk 3: 2-19)
5. The Prayer of Isaiah the Prophet (Isaiah 26: 9-20)
6. The Prayer of Jonah the Prophet (Jonah 2: 3-10)
7. The Prayer of the Three Holy Youths (Daniel 3:26-56)*
8. The Song of the Three Holy Youths (Daniel 3:57-88)*

*These odes are found only in the Septuagint.

9. The Song of the Theotokos (The ***Magnificat***, Luke 1: 46-55) and the Prayer of Zechariah, the father of John the Baptist (The ***Benedictus***, Luke 1: 68-79)

These biblical canticles are normally found in the back of the Psalter used by Orthodox churches, where they are often printed with markings to indicate where to begin inserting the irmos and troparia of the canons.

Ode 2 (from Moses in Deuteronomy) is a penitential ode, so it is **only** sung during Great Lent. Therefore, during the rest of the year, the order of the odes sung is ode 1, then odes 3 through 9.

After ode 3, a Kathisma Hymn is sung. In the Greek practice, however, after ode 3, the Resurrectional Matins Gospel is chanted by the celebrant standing on the south (right-hand) side of the altar. After ode 6, the Kontakion and Oikos are celebrated. The Oikos (pronounced, "EE-kose," from the Greek word meaning "house") was originally a set of eighteen to twenty-four metrically identical stanzas. In modern practice, it consists of only one stanza, which ends with the last verse of the

Kontakion. So, after the 6th ode, the Kontakion is sung. Then, a reader chants the text of the Oikos, stopping just before the last verse of the Kontakion, which is then again sung by the people. In the Greek tradition, both the Kontakion and the Oikos are chanted by a reader, rather than sung by the people. In the Byzantine practice, a reading from the Synaxarion, about the lives of saints, is read. After this, the Kanon continues with ode 7.

In the Byzantine tradition, before the 9th ode, the deacon comes out and, standing on the solea in front of the icon of the Theotokos, he chants, "The Theotokos and the Mother of the Light, let us honor and magnify in song!". After the 9th ode and troparia, the 9th ode is usually then repeated as a **Katavasia** (pronounced, "kaht-ah-vah-SEE-ah"). This is from the Greek word meaning "descent," so called because, in the early Church, the cantors used to go down from their stalls and unite in the middle of the choir to sing them. There are Katavasia at the end of every ode. They usually anticipate the next feast. Therefore, Katavasia for Christmas are chanted from 21 November until the feast. In modern parish practice, however, **only** ode 9 is repeated as a Katavasia after its troparia are chanted.

The usual order, then, for the Kanon, is as follows:

- Ode 1
- Ode 3
- [Little Litany, usually omitted]
- Kathisma Hymn
- Ode 4
- Ode 5
- Ode 6
- [Little Litany, usually omitted]
- Kontakion and Oikos
- Synaxarion reading  (Byzantine practice)
- Ode 7
- Ode 8
- Ode 9
- Katavasia of Ode 9
- Little Litany [usually *__not__* omitted]

## "Holy is the Lord our God"

"Holy is the Lord our God" is then chanted by the deacon (or priest) in the Slavic tradition and by a reader in the Byzantine tradition, and responded to by the people. The final singing of it by the people usually has a cadential ending, to signify its conclusion.

**Deacon:** Holy is the Lord our God!

**People:** Holy is the Lord our God!

**Deacon:** For, Holy is the Lord our God!

**People:** Holy is the Lord our God!

**Deacon:** Over all people is our God!

**People:** Holy is the <u>Lord</u> our <u>God</u>!

In the Greek practice, readers chant "Holy is the Lord our God!", rather than a deacon. Also, for the third time, instead of, "Over all people is our God!", the verse is, "Exalt the Lord our God, and worship at His footstool!  For, He is holy!".

## The Exapostilarion (Hymn of Light)

The Exapostilarion (Hymn of Light) is then sung. The term "exapostilarion" is related to the word Apostle, which itself is derived from a Greek word meaning "sent out." It has this name because in ancient times a chanter was sent out from the choir into the center of the church to chant this hymn. The exapostilarion asks God to enlighten the minds of the faithful that they might worthily praise the Lord in the verses of the Praises that follow, and in the Great Doxology. On Sundays, the theme of the Exapostilarion reflects the concept of the Myrrh-Bearing Women sent to bring the Good News (Gospel) of the Resurrection of Christ to the Apostles, and is drawn from the Resurrection Gospel that was chanted before the Kanon.

## The Praises, with Stikhera

The Praises (Psalms 148, 149, and 150) are an integral part of Matins. The intent is that the Praises will be chanted as the sun begins to arise, culminating with either the Great Doxology or the

Lesser Doxology, and the Apolytikion (troparion of the day). The praises start with the singing of "Let every breath praise the Lord! Praise the Lord in Heaven! Praise Him in the highest! To You, O God, is due a song!" and "Praise Him, all you angels of His! Praise Him, all His hosts! To You, O God, is due a song!".

On Sundays and feast days, there are special stikhera that are chanted between the Psalm verses of the Praises. In these cases the Psalm verses and their stikhera will be chanted (sung). On days when there are no troparia appointed, the Psalms will be read simply by the reader.

### *The Great Doxology*

The Great Doxology is an ancient hymn of praise to the Trinity that is chanted or read daily. In Resurrectional Matins, it is chanted. It begins with the exclamation, "Glory to You, Who have shone us the Light!" In the Slavic tradition, this is done by the priest or the bishop. In the Byzantine tradition, this is done by a reader. The people then sing the Great Doxology, which begins with the words, "Glory to

God in the highest, and, on Earth, peace, good will towards men!" The Great Doxology ends with the Trisagion.

## Resurrectional Troparion

At this point, one of two special troparia for the Resurrection is sung. The determining factor for which troparion is sung is whether the tone of the week is an odd-numbered or even-numbered tone.
Therefore, when the tone of the week is tone 1, 3, 5, or 7 in the Slavic tradition or tone 1, 2, 3, or 4 in the Byzantine tradition, the following troparion (in tone 4) will be sung:

> Today, salvation has come to the world! Let us sing praises to Him Who arose from the grave, the Author of our life! For, by death, He has destroyed death! He gives us the victory and grants us great mercy!

When the tone of the week is tone 2, 4, 6, or 8 in the Slavic tradition or tone 5, 6, 7, or 8 in the Byzantine tradition, the following troparion (in tone 8) will be sung:

> When You arose from the tomb and had burst the bonds of hell, You loosed the condemnation of death, O Lord, redeeming all from the snares of the enemy! When You revealed Yourself to Your Apostles, You sent them forth to proclaim You! Through them, You have granted peace to the world, O only merciful One!

In the Greek practice, regardless of the tone of the week, **only** the troparion "Today, salvation has come to the world!" is sung. The other troparion ("When You arose from the tomb...!") is **never** sung.

### Augmented Litany

The correct practice for the Augmented Litany at Matins is to begin with the petition, "Have mercy on us, O God, according to Your steadfast love, we pray You: Hear us and have mercy," with the people responding with a "***triple*** 'Lord, have mercy'" for each petition.  ***Note:***  In the Byzantine tradition, ***if*** the Divine Liturgy follows Resurrectional Matins, these litanies and the Dismissal are ***not*** done aloud.  Instead, the clergy do them silently during the singing of the Great Doxology, which is then ***immediately*** followed by the beginning of the Divine Liturgy.  However, ***if*** the Divine Liturgy does ***not*** follow Resurrectional Matins, then the litanies and Dismissal ***are*** done as presented here.

Each petition is responded to by singing a "***triple*** 'Lord, have mercy'."  As with the Great Litany, when the priest or deacon gets to the petition that begins, "Commemorating our most holy...," the people respond with, "To You, O Lord."  After the exclamation chanted by the priest, the people respond with, "Amen."


**Litany of Supplication**


The Litany of Supplication is chanted.  The first two petitions of the Litany are responded to by the people with the singing of  "Lord, have mercy."

When the priest or deacon chants the petition, "That the whole evening may be perfect, holy, peaceful, and sinless, let us ask of the Lord," the people respond with singing, "Grant it, O Lord." This is done for the remaining petitions until, again, the petition that begins, "Commemorating our most holy,…," with the people responding, "To You, O Lord." After an exclamation by the priest and the "Amen" by the people, the priest faces the people and, blessing them, says, "Peace be with you all!" The people then respond by singing, "And with your spirit!" The priest or deacon then says, "Bow your heads unto the Lord." The people sing, "To You, O Lord." The priest reads a prayer, ending with an exclamation, to which the people respond with, "Amen."

### *Dismissal*

The Dismissal begins with the priest or deacon chanting, "Wisdom!" Then, the people respond with "Father, bless!" (or, if a bishop is present, "Master, bless!" If the Metropolitan is present, the people will sing, "Most blessed Master, bless!") The priest says, "Christ, the One Who Is, is blessed always, now and ever and unto ages of ages!" The people respond with "Amen. Preserve, O God, the Holy Orthodox Faith and Orthodox Christians, now and ever and unto ages of ages."

The priest then chants, "Most Holy Theotokos, save us!" The people respond with, "More honorable than the Cherubim and more glorious beyond compare than the Seraphim! Without defilement, you gave Birth to God the Word! True Theotokos, we magnify you!"

During most of the year, the priest then says, "Glory to You, Christ our God and our Hope, glory to You!" The people then respond with "Glory...now and ever...Amen. Lord, have mercy (**three** times). Father, bless!" (or, if a bishop is present, "Master, bless!" If the Metropolitan is present, the people will sing, "Most blessed Master, bless!") If it is Pascha or Bright Week, the priest will sing "Christ is Risen!" **three** times, and the people will respond also by singing "Christ is Risen!" **three** times. If it is between Bright Week and Ascension, the priest will sing "Christ is Risen!" **two-and-a-half** times, with the people responding with the **final half**, "and, upon those in the tombs, bestowing life!" In the Greek practice, the clergy and people sing "Christ is Risen!" **together three** times, with the priest coming out of the sanctuary to bless the people with the paschal candle during the third singing.

In any case, the priest will then chant the Dismissal. The people respond with "Amen," sung either once or twice, according to the parish practice. If it is during the time between Pascha and Ascension, the people then sing, "And, unto us, He has given eternal life! Let us worship His Resurrection on the third day!"

As the people come forward to venerate the Holy Cross and the icons, the Resurrectional and/or festal troparia may be sung, according to the parish practice. Then, before closing the Royal Doors, the priest chants, "Through the prayers of our holy fathers, O Lord, Jesus Christ, have mercy on us and save us!". The people then sing "Amen." and, usually, a ***triple*** "Lord, have mercy.". If it is during the Pascha season, after the "Amen.", the people will sing the Paschal troparion ("Christ is Risen from the dead!").

## B. FESTAL MATINS

When it comes to Matins, there is a difference in practice between the Byzantine (Greek) and Slavic (Russian) styles. When both Vespers ***and*** Matins are to be celebrated (either for a Sunday or for a feast), they are usually celebrated *separately* in the Byzantine practice, but usually celebrated *together* (as a *Vigil* service) in the Slavic practice.[7]

## Doxology

If a Vigil (both Great Vespers and Festal Matins together) is to be celebrated according to the Slavic practice, there is **_no_** Doxology at the beginning of Festal Matins.  The Doxology for the Vigil is exclaimed *at the beginning of Great Vespers*.[8]  In this case, the reader will begin the Matins at the beginning of the Six Psalms, with no introductory exclamation by the clergy.

If, however, Festal Matins *is* to be celebrated separately from Great Vespers (as per the Byzantine practice), then the Matins will begin with the exclamation by the priest (or bishop), "Blessed is our God, always now and ever and unto ages of ages!" The reader then chants, "Amen," followed by Psalms

---

[7] Cf. Mother Mary and Ware, Archimandrite Kallistos, *The Festal Menaion*, Faber and Faber, London, 1977, p. 70, footnote 1.

[8] Cf. "Doxology" in chapter 1, "Vespers", p. 1.

19 and 20 (these Psalms are **not** done at this point in the Byzantine practice, but only during Daily Lenten Matins). After this, the reader chants "Glory to You, our God, glory to You!", "O Heavenly King!", the Trisagion Prayers ("Holy God!..." **three** times; "Glory,...now and ever...;" "Most Holy Trinity, have mercy on us!...;" "Lord, have mercy" **three** times; "Glory,...now and ever...;" "Our Father,...!"). This is followed by special troparia (the same troparia that the clergy use in their Entrance Prayers before the Divine Liturgy) that, in the Slavic tradition, are: "O Lord, save Your people,...;" "Glory... Spirit!"; "We venerate Your most pure image,...!"; "now and ever..."; "Blessed Theotokos, open the doors of compassion to us...!". In the Byzantine tradition, after "O Lord, save Your people,...!" and "Glory... Spirit!", the troparion is "Do You, Who, of Your own good will,...!", then "Now and ever...Amen.", then "O dread champion, who cannot be put to confusion,...!". Then, there is an abbreviated Augmented Litany, consisting of the first three petitions, the response for each being "Lord, have mercy" sung **three** times, then an exclamation, and an "Amen." After this, the reader chants, "In the Name of the Lord, Father (or, if it be a bishop, "Master"; or, if it be the Metropolitan, "Most

blessed Master"), bless!", and then the priest (or bishop) exclaims, "Glory to the Holy, consubstantial, life-creating and undivided Trinity, always now and ever and unto ages of ages!"  The reader responds with "Amen."  The reader then continues by chanting "Glory to God in the highest and, on Earth, peace, good will towards men!" **three** times, and "Lord, open my lips, and my mouth will show forth Your praise!" **two** times.  The reader then proceeds to chant the Six Psalms.  (This entire elaborate opening is a remnant of an imperial office, originating in monasteries founded by the Byzantine emperor.)

    In many parishes, there is an abbreviated version of the above.  When following this celebration of Matins separate from Vespers, these parishes will begin with "Blessed is our God…," followed by the "Amen", "Glory to You, our God, glory to You!", "O Heavenly King!", the Trisagion Prayers, and the Lord's Prayer, with the "Amen" following the Lord's Prayer, the "Amen." and  "In the Name of the Lord, Father (or, if it be a bishop, "Master"; or, if it be the Metropolitan, "Most blessed Master"), bless!"; then, the exclamation, "Glory to the Holy, consubstantial, life-creating and undivided Trinity, always now and ever and unto ages of ages!" The reader responds with "Amen." The reader then continues by chanting "Glory to God in the highest and, on Earth, peace, good will towards men!" *three* times, and "Lord, open my lips, and my mouth will show forth Your praise!" *two* times. The reader then proceeds to chant the Six Psalms.

### The Six Psalms

The reader chants the Six Psalms of Matins, Psalms 3, 37, 62, 87, 102, and 143. After the third Psalm (62) is chanted, it is customary to chant, "Glory,…now and ever…," "Alleluia! Alleluia! Alleluia! Glory to You, O God!" *three* times, "Lord, have mercy" *three* times, and then, once again, "Glory,…now and ever."

Also, it is customary in many parishes to have *two* readers chant the Six Psalms. In that case, the practice is for the *first* reader to chant the *first* three Psalms (through Psalm 62), then the "Glory,…now and ever," the "Alleluia!" and "Lord, have mercy" elements, each *three* times, then a *"split* 'Glory'," with the first reader chanting the final "Glory" through the words, "the Holy Spirit." The **second** reader then takes up the second half of this final "Glory" with the words, "now and ever and unto ages of ages. Amen." The **second** reader then proceeds with chanting the **second** three of the Six Psalms, beginning with Psalm 87. In the Greek practice there is **no** "split 'Glory'": The first reader would chant the full "Glory,... now and ever...!", and the second reader would begin chanting Psalm 87.

**The Great Litany**

As with **all** forms of Matins, the Great Litany is then chanted by the clergy, with responses sung by the people. There are eleven petitions, with the people singing, "Lord, have mercy" after each one. However, in some Greek parishes, there are twelve petitions of the Great Litany: Between what is usually the fourth petition ("For this holy house,...!") and the fifth petition ("For His Beatitude, our Metropolitan...!"), there is a petition that states, "For pious and Orthodox Christians, let us pray to the Lord!". When the priest or deacon chants the petition that begins, "Commemorating our most holy, most pure, most blessed and glorious Lady,...," the people respond to that petition with, "To You, O Lord!" The priest then chants the exclamation, to which the people respond by singing, "Amen."

### "God is the Lord" and Troparia

The singing of "God is the Lord" and the troparion or troparia for the day is then sung. "God is the Lord" is chanted in the tone of **_the first troparion to be sung_**. The singing of "God is the Lord" is interspersed with verses Psalm 117, chanted by the deacon (or priest, if there is no deacon serving). Once the Six Psalms are concluded, the chanting between the deacon and the people is as follows (in the Byzantine tradition, the deacon does **not** start the "God is the Lord". Rather, a reader chants, "O give thanks to the Lord, for He is good! For, His steadfast love endures forever!", and the rest proceeds as presented below, with a reader being substituted for the deacon):

*Matins*

*Deacon:* God is the Lord, and has revealed Himself to us. Blessed is He Who comes in the Name of the Lord! O give thanks to the Lord, for He is good! For, His steadfast love endures forever!

*People:* God is the Lord, and has revealed Himself to us. Blessed is He Who comes in the Name of the Lord!

*Deacon:* All nations surrounded me! But, in the Name of the Lord, I destroyed them!

*People:* God is the Lord, and has revealed Himself to us. Blessed is He Who comes in the Name of the Lord!

*Deacon:* I will not die, but live, and recount the deeds of the Lord!

*People:* God is the Lord, and has revealed Himself to us. Blessed is He Who comes in the Name of the Lord!

*Deacon:* The stone that the builders has become the head of the corner! This is the Lord's doing, and it is marvelous in our eyes!

**People:** God is the Lord, and has revealed Himself to us. Blessed is He Who comes in the Name of the Lord!

In the Greek tradition, instead of four interspersed verses from Psalm 117, *some* parishes celebrate ***only three***! The one that is ***omitted*** is, "I will not die, but live, and recount the deeds of the Lord!".

## Kathisma, Kathisma Hymns, Polyeleos, Magnification and Hymns of Degrees

For Festal Matins, Kathismata for the day are read. These are interspersed with Kathisma Hymns in the tone of the week, along with the Polyeleos (meaning, "many praises," verses taken from Psalms 134 and 135), and the Magnification (or, "Megalynarion"). Kathisma Hymns are also known as "Sedalen" or "Sessional Hymns."

The Polyeleos is prescribed to be sung on all Sundays from the Leavetaking of the Exaltation of the Holy Cross (22 September) through Forgiveness (Cheesefare) Sunday. However, in parish practice, the Polyeleos is *usually* sung all year round. Furthermore, in the Byzantine tradition, the Polyeleos is sung *only* for certain feasts.

Little Litanies are also interspersed here. The content of a Little Litany is as follows:

**Deacon:** Again and again, in peace, let us pray to the Lord.

**People:** Lord, have mercy.

**Deacon:** Help us, save us, have mercy on us, and keep us, O God, by Your grace.

**Deacon:** Commemorating our most holy, most pure, most blest and glorious Lady, the Theotokos and ever-Virgin Mary, with all the saints, let us commend ourselves and each other and all our life unto Christ our God.

**People:** To You, O Lord.

**Priest:** For, to You are due all glory, honor, and worship: to the Father, and to the Son, and to the Holy Spirit, now and ever and unto ages of ages.

**People:** Amen.

In the Slavic practice, the Magnification is chanted once by the clergy. Then, as the clergy perform a great censing of the church, the people sing the Magnification numerous times, with Psalm verses interspersed between each singing of the Magnification. At the conclusion of the censing, the clergy sing the Magnification one last time.

In the Byzantine practice, the Magnification is **_not_** sung, but the Psalm verses alone are chanted. In this usage, these Psalm verses are referred to as "Eclogarion."

After the Magnification or Eclogarion, the First Antiphon of the Hymn of Degrees (beginning with the words, "From My Youth") is sung in the $4^{th}$ tone.

The order, then, for this entire "block" of liturgical elements is as follows:

- 1st Kathisma reading from the Psalter
- Little Litany
- Kathisma Hymn
- 2nd Kathisma reading from the Psalter
- Little Litany
- Kathisma Hymn
- Polyeleos
- Magnification
- Little Litany
- Hypakoe
- Hymn of Degrees: First Antiphon in Tone 4

In the Greek practice, however, the order for this entire "block" of liturgical elements is as follows:

- 1ˢᵗ Kathisma Hymns (3 per set)
- "Glory,… now and ever…!"
- 2ⁿᵈ Kathisma Hymns (3 per set)
- "Glory,… now and ever…!"
- 3ʳᵈ Kathisma Hymns (3 per set)
- Hymn of Degrees: First Antiphon in Tone 4

## *Prokeimena and Festal Matins Gospel*

At this point, the Prokeimenon in the tone of the week is chanted. This is followed by a litany petition and exclamation, and then by a fixed Prokeimenon. After this the Festal Matins Gospels is chanted. The order for these elements is as follows (again, in the Byzantine tradition, a reader takes the place of the deacon in this liturgical element):

***Deacon:*** Wisdom!  Let us be attentive!

***Priest:*** Peace be with you all!

***Deacon:*** And with your spirit!

***Priest:*** Wisdom!

***Deacon:*** The Prokeimenon is in the [1ˢᵗ – 8ᵗʰ] tone:  [chants ***first*** Prokeimenon verse].

***People:*** [sing ***first*** Prokeimenon verse].

***Deacon:*** [chants ***second*** Prokeimenon verse].

***People:*** [sing ***first*** Prokeimenon verse].

***Deacon:*** [chants ***first half*** of ***first*** Prokeimenon verse].

***People:*** [sing ***second half*** of ***first*** Prokeimenon verse].

***Deacon:*** Let us pray to the Lord.

***People:*** Lord, have mercy.

**Priest:** For, You are holy, our God, Who rest in the saints, and unto You do we ascribe glory: to the Father, and to the Son, and to the Holy Spirit, now and ever and unto ages of ages.

**People:** Amen.

**Deacon:** Let every breath praise the Lord!

**People:** Let every breath praise the Lord! [sung in the tone of the week]

**Deacon:** Praise God in His sanctuary! Praise Him in His mighty firmament!

**People:** Let every breath praise the Lord!

**Deacon**: Let every breath!

**People:** Praise the Lord!

**Deacon:** And that we may be made worthy to listen to the Holy Gospel, let us pray to the Lord our God!

**People:** Lord, have mercy. *(3)* [meaning, sung *three* times]

**Deacon:** Wisdom! Let us be attentive! Let us listen to the Holy Gospel!

**Priest:** Peace be with you all!

**People:** And with your spirit!

**Priest:** The Reading is from the Holy Gospel according to Saint [Matthew, Mark, Luke, *or* John the Theologian]!

**People:** Glory to You, our God, glory to You!

**Deacon:** Let us be attentive!

**Priest:** [reads the prescribed Resurrectional Matins Gospel.]

**People:** Glory to You, our God, glory to You!

In the Greek practice, at the beginning of the Prokeimenon, the deacon will intone, "Evening! Prokeimenon!", and the singers will intone and sing the entire Prokeimenon themselves. Also, in the Greek practice, **only two** verses from the Psalm are intoned.

## Psalm 50 and Troparion

After the Festal Matins Gospel, a reader chants Psalm 50, concluding with, "Glory...now and ever...," and then, "Alleluia! Alleluia! Alleluia! Glory to You, O God!" **three** times. The people then sing the festal troparion. In the Byzantine tradition, Psalm 50 is chanted antiphonally, in tone 6, with**out** concluding with the "Glory,... now and ever...!" or "Alleluia!" elements.

Furthermore, in the Byzantine tradition, there are stikhera sung at this point, in tone 2: "Glory...Spirit!", "Through the intercessions of the Apostles,...!", "Now and ever...Amen.", and "Through the intercessions of the Theotokos,...!". Then, "Have mercy on me, O God,...!" and "Jesus has Risen from the tomb,...!".

## Litany of Intercession

The Litany of Intercession is now chanted, with the deacon chanting the petition that begins, "O God, save Your people and bless Your inheritance." This long petition, asking for the prayers of numerous saints, is responded to by the people singing "Lord, have mercy" **twelve** times. The priest then gives an exclamation that begins, "Through the mercy and compassion...," to which the people respond by singing "Amen."

**[Hypakoe, Kontakion, Oikos, and Synaxarion]**

At this point, in the Greek tradition, the following are then chanted by a reader: the Hypakoe, the Kontakion, the Oikos, and the reading from the Synaxarion.

**The Kanon**

The Kanon is a structured hymn, consisting of nine **odes**, sometimes called **canticles** or **songs** depending on the translation, based on the Biblical canticles. Most of these are found in the Old Testament, but the final ode is taken from the Magnificat and the Song of Zechariah in the New Testament. For clarity, we will use the term "canticle" to refer to the original biblical text, and "ode" to refer to the composed liturgical hymns. An ode is also referred to as an "heirmos" or "irmos" (pronounced, "EAR-mose"). After each heirmos, troparia and refrains are chanted, usually by two different readers. In this case, the troparia are verses that expound the theme of the heirmos being sung. After the heirmos, a reader will chant a refrain appropriate for the day, such as, "Glory to You, our God, glory to You!" or "Glory to Your Holy Resurrection, O Lord!" The other reader will then chant a troparion. The first reader will then alternately chant the same refrain between the remaining troparia. However, before the final troparion, the "refrain" reader will chant a "Glory,…now and ever….". In the Antiochian practice, the troparia for Resurrectional Matins are **not** celebrated, but only the heirmos and the Katavasia. Furthermore, in the Greek tradition, the troparia and Katavasia are **not** celebrated, and the heirmos is chanted by a reader, **not** sung by the people.

    The Kanon dates from the 7th century and was either devised or introduced into the Greek language by St. Andrew of Crete, whose penitential Great Kanon is still used in Grand Compline during Great Lent. It was further developed in the 8th century by Ss. John of Damascus and Cosmas of

Jerusalem, and in the 9th century by Ss. Joseph the Hymnographer and Theophanes the Branded.

Over time the Kanon (coming from Palestinian monastic usage) came to replace the Kontakion (which grew out of the cathedral practice of Constantinople), a form of which is still used on several occasions and that has been incorporated into the performance of the Kanon (after the 6$^{th}$ ode). Each Kanon develops a specific theme, such as repentance or honouring a particular saint. Sometimes more than one Kanon can be chanted together, as frequently happens at Matins. However, in parish practice, usually just one Kanon is celebrated.

The nine biblical canticles are:

1. The Song of Moses in Exodus (Exodus 15: 1-19)
2. The Song of Moses in Deuteronomy (Deuteronomy 32: 1-43)
3. The Prayer of Anna the mother of Samuel the Prophet (1 Samuel 2: 1-10)
4. The Prayer of Habakkuk the Prophet (Habakkuk 3: 2-19)

5. The Prayer of Isaiah the Prophet (Isaiah 26: 9-20)

6. The Prayer of Jonah the Prophet (Jonah 2: 3-10)

7. The Prayer of the Three Holy Youths (Daniel 3:26-56)*

8. The Song of the Three Holy Youths (Daniel 3:57-88)*

9. The Song of the Theotokos (The **Magnificat**, Luke 1: 46-55) and the Prayer of Zechariah, the father of John the Baptist (The **Benedictus**, Luke 1: 68-79)

*These odes are found only in the Septuagint.

These biblical canticles are normally found in the back of the Psalter used by Orthodox churches, where they are often printed with markings to indicate where to begin inserting the irmos and troparia of the canons.

Ode 2 (from Moses in Deuteronomy) is a penitential ode, so it is **only** sung during Great Lent. Therefore, during the rest of the year, the order of the odes sung is ode 1, then odes 3 through 9.

After ode 3, an Hypakoe or Kathisma Hymn is sung. After ode 6, the Kontakion and Oikos are celebrated. The Oikos (pronounced, "EE-kose," from the Greek word meaning "house") was originally a set of eighteen to twenty-four metrically identical stanzas. In modern practice, it consists of only one stanza, which ends with the last verse of the Kontakion. So, after the 6th ode, the Kontakion is sung. Then, a reader chants the text of the Oikos, stopping just before the last verse of the Kontakion, which is then again sung by the people. In the Byzantine practice, a reading from the Synaxarion, about the lives of saints, is read. After this, the Kanon continues with ode 7.

In the Byzantine tradition, before the 9th ode, the deacon comes out and, standing on the solea in front of the icon of the Theotokos, he chants, "The Theotokos and the Mother of the Light, let us honor and magnify in song!". After the 9th ode and troparia, the 9th ode is usually then repeated as a **Katavasia** (pronounced, "kaht-ah-vah-SEE-ah"). This is from the Greek word meaning "descent," so called because, in the early Church, the cantors used to go down from their stalls and unite in the middle of the choir to sing them. There are Katavasia at the end of every ode. They usually anticipate the next feast. Therefore, Katavasia for Christmas are chanted from 21 November until the feast. In modern parish practice, however, **only** ode 9 is repeated as a Katavasia after its troparia are chanted.

The usual order, then, for the Kanon, is as follows:

- Ode 1
- Ode 3
- [Little Litany, usually omitted]
- Hypakoe or Kathisma Hymn
- Ode 4
- Ode 5
- Ode 6
- [Little Litany, usually omitted]
- Kontakion and Oikos
- Synaxarion reading (Byzantine practice)

- Ode 7
- Ode 8
- Ode 9
- Katavasia of Ode 9
- Little Litany [usually ***not*** omitted]

## The Exapostilarion (Hymn of Light)

The Exapostilarion (Hymn of Light) is then sung. The term "exapostilarion" is related to the word Apostle, which itself is derived from a Greek word meaning "sent out." It has this name because in ancient times a chanter was sent out from the choir into the center of the church to chant this hymn. The Exapostilarion asks God to enlighten the minds of the faithful that they might worthily praise the Lord in the verses of the Praises that follow, and in the Great Doxology.

## *The Praises, with Stikhera*

The Praises (Psalms 148, 149, and 150) are an integral part of Matins. The intent is that the Praises will be chanted as the sun begins to arise, culminating with either the Great Doxology or the Lesser Doxology, and the Apolytikion (troparion of the day). The praises start with the singing of "Let every breath praise the Lord! Praise the Lord in Heaven! Praise Him in the highest! To You, O God, is due a song!" and "Praise Him, all you angels of His! Praise Him, all His hosts! To You, O God, is due a song!".

On feast days, there are special stikhera that are chanted between the Psalm verses of the Praises. In these cases the Psalm verses and their stikhera will be chanted (sung). On days when there are no troparia appointed, the Psalms will be read simply by the reader.

## The Great Doxology

The Great Doxology is an ancient hymn of praise to the Trinity that is chanted or read daily. In Festal Matins, it is chanted. It begins with the exclamation, "Glory to You, Who have shone us the Light!" In the Slavic tradition, this is done by the priest or the bishop. In the Byzantine tradition, this is done by a reader. The people then sing the Great Doxology, which begins with the words, "Glory to God in the highest, and, on Earth, peace, good will towards men!" The Great Doxology ends with the Trisagion.

## Festal Troparion

After the Great Doxology, the festal troparion is sung **_once_** only.

## Augmented Litany

The correct practice for the Augmented Litany at Matins is to begin with the petition, "Have mercy on us, O God, according to Your steadfast love, we pray You: Hear us and have mercy," with the people responding with a "***triple*** 'Lord, have mercy'" for each petition. <u>**Note:**</u> In the Byzantine tradition, ***if*** the Divine Liturgy follows Resurrectional Matins, these litanies and the Dismissal are ***not*** done aloud. Instead, the clergy do them silently during the singing of the Great Doxology, which is then ***immediately*** followed by the beginning of the Divine Liturgy. However, ***if*** the Divine Liturgy does ***not*** follow Resurrectional Matins, then the litanies and Dismissal ***are*** done as presented here.

Each petition is responded to by singing a "***triple*** 'Lord, have mercy'." As with the Great Litany, when the priest or deacon gets to the petition that begins, "Commemorating our most holy…," the people respond with, "To You, O Lord." After the exclamation chanted by the priest, the people respond with, "Amen."

## Litany of Supplication

The Litany of Supplication is chanted. The first two petitions of the Litany are responded to by the people with the singing of "Lord, have mercy." When the priest or deacon chants the petition, "That the whole evening may be perfect, holy, peaceful, and sinless, let us ask of the Lord," the people respond with singing, "Grant it, O Lord." This is done for the remaining petitions until, again, the petition that begins, "Commemorating our most holy,…," with the people responding, "To You, O Lord." After an exclamation by the priest and the "Amen" by the people, the priest faces the people and, blessing them, says, "Peace be with you all!" The people then respond by singing, "And with your spirit!" The priest or deacon then says, "Bow your heads unto the Lord." The people sing, "To You, O Lord." The priest reads a prayer, ending with an exclamation, to which the people respond with, "Amen."

## Dismissal

The Dismissal begins with the priest or deacon chanting, "Wisdom!" Then, the people respond with "Father, bless!" (or, if a bishop is present, "Master, bless!" If the Metropolitan is present, the people will sing, "Most blessed Master, bless!") The priest says, "Christ, the One Who Is, is blessed always, now and ever and unto ages of ages!" The people respond with "Amen. Preserve, O God, the Holy Orthodox Faith and Orthodox Christians, now and ever and unto ages of ages."

The priest then chants, "Most Holy Theotokos, save us!" The people respond with, "More honorable than the Cherubim and more glorious beyond compare than the Seraphim! Without defilement, you gave Birth to God the Word! True Theotokos, we magnify you!"

During most of the year, the priest then says, "Glory to You, Christ our God and our Hope, glory to You!" The people then respond with "Glory…now and ever…Amen. Lord, have mercy (*three* times). Father, bless!" (or, if a bishop is present, "Master, bless!" If the Metropolitan is present, the people will sing, "Most blessed Master, bless!") If it is Pascha or Bright Week, the priest will sing "Christ is Risen!" *three* times, and the people will respond also by singing "Christ is Risen!" ***three*** times.  If it is between Bright Week and Ascension, the priest will sing "Christ is Risen!" ***two-and-a-half*** times, with the people responding with the ***final half***, "and, upon those in the tombs, bestowing life!"  In the Greek practice, the clergy and people sing "Christ is Risen!" ***together three*** times, with the priest coming out of the sanctuary to bless the people with the paschal candle during the third singing.

In any case, the priest will then chant the Dismissal.  The people respond with "Amen," sung either once or twice, according to the parish practice.  If it is during the time between Pascha and Ascension, the people then sing, "And, unto us, He has given eternal life!  Let us worship His Resurrection on the third day!"

As the people come forward to venerate the Holy Cross and the icons, the Resurrectional and/or festal troparia may be sung, according to the parish practice.  Then, before closing the Royal Doors, the priest chants, "Through the prayers of our holy fathers, O Lord, Jesus Christ, have mercy on us and save us!".  The people then sing "Amen." and, usually, a ***triple*** "Lord, have mercy.".  If it is during the Pascha season, after the "Amen.", the people will sing the Paschal troparion ("Christ is Risen from the dead!").

## C. DAILY MATINS

*Doxology*

The Matins begins with the exclamation by the priest (or bishop), "Blessed is our God, always now and ever and unto ages of ages!" The reader then chants, "Amen," followed by Psalms 19 and 20 (these Psalms are *not* done at this point in the Byzantine practice, but only during Daily Lenten Matins). After this, the reader chants "Glory to You, our God, glory to You!", "O Heavenly King!", the Trisagion Prayers ("Holy God!…" *three* times; "Glory,…now and ever…;" "Most Holy Trinity, have mercy on us!…;" "Lord, have mercy" *three* times; "Glory,…now and ever…;" "Our Father,…!"). This is followed by special troparia (the same troparia that the clergy use in their Entrance Prayers before the Divine Liturgy) that, in the Slavic tradition, are: "O Lord, save Your people,…;" "Glory… Spirit!"; "We venerate Your most pure image,…!"; "now and ever…"; "Blessed Theotokos, open the doors of compassion to us…!". In the Byzantine tradition, after "O Lord, save Your people,…!" and "Glory… Spirit!", the troparion is "Do You, Who, of Your own good will,…!", then "Now and ever…Amen.", then "O dread champion, who cannot be put to confusion,…!". Then, there is an abbreviated Augmented Litany, consisting of the first three petitions, the response for each being "Lord, have mercy" sung **three** times, then an exclamation, and an "Amen." After this, the reader chants, "In the Name of the Lord, Father (or, if it be a bishop, "Master"; or, if it be the Metropolitan, "Most blessed Master"), bless!", and then the priest (or bishop) exclaims, "Glory to the Holy, consubstantial, life-creating and undivided Trinity, always now and ever and unto ages of ages!" The reader responds with "Amen." The reader then continues by chanting "Glory to God in the highest and, on Earth, peace, good will towards men!" **three** times, and "Lord, open my lips, and my mouth will show forth Your praise!" **two** times. The reader then proceeds to chant the Six Psalms.

In many parishes, there is an abbreviated version of the above. When following this celebration of Matins separate from Vespers, these parishes will begin with "Blessed is our God…," followed by the "Amen", "Glory to You, our God, glory to You!", "O Heavenly King!", the Trisagion Prayers, and the Lord's Prayer, with the "Amen" following the Lord's Prayer, the "Amen." and "In the Name of the Lord, Father (or, if it be a bishop, "Master"; or, if it be the Metropolitan, "Most blessed Master"), bless!"; then, the exclamation, "Glory to the Holy, consubstantial, life-creating and undivided Trinity, always now and ever and unto ages of ages!" The reader responds with "Amen." The reader then continues by chanting "Glory to God in the highest and, on Earth, peace, good will towards men!" **three** times, and "Lord, open my lips, and my mouth will show forth Your praise!" **two** times. The reader then proceeds to chant the Six Psalms.

### The Six Psalms

The reader chants the Six Psalms of Matins, Psalms 3, 37, 62, 87, 102, and 143. After the third Psalm (62) is chanted, it is customary to chant, "Glory,…now and ever…," "Alleluia! Alleluia! Alleluia! Glory to You, O God!" **three** times, "Lord, have mercy" **three** times, and then, once again, "Glory,…now and ever."

Also, it is customary in many parishes to have **two** readers chant the Six Psalms.  In that case, the practice is for the **first** reader to chant the **first** three Psalms (through Psalm 62), then the "Glory,…now and ever," the "Alleluia!" and "Lord, have mercy" elements, each three times, then a "**split** 'Glory'," with the first reader chanting the final "Glory" through the words, "the Holy Spirit."  The **second** reader then takes up the second half of this final "Glory" with the words, "now and ever and unto ages of ages.  Amen."  The **second** reader then proceeds with chanting the **second** three of the Six Psalms, beginning with Psalm 87.  In the Greek practice there is **no** "split 'Glory'":  The first reader would chant the full "Glory,… now and ever…!", and the second reader would begin chanting Psalm 87.

## The Great Litany

As with **all** forms of Matins, the Great Litany is then chanted by the clergy, with responses sung by the people.  There are eleven petitions, with the people singing, "Lord, have mercy" after each one.  However, in some Greek parishes, there are twelve petitions of the Great Litany:  Between what is usually the fourth petition ("For this holy house,…!") and the fifth petition ("For His Beatitude, our Metropolitan…!"), there is a petition that states, "For pious and Orthodox Christians, let us pray to the Lord!". When the priest or deacon chants the petition that begins, "Commemorating our most holy, most pure, most blessed and glorious Lady,…," the people respond to that petition with, "To You, O Lord!" The priest then chants the exclamation, to which the people respond by singing, "Amen."

### "God is the Lord" and Troparia

The singing of "God is the Lord" and the troparion or troparia for the day is then sung. "God is the Lord" is chanted in the tone ***of the first troparion to be sung***. The singing of "God is the Lord" is interspersed with verses Psalm 117, chanted by the deacon (or priest, if there is no deacon serving). Once the Six Psalms are concluded, the chanting between the deacon and the people is as follows:

**Deacon:** God is the Lord, and has revealed Himself to us. Blessed is He Who comes in the Name of the Lord! O give thanks to the Lord, for He is good! For, His steadfast love endures forever!

**People:** God is the Lord, and has revealed Himself to us. Blessed is He Who comes in the Name of the Lord!

**Deacon:** All nations surrounded me! But, in the Name of the Lord, I destroyed them!

**People:** God is the Lord, and has revealed Himself to us. Blessed is He Who comes in the Name of the Lord!

**Deacon:** I will not die, but live, and recount the deeds of the Lord!

**People:** God is the Lord, and has revealed Himself to us. Blessed is He Who comes in the Name of the Lord!

**Deacon:** The stone that the builders has become the head of the corner! This is the Lord's doing, and it is marvelous in our eyes!

***People:*** God is the Lord, and has revealed Himself to us. Blessed is He Who comes in the Name of the Lord!

In the Greek tradition, instead of four interspersed verses from Psalm 117, ***some*** parishes celebrate ***only three***! The one that is ***omitted*** is, "I will not die, but live, and recount the deeds of the Lord!".

### Kathisma and Kathisma Hymns

For Daily Matins, Kathismata for the day are read. These are interspersed with Kathisma Hymns in the tone of the week. Most of the time, there are three readings from the Psalter, although there sometimes may be only two.

The order for this "block" of liturgical elements is as follows (***Note:*** This ***entire*** "block" of liturgical elements is ***omitted*** in the Greek tradition):

- 1st Kathisma reading from the Psalter
- Kathisma Hymn
- 2nd Kathisma reading from the Psalter
- Kathisma Hymn
- 3rd Kathisma reading from the Psalter
- Kathisma Hymn

## [Prokeimenon, Epistle, "Alleluia Verses," and Gospel]

In Daily Matins, there is usually **_not_** a Prokeimenon and Gospel chanted. The Matins service at this point goes from the final Kathisma Hymn into the chanting of Psalm 50 by a reader. However, in some parishes, where Daily Matins is celebrated with**_out_** the celebration of the Divine Liturgy, a Prokeimenon, Epistle, "Alleluia" verses, and Gospel *may* be celebrated, using the Epistle and Gospel readings that are prescribed for the Divine Liturgy being celebrated here in Daily Matins. If this is the case, then the Prokeimenon for the day is chanted. After this the Epistle and "Alleluia" verses are chanted, followed by the Gospel reading. In the Antiochian tradition, if there is to be no 1st Hour and Divine Liturgy following, then the Epistle and Gospel may be celebrated after the Lord's Prayer and Concluding Troparia. These are **not** celebrated in the Greek practice. In any case, the order for these elements is as follows (in the Antiochian tradition, a reader takes the place of the deacon here):

*Deacon:* Wisdom! Let us be attentive!

*Priest:* Peace be with you all!

*Deacon:* And with your spirit!

*Priest:* Wisdom!

*Deacon:* The Prokeimenon is in the [1st – 8th] tone: [chants **first** Prokeimenon verse].

*People:* [sing **first** Prokeimenon verse].

*Deacon:* [chants **second** Prokeimenon verse].

*People:* [sing **_first_** Prokeimenon verse].

*Matins*

| | |
|---|---|
| ***Deacon:*** | [chants ***first*** *half* of ***first*** Prokeimenon verse]. |
| ***People:*** | [sing ***second*** *half* of ***first*** Prokeimenon verse]. |
| ***Deacon:*** | Let us pray to the Lord. |
| ***People:*** | Lord, have mercy. |
| ***Priest:*** | For, You are holy, our God, Who rest in the saints, and unto You do we ascribe glory: to the Father, and to the Son, and to the Holy Spirit, now and ever and unto ages of ages. |
| ***People:*** | Amen. |
| ***Deacon:*** | And that we may be made worthy to listen to the Holy Gospel, let us pray to the Lord our God! |
| ***People:*** | Lord, have mercy. *(3)* [meaning, sung ***three*** times] |
| ***Deacon:*** | Wisdom! Let us be attentive! Let us listen to the Holy Gospel! |
| ***Priest:*** | Peace be with you all! |
| ***People:*** | And with your spirit! |

**Priest:** The Reading is from the Holy Gospel according to Saint [Matthew, Mark, Luke, *or* John the Theologian]!

**People:** Glory to You, our God, glory to You!

**Deacon:** Let us be attentive!

**Priest:** [reads the prescribed Resurrectional Matins Gospel.]

**People:** Glory to You, our God, glory to You!

## *Psalm 50*

After either the Kathisma Hymn or the Gospel, a reader chants Psalm 50, concluding with, "Glory…now and ever…," and then, "Alleluia! Alleluia! Alleluia! Glory to You, O God!" ***three*** times. In the Byzantine tradition, ***only*** Psalm 50 is chanted, with**out** the "Glory!" and "Alleluia!" elements.

## The Kanon

The Kanon is a structured hymn, consisting of nine **odes**, sometimes called **canticles** or **songs** depending on the translation, based on the Biblical canticles. Most of these are found in the Old Testament, but the final ode is taken from the Magnificat and the Song of Zechariah in the New Testament. For clarity, we will use the term "canticle" to refer to the original biblical text, and "ode" to refer to the composed liturgical hymns. An ode is also referred to as an "heirmos" or "irmos" (pronounced, "EAR-mose"). After each heirmos, troparia and refrains are chanted, usually by two different readers. In this case, the troparia are verses that expound the theme of the heirmos being sung. After the heirmos, a reader will chant a refrain appropriate for the day, such as, "Glory to You, our God, glory to You!" or "Glory to Your Holy Resurrection, O Lord!" The other reader will then chant a troparion. The first reader will then alternately chant the same refrain between the remaining troparia. However, before the final troparion, the "refrain" reader will chant a "Glory,…now and ever….".

The Kanon dates from the 7th century and was either devised or introduced into the Greek language by St. Andrew of Crete, whose penitential Great Kanon is still used in Grand Compline during Great Lent. It was further developed in the 8th century by Ss. John of Damascus and Cosmas of Jerusalem, and in the 9th century by Ss. Joseph the Hymnographer and Theophanes the Branded.

Over time the Kanon (coming from Palestinian monastic usage) came to replace the Kontakion (which grew out of the cathedral practice of Constantinople), a form of which is still used on several occasions and that has been incorporated into the performance of the Kanon (after the 6$^{th}$ ode). Each Kanon develops a specific theme, such as repentance or honouring a particular saint. Sometimes more than one Kanon can be chanted together, as frequently happens at Matins. However, in parish practice, usually just one Kanon is celebrated.

The nine biblical canticles are:

1. The Song of Moses in Exodus
    (Exodus 15: 1-19)

2. The Song of Moses in Deuteronomy
    (Deuteronomy 32: 1-43)

3. The Prayer of Anna the mother of Samuel the Prophet (1 Samuel 2: 1-10)

4. The Prayer of Habakkuk the Prophet (Habakkuk 3: 2-19)

5. The Prayer of Isaiah the Prophet (Isaiah 26: 9-20)

6. The Prayer of Jonah the Prophet (Jonah 2: 3-10)

7. The Prayer of the Three Holy Youths (Daniel 3:26-56)*

8. The Song of the Three Holy Youths (Daniel 3:57-88)*

9. The Song of the Theotokos (The *Magnificat*, Luke 1: 46-55) and the Prayer of Zechariah, the father of John the Baptist (The *Benedictus*, Luke 1: 68-79)

*These odes are found only in the Septuagint.

These biblical canticles are normally found in the back of the Psalter used by Orthodox churches, where they are often printed with markings to indicate where to begin inserting the irmos and troparia of the canons.

Ode 2 (from Moses in Deuteronomy) is a penitential ode, so it is **only** sung during Great Lent. Therefore, during the rest of the year, the order of the odes sung is ode 1, then odes 3 through 9.

After ode 3, a Kathisma Hymn is sung. After ode 6, the Kontakion and Oikos are celebrated. The Oikos (pronounced, "EE-kose," from the Greek word meaning "house") was originally a set of eighteen to twenty-four metrically identical stanzas. In modern practice, it consists of only one stanza, which ends with the last verse of the Kontakion. So, after the 6th ode, the Kontakion is sung. Then, a reader chants the text of the Oikos, stopping just before the last verse of the Kontakion, which is then again sung by the people. In the Antiochian practice, a reading from the Synaxarion, about the lives of saints, is read. After this, in the entire Byzantine practice, the Kanon continues with ode 7. Just before the 9th ode, the priest, standing before the icon of the Theotokos on the iconstasis, lifts the censer and says, "The Theotokos and the Mother of the Light, let us honor and magnify in song!" The people then sing the 9th ode.

Before the 9th ode, the deacon comes out and, standing on the solea in front of the icon of the Theotokos, he chants, "The Theotokos and the Mother of the Light, let us honor and magnify in song!". After the 9th ode and troparia, the 9th ode is usually then repeated as a ***Katavasia*** (pronounced, "kaht-ah-vah-SEE-ah"). This is from the Greek word meaning "descent," so called because, in the early Church, the cantors used to go down from their stalls and unite in the middle of the choir to sing them. There are Katavasia at the end of every ode. They usually anticipate the next feast. Therefore, Katavasia for Christmas are chanted from 21 November until the feast. In modern parish practice, however, **only** ode 9 is repeated as a Katavasia after its troparia are chanted.

The usual order, then, for the Kanon, is as follows:

- Ode 1
- Ode 3
- [Little Litany, usually omitted]
- Kathisma Hymn
- Ode 4

- Ode 5
- Ode 6
- [Little Litany, usually omitted]
- Kontakion and Oikos
- Synaxarion reading  (Byzantine practice)
- Ode 7
- Ode 8
- Ode 9
- Katavasia of Ode 9
- "It is Truly Meet" and "More Honorable" (Byzantine practice)
- Little Litany [usually **_not_** omitted]

## The Exapostilarion  (Hymn of Light)

The Exapostilarion (Hymn of Light) is then sung.  The term "exapostilarion" is related to the word Apostle, which itself is derived from a Greek word meaning "sent out." It has this name because in ancient times a chanter was sent out from the choir into the center of the church to chant this hymn. The exapostilarion asks God to enlighten the minds of the faithful that they might worthily praise the Lord in the verses of the Praises that follow, and in the Lesser Doxology.

**The Praises**

The Praises (Psalms 148, 149, and 150) are an integral part of Matins. The intent is that the Praises will be chanted as the sun begins to arise, culminating with the Lesser Doxology. Unlike at the celebration of Resurrectional or Festal Matins, the chanting of the Praises by a reader at Daily Matins is done with**out** any stikhera interspersed. In the Antiochian practice, this element is concluded with a reader chanting, "To You, O Lord our God, belongs glory, and to You we send up glory: to the Father, and to the Son, and to the Holy Spirit, now and ever and unto ages of ages! Amen." In the Greek tradition, the Praises are **_omitted_** altogether from Daily Matins.

## The Lesser Doxology

The Lesser Doxology is an ancient hymn of praise to the Trinity that is chanted by a reader in Daily Matins. It begins with the priest (or bishop) chanting the exclamation, "Glory to You, Who have shone us the Light!" (***except*** in the Byzantine practice). The reader then chants the Lesser Doxology, beginning with the words, "Glory to God in the highest, and, on Earth, peace, good will towards men!" The Lesser Doxology does **_not_** end with the Trisagion.

## Litany of Supplication

Here, the order of service departs from that of Resurrectional or Festal Matins. In those services, at this point, there would be the Augmented Litany, followed by the Litany of Supplication. Here, in Daily Matins, the Litany of Supplication comes ***first***, ***then*** the Apostika, followed by the troparia and Theotokion for the day, ***and then*** the Augmented Litany.

The Litany of Supplication is chanted.  The first two petitions of the Litany are responded to by the people with the singing of  "Lord, have mercy."

When the priest or deacon chants the petition, "That the whole evening may be perfect, holy, peaceful, and sinless, let us ask of the Lord," the people respond with singing, "Grant it, O Lord." This is done for the remaining petitions until, again, the petition that begins, "Commemorating our most holy,…," with the people responding, "To You, O Lord."  After an exclamation by the priest and the "Amen" by the people, the priest faces the people and, blessing them, says, "Peace be with you all!" The people then respond by singing, "And with your spirit!"  The priest or deacon then says, "Bow your heads unto the Lord." The people sing, "To You, O Lord." The priest reads a prayer, ending with an exclamation, to which the people respond with, "Amen."

**The Apostikha**

The stikhera of the Apostikha are then sung. They are a set of hymns (***stikhera***) accompanied by

Psalm verses by a reader that are chanted towards the end of Vespers and Matins.

The Greek term literally means "[hymns] on the verses." The apostikha belong to a family of hymns, known as **stikhera**, which are normally tied to psalm verses. Unlike other stikhera, which normally follow their Psalm verses, the Apostikha are unique in that they precede their psalm verses.

Aposticha are found at Vespers every day, but at Matins they occur **only** in Daily Matins and Daily Lenten Matins, being **omitted** in Resurrectional and Festal Matins.

In the Byzantine practice, the Apostikha is concluded with the priest chanting, "It is good to give thanks to the Lord, to sing praises to Your Name, O Most–High, to declare Your steadfast love in the morning, and Your truth by night!".

*Trisagion Prayers*

A reader then chants the Trisagion Prayers, which consist of the following: "Holy God! Holy Mighty! Holy Immortal! Have mercy on us!" chanted **three** times; "Glory to the Father, and to the

Son, and to the Holy Spirit, now and ever and unto ages of ages. Amen."; "Most Holy Trinity, have mercy on us! Lord, cleanse us from our sins! Master, pardon our transgressions! Holy One, visit and heal our infirmities, for Your Name's sake!"; "Lord, have mercy" **three** times; another "Glory...now and ever..."; then, the Lord's Prayer. In some parish communities, the Lord's Prayer is said by the entire congregation. After the exclamation by the priest, the people respond with, "Amen."

### Concluding Troparia

Then, the troparia for the day are sung. On many days, there is **only one** troparion. In that case, the troparion is sung, followed by "Glory,...now and ever...," and then the Theotokion **sung in the <u>same</u> <u>tone</u> as the troparion**. If there is **more** than one troparion (two, three, etc.), they are all sung, with a "split 'Glory'" ("Glory...the Holy Spirit") before the last troparion, then the final troparion, then the rest of the "split 'Glory'" ("now and ever...Amen."), then the Theotokion **sung in the <u>same</u> <u>tone</u> as the <u>final</u> troparion** for the specific day of the week.

It is at this point, in the Byzantine practice, that the Epistle and Gospel would be celebrated if Daily Matins was *not* to be followed by the 1st Hour and the Divine Liturgy.

### *Augmented Litany*

As previously mentioned, the Augmented Litany is celebrated in Daily Matins at this point, following the concluding troparia and Theotokion.

The correct practice for the Augmented Litany at Matins is to begin with the petition, "Have mercy on us, O God, according to Your steadfast love, we pray You: Hear us and have mercy," with the people responding with a *"triple* 'Lord, have mercy'" for each petition.

Each petition is responded to by singing a *triple* "Lord, have mercy." As with the Great Litany, when the priest or deacon gets to the petition that begins, "Commemorating our most holy…," the people respond with, "To You, O Lord." After the exclamation chanted by the priest, the people respond with, "Amen."

## Dismissal

The Dismissal begins with the priest or deacon chanting, "Wisdom!" Then, the people respond with "Father, bless!" (or, if a bishop is present, "Master, bless!" If the Metropolitan is present, the people will sing, "Most blessed Master, bless!") The priest says, "Christ, the One Who Is, is blessed always, now and ever and unto ages of ages!" The people respond with "Amen. Preserve, O God, the Holy Orthodox Faith and Orthodox Christians, now and ever and unto ages of ages."

The priest then chants, "Most Holy Theotokos, save us!" The people respond with, "More honorable than the Cherubim and more glorious beyond compare than the Seraphim! Without defilement, you gave Birth to God the Word! True Theotokos, we magnify you!"

During most of the year, the priest then says, "Glory to You, Christ our God and our Hope, glory to You!" The people then respond with "Glory…now and ever…Amen. Lord, have mercy (**three** times). Father, bless!" (or, if a bishop is present, "Master, bless!" If the Metropolitan is present, the people will sing, "Most blessed Master, bless!") If it is Pascha or Bright Week, the priest will sing "Christ is Risen!" **three** times, and the people will respond also by singing "Christ is Risen!" **three** times.  If it is between Bright Week and Ascension, the priest will sing "Christ is Risen!" **two-and-a-half** times, with the people responding with the **final half**, "and, upon those in the tombs, bestowing life In the Greek practice, the clergy and people sing "Christ is Risen!" **together three** times, with the priest coming out of the sanctuary to bless the people with the paschal candle during the third singing.

In any case, the priest will then chant the Dismissal.  The people respond with "Amen," sung either once or twice, according to the parish practice.  If it is during the time between Pascha and Ascension, the people then sing, "And, unto us, He has given eternal life!  Let us worship His Resurrection on the third day!"

As the people come forward to venerate the Holy Cross and the icons, the Resurrectional and/or festal troparia may be sung, according to the parish practice.  Then, before closing the Royal Doors, the priest chants, "Through the prayers of our holy fathers, O Lord, Jesus Christ, have mercy on us and save us!".  The people then sing "Amen." and, usually, a **triple** "Lord, have mercy.".  If it is during the Pascha season, after the "Amen.", the people will sing the Paschal troparion ("Christ is Risen from the dead!").

## D.  DAILY LENTEN MATINS

*Doxology*

The Matins begins with the exclamation by the priest (or bishop), "Blessed is our God, always now and ever and unto ages of ages!"  The reader then chants, "Amen," followed by the reader chanting, "Glory to You, our God, glory to You!", "O Heavenly King!" the Trisagion Prayers ("Holy God!..." **three** times; "Glory,...now and ever...;"  "Most Holy Trinity, have mercy on us!...;" "Lord, have mercy" **three** times; "Glory,...now and ever...!"), and the Lord's Prayer.  After the exclamation, the reader chants "Amen.", and then Psalms 19 and 20.  This is followed by special troparia (the same troparia that the clergy use in their Entrance Prayers before the Divine Liturgy) that, in the Slavic tradition, are:  "O Lord, save Your people,...;" "Glory... Spirit!"; "We venerate Your most pure image,...!"; "now and ever..."; "Blessed Theotokos, open the doors of compassion to us...!". In the Byzantine tradition, after "O Lord, save Your people,...!" and "Glory... Spirit!", the troparion is "Do You, Who, of Your own good will,...!", then "Now and ever...Amen.", then "O dread champion, who cannot be put to confusion,…!". Then, there is an abbreviated Augmented Litany, consisting of the first three petitions, the response for each being "Lord, have mercy" sung **three** times, then an exclamation, and an "Amen." After this, the reader chants, "In the Name of the Lord, Father (or, if it be a bishop, "Master"; or, if it be the Metropolitan, "Most blessed Master"), bless!", and then the priest (or bishop) exclaims, "Glory to the Holy, consubstantial, life-creating and undivided Trinity, always now and ever and unto ages of ages!" The reader responds with "Amen." The reader then continues by chanting "Glory to God in the highest and, on Earth, peace, good will towards men!" **three** times, and "Lord, open my lips, and my mouth will show forth Your praise!" **two** times. The reader then proceeds to chant the Six Psalms. In the Greek practice, the Trisagion Prayers are chanted **twice**: once before Psalms 19 and 20, and once before the prayer, "O Lord, save Your people,…!".

In many parishes, there is an abbreviated version of the above. When following this celebration of Matins separate from Vespers, these parishes will begin with "Blessed is our God…," followed by the "Amen", "Glory to You, our God, glory to You!", "O Heavenly King!", the Trisagion Prayers, and the Lord's Prayer, with the "Amen" following the Lord's Prayer, the "Amen." and "In the Name of the Lord, Father (or, if it be a bishop, "Master"; or, if it be the Metropolitan, "Most blessed Master"), bless!"; then, the exclamation, "Glory to the Holy, consubstantial, life-creating and undivided Trinity, always now and ever and unto ages of ages!" The reader responds with "Amen." The reader then continues by chanting "Glory to God in the highest and, on Earth, peace, good will towards men!" ***three*** times, and "Lord, open my lips, and my mouth will show forth Your praise!" ***two*** times. The reader then proceeds to chant the Six Psalms.

### The Six Psalms

The reader chants the Six Psalms of Matins, Psalms 3, 37, 62, 87, 102, and 143. After the third Psalm (62) is chanted, it is customary to chant, "Glory,...now and ever...," "Alleluia! Alleluia! Alleluia! Glory to You, O God!" ***three*** times, "Lord, have mercy" ***three*** times, and then, once again, "Glory,...now and ever."

Also, it is customary in many parishes to have **two** readers chant the Six Psalms. In that case, the practice is for the **first** reader to chant the **first** three Psalms (through Psalm 62), then the "Glory,…now and ever," the "Alleluia!" and "Lord, have mercy" elements, each three times, then a **"split 'Glory',"** with the first reader chanting the final "Glory" through the words, "the Holy Spirit." The **second** reader then takes up the second half of this final "Glory" with the words, "now and ever and unto ages of ages. Amen." The **second** reader then proceeds with chanting the **second** three of the Six Psalms, beginning with Psalm 87. In the Greek practice there is **no** "split 'Glory'": The first reader would chant the full "Glory,… now and ever…!", and the second reader would begin chanting Psalm 87.

### The Great Litany

As with **all** forms of Matins, the Great Litany is then chanted by the clergy, with responses sung by the people. There are eleven petitions, with the people singing, "Lord, have mercy" after each one. However, in some Greek parishes, there are twelve petitions of the Great Litany: Between what is usually the fourth petition ("For this holy house,....!") and the fifth petition ("For His Beatitude, our Metropolitan...!"), there is a petition that states, "For pious and Orthodox Christians, let us pray to the Lord!". When the priest or deacon chants the petition that begins, "Commemorating our most holy, most pure, most blessed and glorious Lady,...," the people respond to that petition with, "To You, O Lord!" The priest then chants the exclamation, to which the people respond by singing, "Amen."

**"Alleluia!"**

During Great Lent, "God is the Lord" *is replaced* with the singing of "Alleluia!", interspersed with verses from Isaiah 26, as follows (in the Byzantine practice, a reader replaces the deacon in the following):

**Deacon:** Alleluia! Alleluia! Alleluia! My spirit arises early for You in the night, O Lord! For, Your commandments are a light upon the Earth!

| | |
|---|---|
| **People:** | Alleluia! Alleluia! Alleluia! |
| **Deacon:** | Learn righteousness, you who dwell upon the Earth! |
| **People:** | Alleluia! Alleluia! Alleluia! |
| **Deacon:** | Jealousy will grasp an untaught people! |
| **People:** | Alleluia! Alleluia! Alleluia! |
| **Deacon:** | Add more evils upon them, O Lord! Add more evils upon those who are glorious upon the Earth! |
| **People:** | Alleluia! Alleluia! Alleluia! |

## Hymns to the Holy Trinity

Then, Hymns to the Holy Trinity are sung, according to the tone of the week.[9] Also, the ending of the hymns varies with each day of the week. After singing, "Holy! Holy! Holy! are You, O our

---

[9] *Triodion*, pp. 662-667.

God!", the endings are as follows: on Monday: "through the protection of Your holy angels"; on Tuesday: "through the prayers of Your Forerunner"; on Wednesday and Friday: "by the power of Your Holy Cross"; on Thursday: "by the prayers of Your Apostles and Saint Nicholas"; then, on **all** the days, it concludes with "have mercy on us!".

**Kathisma and Kathisma Hymns**

For Daily Lenten Matins, Kathismata for the day are read. These are interspersed with Kathisma Hymns in the tone of the week. Most of the time, there are three readings from the Psalter, although there sometimes may be only two.

The order for this "block" of liturgical elements is as follows:

- 1st Kathisma reading from the Psalter
- Kathisma Hymn
- 2nd Kathisma reading from the Psalter
- Kathisma Hymn

- 3ʳᵈ Kathisma reading from the Psalter
- Kathisma Hymn

**Psalm 50**

After the Kathisma and Kathisma Hymns, a reader chants Psalm 50, concluding with, "Glory…now and ever…," and then, "Alleluia! Alleluia! Alleluia! Glory to You, O God!" **three** times. In the Byzantine practice, **only** Psalm 50 is chanted, with**out** the "Glory!" and "Alleluia!" elements.

**The Kanon**

The Kanon is a structured hymn, consisting of nine **odes**, sometimes called **canticles** or **songs** depending on the translation, based on the Biblical canticles. Most of these are found in the Old Testament, but the final ode is taken from the Magnificat and the Song of Zechariah in the New Testament. For clarity, we will use the term "canticle" to refer to the original biblical text, and "ode" to refer to the composed liturgical hymns.  An ode is also referred to as an "heirmos" or "irmos" (pronounced, "EAR-mose").  After each heirmos, troparia and refrains are chanted, usually by two different readers.  In this case, the troparia are verses that expound the theme of the heirmos being sung.  After the heirmos, a reader will chant a refrain appropriate for the day, such as, "Glory to You, our God, glory to You.  The other reader will then chant a troparion.  The first reader will then alternately chant the same refrain between the remaining troparia.  However, before the final troparion, the "refrain" reader will chant a "Glory,…now and ever….".  **Note:** In the Greek practice, the Kanon element is **omitted** altogether at Daily Lenten Matins.

    The Kanon dates from the 7th century and was either devised or introduced into the Greek language by St. Andrew of Crete, whose penitential Great Kanon is still used in Grand Compline during Great Lent.  It was further developed in the 8th century by Ss. John of Damascus and Cosmas of Jerusalem, and in the 9th century by Ss. Joseph the Hymnographer and Theophanes the Branded.

    Over time the Kanon (coming from Palestinian monastic usage) came to replace the Kontakion (which grew out of the cathedral practice of

Constantinople), a form of which is still used on several occasions and that has been incorporated into the performance of the Kanon (after the 6$^{th}$ ode). Each Kanon develops a specific theme, such as repentance or honouring a particular saint. Sometimes more than one Kanon can be chanted together, as frequently happens at Matins. However, in parish practice, usually just one Kanon is celebrated.

The nine biblical canticles are:

1. The Song of Moses in Exodus
   (Exodus 15: 1-19)

2. The Song of Moses in Deuteronomy
   (Deuteronomy 32: 1-43)

3. The Prayer of Anna the mother of
   Samuel the Prophet  (1 Samuel 2: 1-10)

4. The Prayer of Habakkuk the Prophet
   (Habakkuk 3: 2-19)

5. The Prayer of Isaiah the Prophet
   (Isaiah 26: 9-20)

6. The Prayer of Jonah the Prophet
   (Jonah 2: 3-10)

7. The Prayer of the Three Holy Youths (Daniel 3:26-56)*

9. The Song of the Three Holy Youths (Daniel 3:57-88)*

9. The Song of the Theotokos (The **Magnificat**, Luke 1: 46-55) and the Prayer of Zechariah, the father of John the Baptist (The **Benedictus**, Luke 1: 68-79)

*These odes are found only in the Septuagint.

These biblical canticles are normally found in the back of the Psalter used by Orthodox churches, where they are often printed with markings to indicate where to begin inserting the irmos and troparia of the canons.

Ode 2 (from Moses in Deuteronomy) is a penitential ode, so it is **only** sung during Great Lent. Therefore, during the rest of the year, the order of the odes sung is ode 1, then odes 3 through 9.

After ode 3, a Kathisma Hymn is sung. After ode 6, the Kontakion and Oikos are celebrated. The

Oikos (pronounced, "EE-kose," from the Greek word meaning "house") was originally a set of eighteen to twenty-four metrically identical stanzas. In modern practice, it consists of only one stanza, which ends with the last verse of the Kontakion. So, after the 6th ode, the Kontakion is sung. Then, a reader chants the text of the Oikos, stopping just before the last verse of the Kontakion, which is then again sung by the people. In the Antiochian practice, a reading from the Synaxarion, about the lives of saints, is read. After this, the Kanon continues with ode 7. Just before the 9th ode, the priest, standing before the icon of the Theotokos on the iconstasis, lifts the censer and says, "The Theotokos and the Mother of the Light, let us honor and magnify in song!" The people then sing the 9th ode.

After the 9th ode and troparia, the 9th ode is usually then repeated as a **Katavasia** (pronounced, "kaht-ah-vah-SEE-ah"). This is from the Greek word meaning "descent," so called because, in the early Church, the cantors used to go down from their stalls and unite in the middle of the choir to sing them. There are Katavasia at the end of every ode. They usually anticipate the next feast. Therefore, Katavasia for Christmas are chanted from 21 November until the feast. In modern parish practice, however, *only* ode 9 is repeated as a Katavasia after its troparia are chanted.

The usual order, then, for the Kanon, is as follows:

- Ode 1
- Ode 3
- [Little Litany, usually omitted]
- Kathisma Hymn
- Ode 4
- Ode 5
- Ode 6
- [Little Litany, usually omitted]
- Kontakion and Oikos
- Synaxarion reading (Antiochian practice)
- Ode 7
- Ode 8
- Ode 9

- Katavasia of Ode 9
- "It is Truly Meet" and "More Honorable" (Antiochian practice)
- Little Litany [usually ***not*** omitted]

## The Exapostilarion (Hymn of Light)

The Exapostilarion (Hymn of Light) is then sung. The term "exapostilarion" is related to the word Apostle, which itself is derived from a Greek word meaning "sent out." It has this name because in ancient times a chanter was sent out from the choir into the center of the church to chant this hymn. The exapostilarion asks God to enlighten the minds of the faithful that they might worthily praise the Lord in the verses of the Praises that follow, and in the Lesser Doxology. At the end of the Exapostilarion, there are special endings (as there were for the "Alleluia!"). These endings are as follows: on Monday: "through the protection of Your holy angels"; on Tuesday: "through the prayers of Your Forerunner"; on Wednesday and Friday: "by the power of Your Holy Cross"; on Thursday: "by the prayers of Your Apostles and Saint Nicholas"; then, on **all** the days, it concludes with "have mercy on us!". **Note:**  In the Greek practice, the Exapostilarion is **omitted** altogether at Daily Lenten Matins.

### The Praises

The Praises (Psalms 148, 149, and 150) are an integral part of Matins.  The intent is that the Praises will be chanted as the sun begins to arise, culminating with the Lesser Doxology.  Unlike at the celebration of Resurrectional or Festal Matins, the chanting of the Praises by a reader at Daily Lenten Matins is done with**out** any stikhera interspersed.  In the Antiochian practice, this element is concluded with a reader chanting, "To You, O Lord our God, belongs glory, and to You we send up glory:  to the Father, and to the Son, and to the Holy Spirit, now and ever and unto ages of ages!  Amen."  In the Greek tradition, the Praises are **omitted** altogether at Daily Lenten Matins.

## The Lesser Doxology

The Lesser Doxology is an ancient hymn of praise to the Trinity that is chanted by a reader in Daily Matins. It begins with the priest (or bishop) chanting the exclamation, "Glory to You, Who have shone us the Light!" (except in the Byzantine practice). The reader then chants the Lesser Doxology, beginning with the words, "Glory to God in the highest, and, on Earth, peace, good will towards men!" The Lesser Doxology does **_not_** end with the Trisagion. In the Greek practice, the Lesser Doxology is followed by a reading from the Synaxarion and by the Megalynarion.

## Litany of Supplication

Here, the order of service departs from that of Resurrectional or Festal Matins. In those services, at this point, there would be the Augmented Litany, followed by the Litany of Supplication. Here, in Daily Lenten Matins, the Litany of Supplication comes *first*, *then* the Apostika, followed by the troparia and Theotokion for the day, **_and NO_** Augmented Litany.

The Litany of Supplication is chanted. The first two petitions of the Litany are responded to by the people with the singing of "Lord, have mercy." When the priest or deacon chants the petition, "That the whole evening may be perfect, holy, peaceful, and sinless, let us ask of the Lord," the people respond with singing, "Grant it, O Lord." This is done for the remaining petitions until, again, the petition that begins, "Commemorating our most holy,...," with the people responding, "To You, O Lord." After an exclamation by the priest and the "Amen" by the people, the priest faces the people and, blessing them, says, "Peace be with you all!" The people then respond by singing, "And with your spirit!" The priest or deacon then says, "Bow your heads unto the Lord." The people sing, "To You, O Lord." The priest reads a prayer, ending with an exclamation, to which the people respond with, "Amen."

## The Apostikha

The Apostikha are then sung. They are a set of hymns (***stikhera***) accompanied by Psalm verses by a reader that are chanted towards the end of Vespers and Matins.

The Greek term literally means "[hymns] on the verses." The apostikha belong to a family of hymns, known as **stikhera**, which are normally tied to psalm verses. Unlike other stikhera, which normally follow their Psalm verses, the Apostikha are unique in that they precede their psalm verses.

Aposticha are found at Vespers every day, but at Matins they occur **only** in Daily Matins and Daily Lenten Matins, being **omitted** in Resurrectional and Festal Matins.

### Trisagion Prayers

A reader then chants the following prayer, "It is good to give thanks to the Lord, to sing praise to Your Name, O Most High, to declare Your steadfast love in the morning and Your truth by night!", and then immediately the Trisagion Prayers, which consist of the following: "Holy God! Holy Mighty! Holy Immortal! Have mercy on us!" chanted **three** times; "Glory to the Father, and to the Son, and to the Holy Spirit, now and ever and unto ages of ages. Amen."; "Most Holy Trinity, have mercy on us! Lord, cleanse us from our sins! Master, pardon our transgressions! Holy One, visit and heal our infirmities, for Your Name's sake!"; "Lord, have mercy" **three** times; another "Glory...now and ever..."; then, the Lord's Prayer. In some parish communities, the Lord's Prayer is said by the entire congregation. After the exclamation by the priest, the reader responds with, "Amen," and then concludes with, "Standing in the temple of your glory, we think that we are in Heaven, O Theotokos. You, who are the gate of Heaven, open to us the gate of your mercy."

Then, a reader chants the following: "Lord, have mercy." **forty** times, a full "Glory,... now and ever...!", "More honorable...!", and then, "In the Name of the Lord, Father (or, if it be a bishop, "Master"; or, if it be the Metropolitan, "Most blessed Master"), bless!". Then, the celebrant chants, "Christ, the One Who Is, is blest always now and ever and unto ages of ages!". The reader chants an "Amen.", and then, "O Heavenly King, establish the Orthodox Christians! Confirm the Faith! Quiet the heathen! Give peace to the world! Place our departed fathers and brethren in the tabernacles of the righteous, and accept us sorrowers and penitents! For, You are good and the Lover of mankind!".

## The Prayer of St Ephraim

The Prayer of St Ephraim, with interspersed prostrations and metania, is then chanted. In the Greek practice, the complete Prayer of St Ephraim is done only once, with the three accompanying prostrations. Since the Augmented Litany is eliminated from Daily Lenten Matins, the Dismissal immediately follows the conclusion of the Prayer of St. Ephraim.

## Dismissal

The Dismissal begins with the priest or deacon chanting, "Wisdom!" Then, the people respond with "Father, bless!" (or, if a bishop is present, "Master, bless!" If the Metropolitan is present, the people will sing, "Most blessed Master, bless!") The priest says, "Christ, the One Who Is, is blessed always, now and ever and unto ages of ages!" The people respond with "Amen. Preserve, O God, the Holy Orthodox Faith and Orthodox Christians, now and ever and unto ages of ages."

The priest then chants, "Most Holy Theotokos, save us!" The people respond with, "More honorable than the Cherubim and more glorious beyond compare than the Seraphim! Without defilement, you gave Birth to God the Word! True Theotokos, we magnify you!"

In the Byzantine practice, the above is **not** done. **Instead**, it begins at this point, where the Slavic practice continues from the above: The celebrant chants, "Glory to You, O Christ, our God and our Hope, glory to You!". The people then sing a full "Glory,… now and ever…!", a *triple* "Lord, have mercy.", and then, "Father, bless!" (or, if a bishop is present, "Master, bless!" If the Metropolitan is present, the people will sing, "Most blessed Master, bless!").

The priest will then chant the Dismissal. The people respond with "Amen," sung either once or twice, according to the parish practice.

# 3
# THE DIVINE LITURGY

## A.  THE DIVINE LITURGY

*["From the Rising of the Sun," Hymn to the Theotokos, "Ton Dhespotin," Vesting Hymns, "Ton Dhespotin"]*

If a bishop is present and a Hierarchical Divine Liturgy is being celebrated, a set of special hymns is sung before the Divine Liturgy proper begins.

As the clergy and parish dignitaries greet the bishop at the entrance from the narthex into the nave, the people sing "From the Rising of the Sun." (**Note:** In the Byzantine tradition, if Resurrectional Matins precedes the Divine Liturgy on a Sunday morning, this will all be done at Matins.)

In the Greek practice, the bishop usually arrives during the celebration of the Kontakion and the Oikos at Matins, and the priests approach the bishop, each with his phelonion draped over his arm.

As the bishop blesses the priest's cross and phelonion (beginning with the senior priest), that priest then puts his phelonion and cross on (in the Byzantine practice, priests usually do **not** wear crosses). During this same Matins, after "Holy is the Lord our God," the bishop chants the first Exapostilarion, the people sing any other Exapostilaria, and then proceed to the Praises. Then, the people sing the long "Ton Dhespotin", and the deacons and servers exit the sanctuary and escort the bishop to the solea, where the Entrance Prayers are celebrated. Then, when the bishop blesses the people with the trikiri, the people sing, "Eis Polla Eti Dhespota!". The bishop is then vested in the sanctuary. During the singing of the Great Doxology, the clergy exit the sanctuary in reverse senior order (junior priest first, bishop last), and line up in front of the bishop's throne, which, in the Byzantine churches, is on the right side of the church near the kleros. Also, in the Greek practice, for all litanies at a Hierarchical Divine Liturgy, whenever the present bishop is commemorated by name, the deacon or priest turns to the bishop and bows, while the people sing, "Eis Polla Eti Dhespota!".

As the bishop, clergy, and servers come forward into the nave, the bishop ascends the ambo onto the solea for his Entrance Prayers. (**_Note:_** Again, in the Byzantine tradition, this is done at Resurrectional Matins on a Sunday morning.) During this time, the people sing the Hymn to the Theotokos that is appropriate for the season. So, for most of the year, "It is Truly Meet" is sung. If it is during Great Lent or on another occasion where the Divine Liturgy of St Basil the Great is being celebrated, "All of Creation" is sung. During the Paschal season, the people would sing "The Angel Cried." And if it is any feast where there is a special Hymn to the Theotokos (such as the 9$^{th}$ Ode of the Matins Kanon), that would be the hymn prescribed.

At the end of the Entrance Prayers, the bishop turns and faces the people. Having been given the ***dikiri*** (two-branched candle [used only in the Slavic tradition]) and ***trikiri*** (three-branched candle) from a server, he takes these two candles (one in each hand) and, making the sign of the Cross, blesses the people. At this point, "Ton Dhespotin" is sung.

The bishop then proceeds to the center of the church, in the Slavic tradition, to be vested. (He is vested in the sanctuary in the Byzantine tradition.) He usually stands on a raised platform called a ***cathedra***. Servers from the sanctuary then proceed to vest the bishop in his hierarchical vestments.

During this time, the people sing two hymns, "Your Soul Will Rejoice" and "The Prophets Proclaimed" (this last hymn sung **only** in the Slavic tradition, and **omitted** in the Byzantine practice.) These are sung slowly and repeatedly (alternating between the two hymns) until the vesting of the bishop is completed. At this point, servers again hand the bishop the *dikiri* and *trikiri*. In the Slavic practice, when the deacon chants the exclamation, "Let your light so shine before men," the people *again* sing "Ton Dhespotin" as the bishop blesses the people in four directions. In the Byzantine tradition, the deacon exclaims, "Let your light so shine before men" in the sanctuary. The bishop then blesses the main priest, who enters the sanctuary to begin the Divine Liturgy as the bishop remains in the nave.

### *[Tonsuring of Chanters or Readers, Ordination of Sub – Deacons]*

If any lay people are to be tonsured as chanters or readers of the Church or if someone is to be ordained a sub-deacon, the tonsuring or ordination is done at this point in the Slavic tradition, before the Divine Liturgy begins. For those who are singing, the people respond with "Lord, have mercy." and "Amen." where it is appropriate. In the Byzantine practice, this is done after the Great Doxology at Resurrectional Matins, before the singing of the Concluding Troparia.

## *Doxology*

At the beginning of the Divine Liturgy, the clergy usually raise their hands and recite, "O Heavenly King." If it is during Paschatide, they will instead recite, "Christ is Risen!" If it is during the feast and postfeast of Ascension, they will instead recite the troparion for Ascension. In any of the preceding, they will then say "Glory to God in the highest, and, on Earth, peace, good will towards men!" twice, and bless themselves and bow each time. Then, the priest will say, as he venerates the Altar and the Gospel Book, "O Lord, open my lips, and my mouth will show forth Your praise!"

The priest will then raise up the Gospel Book and, while he makes the sign of the cross with it, will give the doxology for **_all_** Divine Liturgies, "Blessed is the Kingdom of the Father, and of the Son, and of the Holy Spirit, now and ever and unto ages of ages!" The people respond with, "Amen."

If it is from Pascha through Bright Saturday, the clergy will sing, "Christ is Risen!" **three** times, followed by the people singing, "Christ is Risen!" **three** times.  If it is from Thomas Sunday to the leavetaking of Pascha, the clergy will sing, "Christ is Risen!" **two-and-a-half** times, the third time stopping with, "trampling down death by death!"  The people will conclude the **final half**, "and, upon those in the tombs, bestowing life!"

The clergy and the people then proceed to the Great Litany.

### The Great Litany

The Great Litany is chanted by the clergy, with responses sung by the people.  There are eleven petitions, with the people singing, "Lord, have mercy" after each one.  When the priest or deacon chants the petition that begins, "Commemorating our most holy, most pure, most blessed and glorious Lady,…," the people respond to that petition with, "To You, O Lord!"  The priest (or bishop) then chants the exclamation, to which the people respond by singing, "Amen."

## *The First Antiphon*

If this is a Hierarchical Divine Liturgy, the bishop and remaining clergy who surround him stay in the nave of the church during the singing of the antiphons.  In the Slavic practice, the bishop is on the cathedra in the middle of the church.  In the Byzantine practice, because of Byzantium's long oppression under the Turkish yoke (whereby the bishop was treated like a secular dignitary of the Empire), the bishop stands in front of his throne on the side of the church.  If there is *no* throne in the church, the bishop will, in the Byzantine tradition, stand on the solea.

In all practices except the Carpatho-Russian and Ukrainian (where only one antiphon is sung), there are three separate antiphons sung at this point of the Liturgy.  What is called for are Psalms alternating with response verses.  However, in America, there are two opposing reductions to this.  In the Slavic practice, the Typika is sung (with *no* response verses).  In the Byzantine practice, the Psalm is omitted but the response verses are sung.  Yet, in more and more parishes of both traditions, the fuller practice of both Psalm and response verses is being restored.

This part of the Liturgy contains some of the most diverse possibilities of the entire service, depending on the day and the Liturgy being celebrated.  There are different antiphons sung on Sunday than on weekdays, and even more different antiphons sung on specific feast days (especially feasts of the Lord).  What is called for at a Sunday Resurrectional Divine Liturgy for the First Antiphon is the chanting (again, with response verses) of Psalm 102.  In the Byzantine tradition, the people sing, instead of the Psalm, "Through the prayers of the Theotokos, O Savior:  Save us!".

**The Little Litany**

As previously mentioned, in both the Carpatho-Russian and Ukrainian traditions, only one antiphon is sung.  So, at this point in the Liturgy, the people of those two practices would immediately go to the singing of "Only-Begotten Son."  In all the other Orthodox traditions, which sing all three antiphons, a Little Litany is celebrated here.  This consists of the following:

**Deacon:** Again and again, in peace, let us pray to the Lord.

**People:** Lord, have mercy.

**Deacon:** Help us, save us, have mercy on us, and keep us, O God, by Your grace.

**People:** Lord, have mercy.

**Deacon:** Commemorating our most holy, most pure, most blest and glorious Lady, the Theotokos and ever-Virgin Mary, with all the saints, let us commend ourselves and each other and all our life unto Christ our God.

**People:** To You, O Lord.

There follows then a prayer chanted by the priest or bishop, concluding with the exclamation, "For, to You are due all glory, honor, and worship: to the Father, and to the Son, and to the Holy Spirit, now and ever and unto ages of ages." The people then respond with "Amen."

## *The Second Antiphon*

After the Little Litany, the Second Antiphon is sung. Again, there are diverse possibilities for this, depending on the day or feast being celebrated. At the Sunday Resurrectional Divine Liturgy, the Psalm (with response verses) is taken from Psalm 145. In the Byzantine practice, instead of singing the Psalm, the people sing the refrain, "O Son of God, Who Arose from the dead: Save us who sing to You: 'Alleluia!'".

A note at this point on the difference in liturgical practice. Many service books mistakenly call for a "split 'Glory'" here. In other words, the rubrics call for singing "Glory to the Father, and to the Son, and to the Holy Spirit," followed by the Second Antiphon, followed by "Now and ever and unto ages of ages. Amen.", and then going on to the singing of "Only-Begotten Son." Again, this is an error in these particular service books. The **correct** practice is to sing the Second Antiphon, **then** a *full* "Glory…, now and ever…," and **then** "Only-Begotten Son." This correct rendering is being restored in many parishes today.

## "Only – Begotten Son"

The singing of "Only-Begotten Son" immediately follows the Second Antiphon, beginning, as stated, with a full "Glory..., now and ever...." This hymn is sung at *all* Divine Liturgies, even on feast days that call for special antiphons to be sung.

## Little Litany

After "Only-Begotten Son," another Little Litany is celebrated. This one, also, ends with a prayer and a concluding exclamation, to which the people respond with "Amen."

## The Third Antiphon

After this second Little Litany, the Third Antiphon is sung. At a Sunday Resurrectional Divine Liturgy, this usually consists in the singing of the Beatitudes. (In some parishes of different traditions [the Antiochian, for example], the Beatitudes are *omitted*.) In many parishes, there are no response verses sung, only the Beatitudes preceded by "In Your Kingdom, remember us, O Lord, when You come in Your Kingdom!" As with other liturgical elements, though, the insertion of response verses in between the verses of the Beatitudes is being restored. During the singing of the Beatitudes, the priest, deacon, and servers exit the sanctuary with the Gospel Book for the Gospel Entrance into the middle of the church.

On feast days that call for special antiphons, the Third Antiphon takes the form of response verses chanted by a reader, interspersed with the singing of the troparion of the feast (***apolytikion***). Once the Gospel Entrance has processed to the middle of the church, the deacon or priest, in addition to chanting, "Wisdom! Let us be attentive!", will intone a final response verse known as the ***little introit***. This is followed by the singing, one last time, of the festal troparion. At a regular Divine Liturgy (non-hierarchical), the clergy and servers enter the sanctuary during this final singing.

### *"Come, Let Us Worship"*

At a regular Divine Liturgy without festal antiphons, the deacon or the priest, once the Gospel

Entrance has processed to the middle of the church, will raise the Gospel Book and intone, "Wisdom! Let us be attentive!" The people then respond with the singing of "Come, Let Us Worship." The first part of the text chants, "Come, let us worship and fall down before Christ." Then, depending on the day, any of a number of verse insertions are sung. If it is a Sunday, after "before Christ" will be added, "Who arose from the dead;" if it is a feast of the Mother of God, the insertion will be "through the prayers of the Theotokos;" if it is a feast of a particular saint, the insertion is "Who is wonderful in His saints;" and, if it is a feast of the Lord (such as Holy Theophany), a special insertion appropriate to the feast is sung (such as, "Who was Baptized in the Jordan"). Whatever the insertion, in **all** cases, this is followed by "Alleluia!"

If it is a Hierarchical Divine Liturgy, the **clergy** begin the singing of "Come, Let Us Worship," with the appropriate insertion and the "Alleluia!" This is followed by the people singing it, but **not** starting at the "Come, Let Us Worship," but **at the insertion** ("Who arose from the dead," etc.) and the "Alleluia!" While the people are singing this, the bishop, clergy, and servers enter the sanctuary. When the people finish singing, the clergy **again** sing, but in the manner just chanted by the people, that is, beginning with the insertion and then the

"Alleluia!" In the Byzantine tradition, while the clergy are singing "Come, Let Us Worship!", the people sing, "Eis Polla Eti Dhespota!", and **then**, <u>*after*</u> the clergy finish singing, the people sing "Save us who sing to You!". Also, in the Byzantine practice, after the people finish singing, the clergy do **not** sing the insertion and the "Alleluia!" again.

### [Elevation of a Proto – Deacon or Archpriest]

If a deacon is to be elevated as a proto-deacon or if a priest is to be elevated as an archpriest, that elevation is done at this point. As with the tonsuring of chanters and readers and the ordination of sub-deacons, for those who are singing, the people respond with "Lord, have mercy." and "Amen." where it is appropriate.

After this, the presiding bishop takes the dikiri and trikiri in his hands and blesses the people, while the people sing a short "Eis Polla Eti Dhespota!"

## ["Eis Polla Eti Dhespota"]

If the service is a Hierarchical Divine Liturgy, the bishop will do a little censing at this point (censing the sanctuary, iconostasis, clergy and servers, and the people). During this censing, the singing of "Eis Polla Eti Dhespota" is done in the Slavic tradition only. This usually consists of a trio setting of the text, followed by a final and elaborate "Eis Polla" being sung by the full choir and people. After this, the clergy in the sanctuary sing the elaborate "Eis Polla" once, followed by a final singing of the elaborate "Eis Polla" by all the people.

## Troparia and Kontakia

The troparia and kontakia of the day are then sung. If there is only one troparion and one Kontakion (for, say, the feast of Holy Theophany), then the troparion is followed by a full "Glory…, now and ever…" before the singing of the Kontakion. If there are three or more elements (in a combination of troparia and kontakia), the following practice holds true: If **the last _two_ elements** are from the **same** "source" (say, both the resurrectional troparion followed by the resurrectional kontakion), then, again, a full "Glory…, now and ever…" is sung between these last two elements.  If, however, the last two elements are from **different** sources (say, a troparion for a saint followed by the resurrectional kontakion), **then** a "**split** 'Glory'" is done.  This consists of singing "Glory to the Father, and to the Son, and to the Holy Spirit;" then, the penultimate (second-to-last) element; then, "Now and ever and unto ages of ages.  Amen."; then, the final element.  This is the correct and proper rendering of full or "split" "Glory's" during the singing of multiple troparia and kontakia.  (In the Byzantine tradition, the singing of either a full "Glory,… now and ever…!" or a "split 'Glory!'" is **not** done, but, rather, all the troparia and kontakia are sung, one right after the other.)

At a Hierarchical Divine Liturgy, the people will sing all elements through the "split 'Glory'" and the penultimate element, and **then stop!**  After this, the **clergy** in the sanctuary will sing the "Now and ever" and the final Kontakion.  In the Byzantine tradition, the clergy **also** sing the first troparion, the one for the Resurrection.

## The Trisagion

In one sense, all that has gone on in the Divine Liturgy up until now has been preparatory. In the early Church, during the time of intense persecution of Christians, the holy items needed for the service (the Gospel Book, the Holy Gifts, etc.) were kept outside the church building and then brought there in a procession, during which the previous hymns (the antiphons, etc.) were sung, followed by the Gospel Entrance (which was the original beginning of the Divine Liturgy, hence the entrance prayer, "Blessed is the entrance of Your saints!") and the thematic hymns of the day (the troparia and kontakia). At this point, the Divine Liturgy proper, the "meat-and-potatoes" of the service, so to speak, begins, and it begins with this victory hymn acknowledging our God in the Holy Trinity: the Father ("Holy God!"), and the Son ("Holy Mighty!"), and the Holy Spirit ("Holy Immortal!"). That is why this hymn is called *the Trisagion*, because the word means "the thrice holy" (from the Greek word "agios" ["*άγιος*"], meaning, "holy").

Along with knowing how the singing of the Trisagion is celebrated, it is also important for choir directors to know what is liturgically occurring during this time, since the reader who is to chant the prokeimenon, the Epistle reading, and the "Alleluia" verses will go to get a blessing at this point and the choir director is usually the person in the parish who oversees the ministry of the readers. The pattern for singing the Trisagion is as follows: the full Trisagion ("Holy God! Holy Mighty! Holy Immortal! Have mercy on us!") is sung **three** times. This is followed by a full "Glory,... now and ever...!" Then, an abbreviated form of the Trisagion, singing **only** "Holy Immortal! Have mercy on us!", is sung. At this point, in the Byzantine practice, the deacon (or, if there is no deacon, the main celebrant) comes out of the sanctuary, stands on the ambo, and intones, "**Dynamis**!" ("δυναμις", which means, "With strength!"), before the final singing of "Holy God!". Then, the full Trisagion is sung one final time. It is at the point where the full "Glory,... now and ever...!" begins that the reader goes to receive a blessing from the priest or bishop. For pastoral reasons, if the reader is a male, he goes into the sanctuary to the High Place to receive his blessing; if the reader is a female, she goes to the foot of the ambo, and the priest or bishop comes out of the sanctuary to give her the blessing. The reader then proceeds to the middle of the church and faces the sanctuary. During the procession, the reader, whether male or female, raises the Epistle book or Holy Bible up in front of his or her face, with the Holy Cross on the front of the book facing outward towards the people. When the reader comes to the priest or bishop, he or she then lays the book flat in the palm of his or her hands, with the Holy Cross facing up, so that, upon receiving the blessing, the reader would then kiss the Cross on the book (if the person giving the blessing is a bishop, the reader would **first** kiss the bishop's hand and **then** the Holy Cross on the book).

This singing of the Trisagion is the standard one sung for most of the liturgical year. However, two other versions may be sung, depending on the particular day. For feasts of the Holy Cross, the regular Trisagion is replaced with the singing of "Before Your Cross!" The order for singing this is: the people sing "Before Your Cross, we bow down in worship, O Master, and Your Holy Resurrection we glorify!" **three** times. This is followed by a full "Glory,... now and ever...!", then an abbreviation ("And Your Holy Resurrection, we glorify!"), and then a final "Before Your Cross!" once more. Again, the reader would proceed to receive a blessing at the sing of the full "Glory,... now and ever...!".

On baptismal feasts (Pascha, Theophany, etc.), the regular Trisagion is replaced with the singing of "As Many as Have Been Baptized". The order for singing this is: the people sing "As many as have been baptized into Christ have put on Christ! Alleluia!" **three** times. This is followed by a full

"Glory,… now and ever…!", then an abbreviation ("Have put on Christ!  Alleluia!"), and then a final "As Many as Have Been Baptized" once more.  Again, the reader would proceed to receive a blessing at the singing of the full "Glory,… now and ever…!".

At a Hierarchical Divine Liturgy, the order for singing the Trisagion is as follows (although there may be numerous variations on this in the Greek practice):

1. The people sing an elaborate "Holy God!".
2. The clergy sing the elaborate "Holy God!".
3. The people sing a plain "Holy God!".
4. The bishop comes out with dikiri and trikiri, chants the prayer, "Lord, Lord, look down upon this vineyard that Your right hand has planted, and establish it!".  He then blesses the people three times (once in each direction), as he says, **separately**, "Holy God!", "Holy Mighty!", "Holy Immortal! Have mercy on us!".  As he says each of these three sections, the people (many times, a trio) repeat the separate sections, singing "Holy God!", "Holy Mighty!", "Holy Immortal!  Have mercy on us!".

5. The people again sing the plain "Holy God!".

6. The clergy sing the elaborate "Holy God!".

7. The people sing a full "Glory,... now and ever...!".

8. The people again sing the elaborate "Holy God!".


## *[Consecration of a Bishop]*

If a priest is to be consecrated a bishop, the consecration takes place after the singing of the Trisagion. As with the tonsuring of chanters and readers and the ordination of sub-deacons, for those who are singing, the people respond with "Lord, have mercy." and "Amen." where it is appropriate.

After the man has been consecrated as a bishop, the presiding bishop (usually the Metropolitan) then brings the newly-consecrated bishop into the royal doorway and, as each vestment that is appropriate to his new office is laid upon him, the presiding bishop intones "Axios! Axios! Axios!" The *clergy* then sing "Axios! Axios! Axios!" And

***then*** the ***people*** sing "Axios! Axios! Axios!" Again, this is done after each and every vestment is put on the man.

After this, the presiding bishop takes the dikiri and trikiri in his hands and blesses the people, while the people sing a short "Eis Polla Eti Dhespota!"

## The Prokeimenon

With the celebration of the prokeimenon, there may be either one or two prokeimena chanted, depending on whether or not two Epistle readings are called for. When there is one reading, there is one prokeimenon; when there are two readings, there are two prokeimena. The pattern for each of these is different.

With the singing of ***one*** prokeimenon, the order for its chanting is as follows (in what follows, the priest may be replaced by the bishop at a Hierarchical Divine Liturgy):

| | |
|---|---|
| ***Deacon:*** | Wisdom! Let us be attentive! |
| ***Priest:*** | Peace be with you all! |
| ***Reader:*** | And with your spirit! |

| | |
|---|---|
| ***Deacon:*** | Wisdom! |
| ***Reader:*** | The prokeimenon is in the [1st through 8th] tone: [Prokeimenon verse is chanted]. |
| ***People:*** | [Prokeimenon verse is sung]. |
| ***Reader:*** | [Psalm verse is chanted]. |
| ***People:*** | [Prokeimenon verse is sung]. |
| ***Reader:*** | [***1st half*** of prokeimenon verse is chanted]. |
| ***People:*** | [***2nd half*** of prokeimenon verse **is sung**]. |

In the Greek practice, however, the reader chants the prokeimenon ***once*** and the Psalm verse ***once***, with ***no*** responses sung.

When there are ***two*** prokeimena, the order for their chanting is as follows (again, in what follows, the priest may be replaced by the bishop at a Hierarchical Divine Liturgy):

| | |
|---|---|
| ***Deacon:*** | Wisdom! Let us be attentive! |
| ***Priest:*** | Peace be with you all! |
| ***Reader:*** | And with your spirit! |

| | |
|---|---|
| ***Deacon:*** | Wisdom! |
| ***Reader:*** | The prokeimenon is in the [1st through 8th] tone: [***1st*** prokeimenon is chanted]. |
| ***People:*** | [***1st*** prokeimenon is sung]. |
| ***Reader:*** | [Psalm verse is chanted]. |
| ***People:*** | [***1st*** prokeimenon is sung]. |
| ***Reader:*** | [***2nd*** prokeimenon is chanted]. |
| ***People:*** | [***2nd*** prokeimenon is sung]. |

There is ***no*** "announcement" of the 2nd prokeimenon as there was with the 1st prokeimenon. Instead, as per above, the reader just immediately chants the 2nd prokeimenon with ***no*** "introduction" as such.

### The Epistle

Even though there is no singing during the chanting of the Epistle, still, as previously mentioned, the choir director is usually the person in the parish who trains and instructs the readers in their ministry. For the beginning of the Epistle reading, the priest or bishop says, "Wisdom!" The reader then responds with one of the following intonation formulae:

- "The Reading is from the Acts of the Holy Apostles!"

- "The Reading is from the Epistle of the Holy Apostle Paul to [the Romans; the Galatians; the Ephesians; the Philippians; the Colossians; Titus; Philemon]."

- "The Reading is from the [1st; 2nd] Epistle of the Holy Apostle Paul to [the Corinthians; the Thessalonians; Timothy]."

- "The Reading is from the Epistle to the Hebrews."

- The Reading is from the [1st; 2nd; 3rd] Catholic Epistle of the Holy Apostle [Peter; John the Theologian]."

The deacon then says, "Let us be attentive!" The reader then commences with the Epistle reading, starting with one of the following introductions:

- If the reading is from the Acts of the Apostles, the introduction is, "In those days,".

- If the reading is from one of the two Epistles to Timothy, the introduction is, "My son, Timothy,".

- If the reading is from the Epistle to Titus, the introduction is, "My son, Titus,".

- If the reading is from any other Epistle, the introduction is, "Brethren,".

If **two** Epistle readings are called for, the reader does **not** "announce" the second reading. Rather, he or she makes a very slight pause, then begins the second reading with the appropriate introduction ("Brethren," etc.).

## *"Alleluia" Verses*

At the conclusion of the Epistle reading, the priest or bishop will bless the reader with the sign of the Cross, saying, "Peace be with you, Reader!" The reader then responds with, "And with your spirit! Alleluia! Alleluia! Alleluia! The people then sing a triple "Alleluia!" The reader then chants the **first** "Alleluia" verse. The people then sing another triple "Alleluia!" The reader then chants the **second** "Alleluia" verse. The people then sing a final triple "Alleluia!"

Many times, when there are **two** Epistle readings called for, there is a **third** "Alleluia" verse that is chanted. In that case, once the priest or bishop says, "Peace be with you, Reader!", the reader responds with **both** "And with your spirit! Alleluia! Alleluia! Alleluia!" **and** the **first** "Alleluia" verse! The people then sing a triple "Alleluia!" The reader then chants the **second** "Alleluia" verse, with the people responding again with a triple "Alleluia!" The reader then chants the **third** "Alleluia" verse, and the people respond with a final triple "Alleluia!"

In **many** Greek parishes, however, the people sing "Alleluia!" **three** times, with **no** "Alleluia!" verses chanted by the reader.

However many "Alleluia" verses there may be, the reader **stays** in the center of the church until the final triple "Alleluia!" is **completely** sung through. **Then**, he or she raises the Epistle book or Holy Bible again (with the Holy Cross facing outward) and processes out of the center of the church.

### *The Gospel*

In many parishes, the priest or bishop will intone aloud the prayer before the Gospel reading, which begins "Illumine our hearts, O Master, Who love mankind, with the pure light of Your knowledge!" In some of these parishes, the people, after the priest concludes with "...now and ever and unto ages of ages!", will sing an "Amen."

In all cases, at this point, the priest or bishop will come out from the sanctuary and bless the people with the sign of the Cross as he says, "Wisdom! Let us be attentive! Let us listen to the Holy Gospel! Peace be with you all!" The people then sing "And with your spirit!" The priest or bishop then chants "The reading is from the Holy Gospel according to Saint [Matthew; Mark; Luke; John the Theologian]!" The people then sing "Glory to You, O Lord! Glory to You!" The deacon then intones "Let us be attentive!", and the priest or bishop then chants the Gospel reading.  If a deacon is chanting the Gospel reading, he does so in the center of the church.  However, in the Greek practice, at a Hierarchical Divine Liturgy, the deacon will chant the Gospel reading from before the bishop's throne on the right hand side of the church.

At the conclusion of the Gospel reading, the people again sing "Glory to You, O Lord!  Glory to You!"  If a bishop or a Metropolitan is serving, then, after singing the "Glory to You, O Lord!", the people would sing "Eis Polla Eti Dhespota!" as the bishop or Metropolitan blesses the people.

**The Sermon**

At the start of the sermon, the people wait until the person giving the sermon begins with "In the Name of the Father, and of the Son, and of the Holy Spirit!  Amen." before sitting down to listen to the sermon.  (In many parishes, the people sit down before the doxology for the sermon is given.)

## Augmented Litany

As with the celebration at Resurrectional and Great Vespers, the correct practice for the Augmented Litany at the Divine Liturgy is to begin with two petitions that are responded by "single 'Lord, have mercy's", the first of which is "Let us say with all our soul and with all our mind, let us say." Then comes the petition beginning, "Have mercy on us, O Lord,…," which is responded to by a *triple* "Lord, have mercy," that is, "Lord, have mercy" sung *three* times. Each subsequent petition is responded to by singing a "*triple* 'Lord, have mercy'." As with the Great Litany, when the priest or deacon gets to the petition that begins, "Commemorating our most holy…," the people respond with, "To You, O Lord." After the exclamation chanted by the priest, the people respond with, "Amen." **Many** times, in the Byzantine tradition, the Augmented Litany is **omitted**.

Some parishes, however, follow the practice of celebrating the Augmented Litany as is done at Daily Vespers and Daily Lenten Vespers, that is, to eliminate the first two "single" petitions and begin with "Have mercy on us, O Lord,…," which is responded to by the *triple* "Lord, have mercy." The choir director and singers should observe whatever is in place by the bishop and the parish priest.

## Litany of the Catechumens

The Augmented Litany is followed by the Litany of the Catechumens. Here, the petitions are responded to with the usual "Lord, have mercy" until the petition, "Bow your heads to the Lord, you catechumens," to which the people respond "To You, O Lord." After the concluding prayer and benediction, the people respond with "Amen."

Some parishes eliminate altogether the celebration of the Litany of the Catechumens. Many parishes eliminate it only during the time between Pascha and Pentecost. This is because, in the early Church, Pascha was the main occasion for Baptism. Therefore, following Pascha, there would not be any catechumens to pray for. Whatever the case, the choir director and singers should observe whatever practice is in place by the bishop and the parish priest.

## Litanies of the Faithful

The Litany of the Catechumens is followed by two Litanies of the Faithful. These are usually **not** omitted in parish practice, but they **may** be abbreviated in their celebration; that is, **only** one or two petitions may be taken, followed by a prayer and the exclamation, or just the exclamation itself. Again, the choir director and singers should observe whatever practice is in place by the bishop and the parish priest. In the Greek practice, **only** the second Litany of the Faithful is celebrated.

In many parishes, to show liturgically that the final litany in this group concludes the sets of petitions that began with the Augmented Litany, the exclamation that begins "that, guarded by Your might, we may ascribe glory,…" is usually responded to with **two** "Amen's."

## The Cherubic Hymn

The Cherubic Hymn is now sung for the Eucharistic Entrance (often called "The Great Entrance"), whereby the Eucharistic Gifts are processed and transferred from the Table of

Oblation to the Altar. At other types of Divine Liturgy (the Liturgy of the Presanctified Gifts, the Vesperal Liturgy of Holy Thursday, the Vesperal Liturgy of Holy Saturday, etc.), other hymns for the Eucharistic Entrance are sung. Whatever type of Liturgy and Entrance hymn are celebrated, the hymn itself is divided into two parts, the first part sung as a censing is done and the procession of the Entrance begins, the second part sung as the Entrance is concluded and the clergy, accompanied by the servers, proceed with the Holy Gifts into the sanctuary.

At this regular Divine Liturgy, the Entrance hymn is, again, the Cherubic Hymn. The first part of the hymn that is sung is "Let us who mystically represent the Cherubim and sing the thrice-holy hymn to the life-creating Trinity now lay aside all earthly cares!" The clergy and servers, with the Holy Gifts, proceed from the Table of Oblation out into the nave of the church, up to the solea, and into the sanctuary. During this procession, it is customary in most parishes for commemorations to be chanted by the clergy. These commemorations may be for our hierarchy, clergy, civil authorities and armed forces, those in the Church with various ministries (singers, servers, teachers, administrators, etc.), our departed members, sick and suffering members, and/or those celebrating specific events (birthdays, name's days, anniversaries, those being married, baptized, or chrismated, etc.).  As the clergy and servers come to the ambo, the celebrants ascend the steps and turn, in the Slavic tradition, to face the people as they stand on the solea (in the Byzantine practice, the clergy would still face the Altar).  At the conclusion of the commemorations, the final commemoration by the main celebrant is usually, "You, and all Orthodox Christians, may the Lord God remember in His Kingdom, always now and ever and unto ages of ages!"  At this point, the people sing "Amen" and then the following as the second part of the Cherubic Hymn:  "that we may receive the King of all Who comes, invisibly upborne by the angelic hosts!  Alleluia!"  (If it is a Hierarchical Divine Liturgy, the bishop will then stand on the solea, holding the dikiri and trikiri, blessing the people with them.  When this occurs, the people sing a short "Eis Polla Eti Dhespota!")  This concludes the Eucharistic Entrance.

### *[Ordination of a Priest]*

If this is a Hierarchical Divine Liturgy at which there will be the ordination of a deacon to the Holy Priesthood, the said ordination occurs at this point.  Other priests go with the candidate who will be ordained to the center of the church.  The candidate bows while the priests accompanying him chant, "Command!"  This is done **three** times, once in front of the center analoi on which an icon is placed, once at the foot of the ambo, and once through the royal doorway in front of the Altar.  The presiding bishop is seated in a chair at the left front corner of the Altar.  The bishop makes the sign of the Cross over the candidate, who is then led around the Altar three times by the concelebrating clergy.  At the **first** encircling of the Altar, all of the **clergy** sing, "O holy martyrs, who fought the good fight and have received your crowns, entreat the Lord that He may have mercy upon us!"  The **people** then respond, in the Slavic tradition, singing this same hymn ("O Holy Martyrs!").  At the **second** encircling of the Altar, all of the **clergy** then sing, "Glory to You, O Christ God, the Apostles' Boast, the martyrs' Joy, whose preaching was the consubstantial Trinity!"  The **people** then respond, again in the Slavic tradition, singing this same hymn ("Glory to You, O Christ God!").  At the **third** encircling of the Altar, all of the **clergy** then sing, "Rejoice, O Isaiah!  A Virgin is with Child, and will bear a Son, Emmanuel, both God and Man!  And 'Orient' is His Name, Whom, magnifying, we called the Virgin 'Blessed!'"  The **people** then respond, again in the Slavic tradition, singing this same final hymn ("Rejoice, O Isaiah!").

The candidate then bows on his knees at the right front corner of the Altar, while the bishop, laying his stole on the head of the candidate, bends over him and quietly gives him words of exhortation. When this is done, the bishop then chants the prayers of ordination, beginning with "The grace divine, which always heals that which is infirm,…!" During these prayers, the people respond with the usually "Lord, have mercy." and, at the exclamation, with "Amen." After this, the senior **priest** intones an augmented version of the Great Litany, containing petitions for the candidate being ordained and for his ministry. As with the regular Great Litany, "Lord, have mercy." is sung in response, with "To You, O Lord" following the petition beginning "Commemorating our most holy,…," and with "Amen." following the exclamation.

When this is done, the bishop takes the newly-ordained priest and presents him to the people in the royal doorway. He then takes each vestment of the new ministry of the priest and, presenting it to the people, exclaims "Axios!" (meaning, "He is worthy!"). The **clergy** then sing a triple "Axios!" ("Axios! Axios! Axios!"). The **people** then respond with this same triple "Axios!" This procedure is done for **each** and **every** vestment presented, as well as the priest's cross and Divine Liturgy service book presented. After all of this, the bishop blesses the newly-ordained priest, kisses him three times, and then, taking the dikiri and trikiri in his hands, blesses all of the people, as the people sing a short "Eis Polla Eti Dhespota!" The rest of the Divine Liturgy then continues.

## Litany of Supplication

The Litany of Supplication is then intoned. For the first few petitions, the response sung by the people is "Lord, have mercy." When the priest or deacon chants the petition, "That the whole evening may be perfect, holy, peaceful, and sinless, let us ask of the Lord," the people respond with singing, "Grant it, O Lord." This is done for the remaining petitions until, again, the petition that begins, "Commemorating our most holy,...," with the people responding, "To You, O Lord." After an exclamation by the priest and the "Amen" by the people, the priest faces the people and, blessing them, says, "Peace be with you all!" The people then respond by singing, "And with your spirit!" The priest or deacon then says, "Bow your heads unto the Lord." The people sing, "To You, O Lord." The priest reads a prayer, ending with an exclamation, to which the people respond with, "Amen."

## The Peace

The priest or bishop then comes out of the sanctuary and blesses the people, chanting, "Peace be with you all!" The people respond with, "And with your spirit!" The celebrant then chants, "Let us love one another, that, with one mind and one heart, we may confess:" The people then sing, "Father, Son, and Holy Spirit! The Trinity, one in essence, and undivided!"

## The Creed

At this point, the deacon, standing on the solea, gestures with his orarion and intones, "The doors! The doors! In wisdom, let us be attentive!" The people then sing the Creed. In some parishes that have a kleros rather than a choir loft, to encourage more congregational singing, the choir director turns and faces the people in the nave, directing them in the singing of the Creed being led by the choir. In the Byzantine tradition, the Creed is often chanted by the people as a reader would, rather than being sung.

## The Anaphora

We now come to **_the central_** section of the Divine Liturgy, the Anaphora, which means "lifting up," since the Holy Gifts of bread and wine are lifted up as an offering to God the Father, to become the Body and Blood of Christ through the descent of the Holy Spirit! As such, being not only the central part of the service, but **a _corporate_ act** (the Eucharistic prayers of both St John Chrysostom and St Basil the Great are in the plural, saying "we" and "us", meaning **both** clergy **_and_** laity), **the Eucharistic prayers _must_ be said aloud for _all_ to hear and offer, in (again) this corporate worship!** The word "**liturgy**" means "**common** work" or "**common** action," and, as such, precludes the involvement of _**all**_ the people of God, "[the] royal priesthood, [the] holy nation" (1 Peter 2:9).

The deacon, still standing on the solea, intones, "Let us stand aright! Let us stand with fear! Let us be attentive, that we may offer the Holy Oblation in peace!" The people respond by singing, "A mercy of peace! A sacrifice of praise!"

The deacon returns to the sanctuary as the main celebrant comes out to stand on the ambo, blessing the people as he chants, "The grace of our Lord, Jesus Christ, the love of God the Father, and the communion of the Holy Spirit, be with all of you!" The people then sing, "And with your spirit!"

The celebrant then turns, faces the Altar, and raises his arms, as he intones, "Let us lift up our hearts!" The people respond with, "We lift them up unto the Lord!"

The celebrant chants, "Let us give thanks to the Lord!", as he goes through the royal doorway and stands before the Altar. At this point, two different styles come to the fore. The Byzantine practice is to sing only, "It is meet and right!" or "It is proper and right!" **However**, this abbreviated form is **only** done in Greek parishes. Antiochian parishes follow the Slavic practice, which is more expanded by singing, "It is meet and right to worship the Father, and the Son, and the Holy Spirit: the Trinity, one in essence, and undivided!"

When this is sung, the Eucharistic Prayer proper begins. The text of the two Liturgies diverges here. St John Chrysostom's Prayer begins, "It is meet and right to hymn You, to bless You, to praise You, to give thanks to You, and to worship You in every place of Your dominion!" St Basil the Great's Prayer begins, "O Existing One [or, "O Living One"], Master, Lord God, Father Almighty and adorable!" Since there is no singing at this point and, when the singing commences, there is no difference in the responses for the two different Anaphoras, it is not necessary to elucidate the full text of either service here.  In **both** Anaphoras, this first section of the Eucharistic Prayer concludes with, "singing the triumphant hymn, shouting, proclaiming, and saying:".  At this point, whichever Liturgy is being celebrated, the people sing, "Holy!  Holy!  Holy!  Lord of Sabaoth!  Heaven and Earth are full of Your glory!  Hosanna in the highest!  Blessed is He Who comes in the Name of the Lord!  Hosanna in the highest!"

In the next section of the Eucharistic Prayer, **both** St John Chrysostom **and** St Basil begin, "With these blessed Powers, O Master Who love mankind, we also cry aloud and say!"  They differ after this for quite a bit, but then conclude the same way:  "Take!  Eat!  This is My Body, Which is broken for you for the remission [or, "forgiveness"] of sins!"  The people respond with, "Amen."

The next section also concludes in the same way in both Liturgies:  "Drink of It, all of you!  This is My Blood of the New Testament, Which is shed for you and for many, for the remission [or, "forgiveness"] of sins!"  Again, the people respond with, "Amen!"

The following part of the Eucharistic Prayer begins differently with the two Liturgies, but concludes in the same way: The deacon lifts the Holy Gifts, as the main celebrant intones, "Your Own of Your Own, we offer unto You, on behalf of all and for all!" The people then sing, "We praise You! We bless You! We give thanks to You, O Lord! And we pray unto You, O our God!"

The wording of the next section differs slightly, but is essentially the same. St John Chrysostom says, "And make this Bread the precious Body of Your Christ!" St Basil says, "Show this Bread to be the precious Body of our Lord and God and Savior, Jesus Christ!" In both instances, the people respond with, "Amen!"

Likewise, the following differs slightly, but is essentially the same. St John Chrysostom says, "And That Which is in this Cup, the precious Blood of Your Christ!" St Basil says, "And show this Cup to be the precious Blood of our Lord and God and Savior, Jesus Christ!" Again, in both instances, the people respond with, "Amen!"

The following **does** conclude the same in both Liturgies in the Slavic practice: "Making the change by Your Holy Spirit!" The people then respond, "Amen! Amen! Amen!" In the Byzantine practice, it is **only** done at the Liturgy of St John Chrysostom.

## The Hymn to the Theotokos

The next section diverges again in both Liturgies, but then concludes the same way: "Especially for [or, "with"] our most holy, most pure, most blessed and glorious Lady, the Theotokos and ever-Virgin Mary!" Here, the singing response is different between the two services: For St John Chrysostom's Liturgy, the people sing, "It is Truly Meet!"; and for St Basil's Liturgy, the people sing, "All of Creation!" For other feast days, there may be special Hymns to the Theotokos, many times the 9th Ode of the Kanon from Matins.

## "And All Mankind"

The next section of prayers chanted by the celebrant, commemorating other saints and praying for departed and living members of the Church, differ in their wording. Both Liturgies, however, conclude this section the same way: The celebrant chants, "Among the first, remember, O Lord, His Beatitude, our Metropolitan [name], and His Grace, our Bishop [name]. Grant them for Your holy churches in peace, safety, honor, health, and length of days, to rightly divide the Word of Your Truth!" The people respond by singing, "And all mankind!"

    If it is a Hierarchical Divine Liturgy, the deacon comes out onto the solea, returning to the sanctuary and gesturing to the presiding bishop with his orarion as he commemorates the hierarch. (This is **sometimes omitted** in the Byzantine tradition.) He then comes back out onto the solea, chanting other commemorations, which conclude with his intoning, "And for all mankind!" The people then respond by singing, "And for all mankind!" (**Note:** In this Hierarchical Divine Liturgy, these two responses are similar, **yet different**! The first response is, "And all mankind!", and the second response is, "And **for** all mankind!")

    In either case, the celebrant continues by chanting, "And grant that, with one mouth and one heart, we may praise Your all-honorable and majestic Name: of the Father, and of the Son, and of the Holy Spirit, now and ever and unto ages of ages!" The people respond, singing, "Amen!"

    The celebrant then comes out to stand on the solea, as he intones, "And the mercies of our great God and Savior, Jesus Christ, be with all of you!" The people then sing, "And with your spirit!"

## [Ordination of a Deacon]

If this is a Hierarchical Divine Liturgy at which there will be the ordination of a man to the Holy Diaconate, the said ordination occurs at this point. Other deacons go with the candidate who will be ordained to the center of the church. The candidate bows while the priests accompanying him chant, "Command!" This is done **three** times, once in front of the center analoi on which an icon is placed, once at the foot of the ambo, and once through the royal doorway in front of the Altar. The presiding bishop is seated in a chair at the left front corner of the Altar. The bishop makes the sign of the Cross over the candidate, who is then led around the Altar three times by the concelebrating clergy. At the **first** encircling of the Altar, all of the **clergy** sing, "O holy martyrs, who fought the good fight and have received your crowns, entreat the Lord that He may have mercy upon us!" The **people** then respond, in the Slavic tradition, singing this same hymn ("O Holy Martyrs!"). At the **second** encircling of the Altar, all of the **clergy** then sing, "Glory to You, O Christ God, the Apostles' Boast, the martyrs' Joy, whose preaching was the consubstantial Trinity!" The **people** then respond, again in the Slavic tradition, singing this same hymn ("Glory to You, O Christ God!"). At the **third** encircling of the Altar, all of the *clergy* then sing, "Rejoice, O Isaiah!  A Virgin is with Child, and will bear a Son, Emmanuel, both God and Man!  And 'Orient' is His Name, Whom, magnifying, we called the Virgin 'Blessed!'"  The **people** then respond, again in the Slavic tradition, singing this same final hymn ("Rejoice, O Isaiah!").

The candidate then bows on his knees at the right front corner of the Altar, while the bishop, laying his stole on the head of the candidate, bends over him and quietly gives him words of exhortation.  When this is done, the bishop then chants the prayers of ordination, beginning with "The grace divine, which always heals that which is infirm,…!"  During these prayers, the people respond with the usually "Lord, have mercy." and, at the exclamation, with "Amen."  After this, the senior **priest** intones an augmented version of the Great Litany, containing petitions for the candidate being ordained and for his ministry.  As with the regular Great Litany, "Lord, have mercy." is sung in response, with "To You, O Lord" following the petition beginning "Commemorating our most holy,…," and with "Amen." following the exclamation.

When this is done, the bishop takes the newly-ordained deacon and presents him to the people in the royal doorway.  He then takes each vestment of the new ministry of the deacon and, presenting it to the people, exclaims "Axios!" (meaning, "He is worthy!"). The **clergy** then sing a triple "Axios!" ("Axios! Axios! Axios!"). The **people** then respond with this same triple "Axios!" This procedure is done for **each** and **every** vestment presented, as well as a liturgical fan with an angel on it. After all of this, the bishop blesses the newly-ordained deacon, kisses him three times, and then, taking the dikiri and trikiri in his hands, blesses all of the people, as the people sing a short "Eis Polla Eti Dhespota!" The rest of the Divine Liturgy then continues.

### Litany Before the Lord's Prayer

In structure, the Litany Before the Lord's Prayer is very similar to the Litany of Supplication celebrated earlier. The first five petitions chanted by the priest or deacon are responded to by singing, "Lord, have mercy." When the priest or deacon chants the petition, "That the whole evening may be perfect, holy, peaceful, and sinless, let us ask of the Lord," the people respond with singing, "Grant it, O Lord." This is done for the remaining petitions until the one that says, "Having asked for the unity of the Faith, and the communion of the Holy Spirit, let us commend ourselves and each other, and all our life unto Christ our God." The people respond to this by singing, "To You, O Lord."

Unlike the Litany of Supplication, there is **no** exclamation after the prayer that follows. Hence, there is **no** "Amen." to be sung. Rather, the service proceeds directly to the Lord's Prayer.

**The Lord's Prayer**

After the prayer that follows the litany just celebrated, the main celebrant chants, "And make us worthy, O Master, that, with boldness and without condemnation, we may dare to call on You, the supra-heavenly God, as Father, and to say:" Everyone stands and the people sing the Lord's Prayer. (In the Byzantine tradition, this is often chanted by the people as a reader would do, rather than being sung.) Again, as with the singing of the Creed, in some parishes that have a kleros rather than a choir loft, to encourage more congregational singing, the choir director turns and faces the people in the nave, directing them in the singing of the Lord's Prayer being led by the choir. The celebrant chants the exclamation, "For, Yours is the Kingdom,…!", to which the people respond by singing, "Amen."

The celebrant then comes out, stands on the ambo, and blesses the people, while intoning,

"Peace be with you all!" The people sing, "And with your spirit!" The deacon then says, "Bow your heads unto the Lord." The people sing, "To You, O Lord." A prayer follows, concluding with the exclamation that begins, "through the grace and compassion and love toward mankind of Your only-begotten Son,….", to which the people respond with, "Amen."

**"One is Holy!"**

A prayer then follows, with *no* exclamation and *no* responding "Amen." The celebrant lifts the Holy Bread off of the discos, and elevates it above the Altar, as the deacon intones, "Let us be attentive!" The celebrant then chants, "The Holy Things for the holy!" The people then sing, "One is Holy! One is the Lord, Jesus Christ, to the glory of God the Father! Amen."

**The Communion Hymn**

The people then ***immediately*** sing the Communion Hymn. If it is a Sunday, the Communion Hymn is, "Praise the Lord from the Heavens! Praise Him in the highest!", followed by a ***triple*** "Alleluia!"

("Alleluia! Alleluia! Alleluia!").  If it is a Sunday with festal overtones that call for special Communion Hymn verses, the people *first* sing, "Praise the Lord from the Heavens!  Praise Him in the highest!", *then* the festal Communion Hymn verse(s), *then*, finally, the *triple* "Alleluia!"  (In the Byzantine tradition, if a feast of the Lord or the Theotokos falls on a Sunday, the special Communion Hymn will be sung with***out*** first singing, "Praise the Lord from the Heavens!".)  If it is a festal Liturgy on any other day of the week, "Praise the Lord from the Heavens!" is *not* sung, *but only* the festal Communion Hymn verse(s) and the *triple* "Alleluia!"  If it is a Divine Liturgy celebrated between Pascha and Ascension, the Communion Hymn is *first*, "Receive the Body of Christ!  Taste the Fountain of Immortality!", *then*, "Praise the Lord from the Heavens!  Praise Him in the highest!", *then* the *triple* "Alleluia!"

### Clergy Communion Hymns

Following the singing of the Communion Hymn, before the clergy receive the Eucharist, everyone in the church together chants the Prayer Before Communion that begins, "I believe, O Lord, and I confess, that You are truly the Christ, the Son of the Living God, Who came into the world to save sinners, of whom I am the first!" (This is the common practice, even though the service books call for the clergy to chant this to themselves silently before their Communion, and then for it to be chanted aloud before the Communion of the faithful.) After this prayer is completed, the Royal Doors are closed, and the clergy proceed to receive the Eucharist and then prepare the Holy Gifts to be received by the people. During this time, the people sing hymns appropriate for the day. There is no liturgical directive concerning this, and there is a wide range of hymns that may be sung (although, the most appropriate thing would be to sing the entire Communion Psalm with an "Alleluia!" refrain). On Sundays, some parishes find it appropriate to sing the Prokeimenon from that day, interspersed with a reader chanting the full Psalm from which the Prokeimenon is taken. On a feast day, the stikhera from "Lord, I Call," the Litya, and/or the Apostikha may be sung. During Great Lent, some parishes sing "Open the Doors of Repentance" or "By the Waters of Babylon." Again, there is no hard-and-fast set of guidelines on what may be sung, and it behooves the choir director to discuss this aspect of the service with the main celebrant, so that, as St Paul says, everything may be done "decently and in order" (1 Corinthians 14:40). In the Byzantine tradition, the Communion Hymn of the day is sung repeatedly, with the other verses of the Psalm that it is from being chanted.  Before the clergy emerge from the sanctuary for the Communion of the Faithful, the people would sing a **triple** "Alleluia!".

During Great Lent, it is good to remember that the time needed at this point is extended, because, along with receiving the Eucharist and preparing the Holy Gifts for the Communion of the people, the clergy **also** need to prepare the Holy Gifts that have been pre-sanctified and will be used later in the week at the celebration of the Liturgy of the Pre-Sanctified Gifts.  Therefore, the choir director, keeping this in mind, needs to have **more hymns** ready to be sung during this time.  The same is true whenever a Hierarchical Divine Liturgy takes place.  When a bishop is present, usually accompanied by his own entourage of clergy, the Communing of the clergy will take longer, since there are more clergy to receive the Eucharist.  Again, the choir director needs to be mindful of this and have **more hymns** ready to be sung.

"Blessed is He"

When the Royal Doors are opened, the clergy come out of the sanctuary with the chalice(s) to Commune the people, and the deacon, raising the chalice he is holding, chants, "In the fear of God, with faith and love, draw near!" The people then sing, "Blessed is He Who comes in the Name of the Lord! God is the Lord, and has revealed Himself to us!" In *some* Greek parishes, however, the people do *not* sing, "Blessed is He Who comes in the Name of the Lord!" in response to "In the fear of God...!".

**"Receive the Body of Christ!"**

As the people come forward to receive the Eucharist, the following Communion Hymn is sung: "Receive the Body of Christ! Taste the Fountain of Immortality!" (Some Byzantine parishes will instead sing "O Son of God, receive me today as a communicant!".) Since it takes a while for all of the people to receive the Eucharist, this Communion Hymn is sung slowly and repeatedly.

In many parishes, when all of the people have finished receiving the Eucharist, the celebrant stands on the ambo, raises the chalice, and says, "Lo! This has touched your lips, and will take away your iniquities, and cleanse your sins!" If this is the local practice, the people *wait* until this prayer is said, and *then* sing a triple "Alleluia!" If this prayer is *not* said, the people sing a triple "Alleluia!" after the last person has received the Eucharist and the clergy return to the sanctuary.

### ["Having Beheld the Resurrection of Christ"]

At this point, the service books call for the deacon in the sanctuary, during the time that the clergy are getting the Holy Gifts ready to be transferred back to the Table of Oblation, to chant a prayer. This "prayer," however, is actually a **hymn** that is sung as Post-Gospel Stikhera at Resurrectional Matins. Therefore, in **some** parishes, the practice is for the people to sing these stikhera in the prescribed tone 6. The stikhera are as follows:

> Having beheld the Resurrection of Christ,
> let us worship the holy Lord, Jesus,
> the only sinless One!
> We venerate Your Cross, O Christ,
> and Your holy Resurrection we praise
>     and glorify!
> For, You are our God,
> and we know no other but You.
> We call on Your Name.
> Come, all you faithful!
> Let us venerate Christ's holy Resurrection!

For, behold, through the Cross joy has come
    into all the world!
Let us ever bless the Lord,
praising His Resurrection!
For, by enduring the Cross for us,
He has destroyed death by death!

Shine! Shine, O new Jerusalem!
The glory of the Lord has shone on you!
Exult now and be glad, O Zion!
Be radiant, O pure Theotokos, in the
    Resurrection of your Son!

O Christ, great and most-holy Pascha!
O Wisdom, Word, and Power of God!
Grant that we may more perfectly
    partake of You
in the never-ending Day of Your Kingdom!

    Again, in some parishes, it is the practice for the people to sing this hymn. This gives the clergy time to prepare the Holy Gifts to be transferred to the Table of Oblation. As with other liturgical elements, the choir director should check with the bishop, the parish priest, or the main celebrant to follow the local practice in that particular parish.

## Liturgy Ending

At this point, the main celebrant comes out onto the ambo, blesses the people, and says, "O God, save Your people and bless Your inheritance!" The people then sing, "We have seen the true Light!" If it is during the time from Pascha until the leavetaking of Pascha, the Paschal troparion, "Christ is Risen!", is sung **once**. If it is during the postfeast of Ascension, the troparion of Ascension is sung **once**.

The celebrant returns to the sanctuary. When the Holy Gifts are ready to be transferred to the Table of Oblation, the deacon takes the paten over there. The celebrant, holding the chalice, stands in the royal doorway and chants, "Blessed is our God, always now and ever and unto ages of ages!" The people respond with, "Amen." If it is during the time of Pascha through Bright Saturday, the people then sing, again, "Christ is Risen!", once. From Thomas Sunday until the next Pascha, the people, after the "Amen.", would sing, "Let our mouths be filled…!"

## The Litany of Thanksgiving

The deacon comes out and stands on the solea. He intones two petitions to which the people respond, "Lord, have mercy." In the next petition, he chants, "Asking that the whole day may be perfect, holy, peaceful, and sinless, let us commend each other, and all our life unto Christ our God!" The people respond with, "To You, O Lord."

The celebrant reads a prayer that concludes with an exclamation that begins, "For, You are our Sanctification...!" The people sing, "Amen." The celebrant (or, some junior priest) comes out into the middle of the church, and, on his way out there, intones, "Let us depart in peace!" The people respond, "In the Name of the Lord!" The deacon, still on the solea, intones, "Let us pray to the Lord." The people sing, "Lord, have mercy."

## "Blessed Be the Name of the Lord"

The celebrant in the center of the church then chants the Prayer Before the Ambo (there are various versions of this prayer, depending on the feast day involved). When he chants the exclamation, the people respond with, "Amen."

The people then sing, "Blessed be the Name of the Lord, henceforth and forevermore!" They *usually* sing this *three* times. However, there are times when various liturgical activities are inserted here, such as the blessing of candles or flowers, the removal of marriage crowns from a bridal couple, the washing off of Chrism from a newly-baptized Christian, etc. In *those* cases, the people sing, "Blessed Be the Name of the Lord!" *only twice*, *then stop*! The inserted liturgical event is then celebrated (usually with sung responses, such as "Lord, have mercy.", "And with your spirit!", "To You, O Lord!", and/or "Amen."). Once this inserted event is completed, as the celebrant returns to the sanctuary, *then* the people sing the *third* and *final* "Blessed Be the Name of the Lord!" In the Byzantine tradition, however, even when various liturgical activities are inserted here, the people *still* sing "Blessed be the Name of the Lord!" *all three times together* (the service books call for Psalm 33:1-8 ["I will bless the Lord at all times"] to be sung here, but this is *usually omitted*).

## The Dismissal

At the dismissal, the celebrant comes out onto the ambo, blesses the people, and chants, "The blessing of the Lord be upon you through His grace and love for mankind, always now and ever and unto ages of ages!" The people respond with, "Amen."

The celebrant then *usually* chants, "Glory to You, O Christ our God and our Hope, glory to You!" When that occurs, the people sing a full "Glory,… now and ever…!", then a triple "Lord, have mercy.", then, "Father, bless!" (or, if a bishop is present, "Master, bless!"; or, if the Metropolitan is present, "Most blessed Master, bless!"). If it is during the time between Pascha and Bright Saturday, the celebrant sings the Paschal troparion ("Christ is Risen from the dead, trampling down death by death, and, upon those in the tombs, bestowing life!") *three* times, followed by the people singing this same Paschal troparion *three* times. If it is during the time from Thomas Sunday until the leavetaking of Pascha, the celebrant then chants the Paschal troparion *two-and-a-half times*, with the people singing *the final half*. In other words, the celebrant chants the full Paschal troparion twice; for the third time, he *only* chants, "Christ is Risen from the dead, trampling down death by death!" The people then respond with the last half of the third time, "And, upon those in the tombs, bestowing life!" (This Paschal element is often **not** celebrated at this point in the Byzantine practice.)

The celebrant then intones the dismissal, commemorating the saints of the day, of the local church, of the local land, and concluding with an exclamation. The people then sing, "Amen." It is customary in many parishes here for the people to sing a **double** "Amen." ("Amen. Amen."). If it is during the time from Pascha until the leavetaking of Pascha, the people then sing the added Paschal verse, "And, unto us, He has given eternal life! Let us worship His Resurrection on the third day!"

At this point, in most parishes, the people sit while the celebrant reads the appropriate announcements for the week.

### ["Many Years"]

After this, the people stand and, if there are any special events to commemorate (those celebrating birthdays, name's days, anniversaries, marriages, births, Baptisms, etc.), the celebrant will stand on the solea facing the Altar and holding up the Holy Cross. The deacon will intone the formula for the commemorations, concluding with, "...and grant them many years!" The people then sing, "God grant you many years!" as the celebrant blesses the people with the Holy Cross. This is **not** done in the Greek practice.

**[Recessional Hymns]**

During the time that the people come forward to venerate the icons and the Holy Cross, any of a number of recessional hymns may be sung, starting with the troparia and kontakia of the day (although this is **not** done in the Greek practice). The details of this should be discussed beforehand between the choir director and the main celebrant.

## B. VESPERAL LITURGY

Today, in our hectic urban society, where most parishioners have to work during the weekdays of Monday through Friday, **many** parishes are celebrating feast days during the week with a Vesperal Divine Liturgy (although this is **not** done in the Greek practice). Basically, the first half of the service is the Great Vespers portion, which then smoothly transitions into the Divine Liturgy part of the service. Its standard outline is as follows.

The celebrant intones, just as at a regular Divine Liturgy, the doxology, "Blessed is the Kingdom of the Father, and of the Son, and of the Holy Spirit, now and ever and unto ages of ages!" The people respond by singing, "Amen.", and then ***immediately*** singing, "Come, Let Us Worship!" and Psalm 103 ("Bless the Lord, O My Soul!"). During the singing of the Psalm, the clergy make a full censing of the entire church. In the Byzantine tradition, the "Come, Let Us Worship!" and Psalm 103 are chanted by the people, rather than sung. This is then followed by the celebration of the Great Litany.

Because Kathisma 1 from the Psalter (Psalms 1-3), beginning with "Blessed is the Man," is prescribed ***only*** for Saturday evening Resurrectional Vespers, when there is a Great Vespers for any other evening of the week (Sunday through Friday evenings), "Blessed is the Man" is ***not*** sung (although "Blessed is the Man" is sometimes prescribed [not always] for the Vespers of feast days that occur on other weekdays)! If the prescribed Kathisma for the Great Vespers for the particular evening of the week is available (as is the case in most monasteries), that may be sung at this point. Otherwise, the people go directly from the Great Litany to the singing of "Lord, I Call Upon You."

After the singing of "Lord, I Call Upon You" and "Let My Prayer Arise," there is a refrain verse by a reader, and then there are festal **stikhera** (sets of sung verses), with refrain verses in between that are chanted by the reader.  Then, the reader chants the "Glory…now and ever…" and the people sing the stikheron relating to the feast and Christ.  There may be up to ten stikhera sung before the "Glory."

The ten possible verses of the reader that are chanted in between the stikhera are as follows:

10) Bring my soul out of prison that I may give thanks to Your Name!

9) The righteous will surround me until You deal bountifully with me!

8) Out of the depths, I cry to You, O Lord! Lord, hear my voice!

7) Let Your ears be attentive to the voice of my supplications!

6) If You, O Lord, should mark iniquities, Lord, who could stand?  But, there is forgiveness with You!

5) For Your Name's sake, I wait for You, Lord!  My soul waits for Your Word!  My soul has hoped in the Lord!

4) From the morning watch until night, from the morning watch, let Israel hope in the Lord!

3) For, with the Lord there is mercy, and with Him is plenteous redemption! And He will deliver Israel from all his iniquities!

2) Praise the Lord, all nations! Praise Him, all peoples!

1) For, His mercy is confirmed on us, and the truth of the Lord endures forever!

These verses are numbered backwards to match the number of stikhera sung. Therefore, if there are seven stikhera to be sung, the reader will start (after "Let My Prayer Arise" is sung) with #7, "Let Your ears be attentive to the voice of my supplications!"; if there are nine stikhera to be sung, the reader will start with #9, "The righteous will surround me until You deal bountifully with me!"; and so forth. In the Byzantine tradition, before the chanting of any of these 10 verses, the reader would chant the prayer, "Set a guard over my mouth, O Lord! Keep watch over the door of my lips!".

There are certainly exceptions here: The Great Vespers that precede the Liturgy of Chrysostom for Annunciation (designated in the Typikon for March 26 - the service is the "end" of the 25th, a full lenten day of fasting) specifies that eleven stikhera be sung on "Lord, I call." The verse preceding the "extra" 11th stikheron is "added in" (after the usual 10) and is: "He makes His angels spirits, and His ministers a flame of fire!" After this stikheron comes the "Glory,...now and ever..." and the stikheron designated for the Feast. Vespers prior to the last singing of the Kanon of St. Andrew (Thursday of the 5th week of Lent) requires 29 stikhera! Usually, for a feast day, there are not that many stikhera to be sung, so any "extra" stikhera response verses would not be needed.

In any case, before the final stikheron, the reader chants the "Glory,...now and ever..."

During the singing of the "Glory..., now and ever..." stikheron, the clergy and servers process from the sanctuary out into the nave, for the Vesperal Entrance. The priest or deacon then raises the censer and says, "Wisdom! Let us be attentive!" The people then sing the Vesperal Entrance hymn, "Gladsome Light," which is the central hymn of Vespers, acknowledging Christ as the Light of the world! The clergy and servers then process back into the sanctuary.

The clergy go to the high place at the back of the altar, and then the Evening Prokeimenon is chanted.  (In the Byzantine tradition, this Evening Prokeimenon is **usually omitted**, and there is also a great variety of practices in that tradition on how this liturgical element is celebrated.  As always, the local custom should be observed.)  The clergy begin by chanting, "Wisdom!  Let us be attentive!  Peace be with you all!," and then continue, "The Prokeimenon is in the [1$^{st}$ through 8$^{th}$] tone."  The main verse of the Prokeimenon is then chanted.  The people respond by singing the main verse of the Prokeimenon in the prescribed tone.  This is sung by the people after each verse is chanted by the clergy.  After the last verse is chanted, the priest or deacon then chants the first half of the verse.  The people then respond with the second half of the verse to conclude the Prokeimenon.

The various Prokeimena for Great Vespers, Sunday through Friday evenings, are as follows.  The virgule (or slash, "/") within these Prokeimena designates the first and second halves of the Prokeimena for the final rendition by both the clergy and the people.

Sunday evening:  **Tone 8  (Psalm 133)**

> "Come, bless the Lord, / all you
>      servants of the Lord!"*

Monday evening:  **Tone 4  (Psalm 4)**

> "The Lord hears / when I call to Him!"

Tuesday evening:  **Tone 1  (Psalm 22)**

> "Your mercy, O Lord, / will follow me
>      all the days of my life!"

Wednesday evening:  **Tone 5  (Psalm 53)**

> "Save me, O God by Your Name, / and judge
>      me by Your strength!"

Thursday evening:  **Tone 6  (Psalm 120)**

> "My help comes from the Lord, / Who made
>      Heaven and Earth!"

Friday evening:  **Tone 7  (Psalm 58)**

> "You, O God, are my Helper, / and Your
>      steadfast love will go before me!"

*In the Antiochian tradition, this Prokeimenon is, "You who stand in the temple of the Lord, / in the courts of the house of our God!"

After the Evening Prokeimenon, three Old (or, sometimes, New) Testament readings are read at this point. If so, there will usually be three readings, though there can be more. The format for introducing these readings is as follows:

| | |
|---|---|
| **Deacon:** | Wisdom! |
| **Reader:** | The Reading is from [name of Biblical Book from which the reading comes]! |
| **Priest:** | Let us be attentive! |
| **Reader:** | [begins the Reading with no special introduction (like, "Brethren").] |

Then, there is a Little Litany celebrated, followed by the singing of the troparion and Kontakion of the feast, as is done at a regular Divine Liturgy. At this point, the Trisagion is celebrated, and the rest of the Divine Liturgy follows, as usual.

## C. BAPTISMAL DIVINE LITURGY

In some dioceses and parishes, the restoration of the Sacrament of Holy Baptism with the Divine Liturgy is taking place (although this is **not** done in the Greek practice). While the order and specifics for such a service need to be according to the instructions of the local bishop, the following seems to be the widely-practiced order for such a service.[10]

The first part of the baptismal rite is known in the service books as the "Prayers at the Reception of the Catechumens." This section includes the Exorcisms, the Renunciation of Satan, the Conversion to Christ, and the Confession of Faith (the Creed). This section is celebrated in the narthex at the back of the church, and is done **_before_** the Divine Liturgy proper (with the doxology, "Blessed is the Kingdom!") begins. During all of these liturgical elements, the various prayers and exclamations are

---

[10] Cf. Schmemann, Alexander, *Of Water and the Spirit: A Liturgical Study of Baptism*, SVS Press, Crestwood, NY, 1974, pp. 115-121, and especially pp. 169-170. For Holy Baptism and Holy Chrismation served separately from the Divine Liturgy, cf. below, chapter 4, "Sacramental Services," pp. 283-299.

responded to with the appropriate singing of "Lord, have mercy." and "Amen." where called for.

When this initial section has been completed, the clergy, servers, initiate(s)-to-be-baptized, his or her sponsors (godparents), and his or her family members proceed from the narthex into the middle of the nave of the church. At this point, the Divine Liturgy proper begins, starting with the doxology, "Blessed is the Kingdom!" The people sing "Amen." in response, and this is followed by the Great Litany, with petitions appropriate to Baptism being added in. In this Baptismal Divine Liturgy, the singing of all three Antiphons and "Only-Begotten Son" is **omitted!**

After the Great Litany, the baptismal rites are celebrated: the Blessing of Water, the Anointing of Water, and the Anointing of the Initiate (both anointings done with "the oil of gladness"). Again, during all of these liturgical elements, the various prayers and exclamations are responded to with the appropriate singing of "Lord, have mercy.", "To You, O Lord.", and "Amen." where called for.

During the anointing of the water, the celebrant makes the sign of the Cross as he pours the oil over the water **three** times. **Each** of the **three** times, he intones, "Alleluia! Alleluia! Alleluia!" The **people** then respond, **each** of the three times, by singing, "Alleluia! Alleluia! Alleluia!" During the anointing of the initiate, as the celebrant anoints the various parts of the body, he intones a phrase appropriate to that portion of the body ("Unto the hearing of faith!", "Your hands have made and fashioned me!.", "That he may walk in the way of Your commandments!"). As each phrase is intoned, the people respond with "Amen."

The Baptism proper (the triple immersion in water) now takes place. The people respond with an "Amen." at the **three** distinct sections of the baptismal exclamation: "The servant of God, [name], is Baptized, in the Name of the Father," ("Amen!"), "and of the Son," ("Amen!"), and of the Holy Spirit!" ("Amen!"). The reader **then immediately** chants Psalm 31 ("Blessed is he whose transgression is forgiven, whose sin is covered!").

Following this, the white baptismal garment is placed on the newly-baptized, as the celebrant chants, "The servant of God, [name], is clothed with the robe of gladness, in the Name of the Father, and of the Son, and of the Holy Spirit!" The people respond with "Amen!", and **then immediately** sing the following hymn, in tone 8:

Grant unto me the robe of light, O most merciful Christ our God, Who clothe Yourself with light as with a garment!

After this, the Sacrament of Holy Chrismation is celebrated.  This begins with a Prayer of Chrismation, the exclamation to which the people sing, "Amen."  The newly-baptized is then anointed with the Holy Chrism.  Similar to the anointing with the oil of gladness, the person is anointed over their entire body.  At *each* point of anointing, the celebrant intones, "The seal of the gift of the Holy Spirit!", to which the people respond, *each* time, with "Amen."  A final prayer is said, to which the people, again, respond by singing "Amen."

At this point, the Gospel Entrance is made, with the people singing, "Come, Let us Worship!"  This is followed by the troparia and kontakia for the day.

Following these hymns, a special version of the Trisagion is sung.  In place of "Holy God!", the people sing "As Many As Have Been Baptized!"  The text is as follows:  "As many as have been Baptized into Christ have put on Christ!  Alleluia!"  This is sung

***three*** times.  At ***each*** of the ***three*** times, the celebrant leads the newly-chrismated, with his or her sponsors and his or her family members, around the baptismal font and the center icon analoi.  After the third encircling and singing, the people continue by singing a full "Glory,... now and ever...!"  During the singing of the "Glory!", the celebrant enters the sanctuary and the reader, carrying the Epistle book or Holy Bible, goes to receive a blessing.  The newly-chrismated, along with his or her sponsors and his or her family members, then advance forward and stand at the foot of the ambo for the next part of the Divine Liturgy, until the faithful receive the Eucharist.  The people then sing an abbreviation of the hymn ("Have put on Christ!  Alleluia!"), followed by a final full "As Many As Have Been Baptized!"

At this point, the reader is at his or her place in the center of the church.  ***Two*** prokeimena are sung here:  the one for the day, and the following Prokeimenon for Baptism, in tone 3:[11]

> The Lord is my Light and my Salvation!
> Whom should I fear?

---

[11] For the format of chanting ***two*** prokeimena, see above, pp. 207-208.

***Two*** Epistle readings are then chanted: the one for the day, and the one for the Sacrament of Baptism (Romans 6:3-11). This is followed by the ***usual two*** "Alleluia!" verses, since there are ***no*** special "Alleluia!" verses called for in the Sacrament of Baptism.

Then, ***two*** Gospel readings are chanted: one for the day, and one for the Sacrament of Baptism (Matthew 28:16-20). Since the person proclaiming the two Gospel readings only pauses slightly (with ***no*** special announcement) between the first and second readings, this does not affect the choir director and Church singers. The responses sung are done as prescribed at a regular Divine Liturgy.

At the time when the faithful receive the Eucharist, the newly-baptized, his or her sponsors, and his or her family members all receive the Eucharist first, followed by the rest of the faithful. Before this, however, the churching of the newly-baptized takes place, with the celebrant bringing the person from the back to the front of the church, pausing as various places with exclamations ("The servant of God, [name], is churched...!", "In the midst of the congregation, [he, she] will sing praises to You!"), to which there are ***no sung responses***. ***After*** the churching, however, the people sing the

Prayer of St Symeon ("Lord, Now Let Your Servant Depart in Peace!") in tone 6.

The Divine Liturgy continues. At the point where the singing of "Blessed Be the Name of the Lord!" is called for, it is appropriate to sing this hymn **only _twice_**. The tonsuring of the newly-baptized then takes place, with the appropriate responses ("Lord, have mercy.", "Amen.") at the usual places.

This is followed by the Washing Off of the Holy Chrism and the Tonsuring. Again, during these sections, the various prayers and exclamations are responded to with the appropriate singing of "Lord, have mercy.", "To You, O Lord.", and "Amen." where called for. All of this is **_immediately_** followed by the **_third_** and **_final_** singing of "Blessed Be the Name of the Lord!" The rest of the Divine Liturgy concludes in the usual order.

## D.  MATRIMONIAL DIVINE LITURGY

In some dioceses and parishes, the restoration of the Sacrament of Matrimony with the Divine Liturgy is taking place (although this is **not** done in the Greek practice). While the order and specifics for such a service need to be according to the instructions of the local bishop, the following seems to be the widely-practiced order for such a service.[12]

The betrothal takes place at the entrance from the narthex into the nave of the church. For this part of the service, for those who are singing, the people respond with "Lord, have mercy." and "Amen." where it is appropriate. This betrothal **may** take place the evening before, at the end of Vespers.[13]

The priest (or bishop) leads the couple to the center of the church for the crowning. The celebrant intones, "Glory to You, our God, glory to You!" The people then sing "Glory to You, our God, glory to You!" The celebrant then intones a set of verses. **After each verse**, the people respond by singing "Glory to You, our God, glory to You!"

**At this point**, the Divine Liturgy begins with the doxology, "Blessed is the Kingdom!" The Great Litany is then celebrated, with its appropriately sung responses. In this Matrimonial Divine Liturgy, the singing of all three Antiphons and "Only-Begotten

---

[12] Cf. Meyendorff, John, *Marriage: An Orthodox Perspective*, SVS Press, Crestwood, NY, 1984, Chapter VIII, "A Liturgical Suggestion," pp. 42-43. For Holy Matrimony served separately from the Divine Liturgy, cf. below, chapter 4, "Sacramental Services," pp. 299-317.

[13] Meyendorff, *Marriage*, p. 43.

Son" is *omitted!* After the Great Litany, the three wedding prayers are said, with the appropriate singing of "Lord, have mercy." and "Amen."

At this point, the crowning takes place. The celebrant crowns each person of the wedding couple, "In the Name of the Father, and of the Son, and of the Holy Spirit." In both cases, the people respond by singing, "Amen."

After this, the Gospel Entrance is made, with the singing of "Come, Let Us Worship!" The troparia and kontakia for the day are then sung, followed by the singing of the Trisagion. Then, **two** prokeimena are then chanted: the one for the day, followed by the following Prokeimenon for Matrimony, in tone 8:[14]

> You have set upon their heads crowns of precious stones! They asked life of You, and You gave it to them!

**Two** Epistle readings are chanted: the one for the day, and the one for the Sacrament of

---

[14] For the format of chanting **two** prokeimena, see above, pp. 207-208.

Matrimony (Ephesians 5:20-33). This is followed by the **usual two** "Alleluia!" verses, since there are **no** special "Alleluia!" verses called for in the Sacrament of Matrimony.

Then, **two** Gospel readings are chanted: one for the day, and one for the Sacrament of Matrimony (John 2:1-12). Since the person proclaiming the two Gospel readings only pauses slightly (with **no** special announcement) between the first and second readings, this does not affect the choir director and Church singers. The responses sung are done as prescribed at a regular Divine Liturgy.

The rest of the service continues to be celebrated. After the laity have received the Eucharist, the bridal couple **may** partake of a "common cup" (as is done when the Sacrament of Matrimony is separated from the Divine Liturgy), with the usual responses of "Lord, have mercy." and "Amen." being sung.[15]

The Divine Liturgy continues. At the point where the singing of "Blessed Be the Name of the Lord!" is called for, it is appropriate to sing this hymn **only twice**. A **triple** procession then occurs, with the main celebrant leading the bridal couple **three** times

---

[15] Meyendorff, *Marriage*, p. 43.

around the analoi holding the icon in the middle of the church.  During the **first** encircling, the people sing, "Rejoice, O Isaiah!  A Virgin is with Child, and will bear a Son, Emmanuel, both God and Man!  And 'Orient' is His Name, Whom, magnifying, we called the Virgin 'Blessed!'"  During the **second** encircling, the people sing, "O holy martyrs, who fought the good fight and have received your crowns, entreat the Lord that He may have mercy upon us!"  During the **third** encircling, the people sing, "Glory to You, O Christ God, the Apostles' Boast, the martyrs' Joy, whose preaching was the consubstantial Trinity!"

The removal of the crowns by the main celebrant then takes place, with the usual responses of "Lord, have mercy." and "Amen." being sung.  This is **immediately** followed by the **third** and **final** singing of "Blessed Be the Name of the Lord!"  The rest of the Divine Liturgy concludes in the usual order.

This Matrimonial Divine Liturgy would **not**, of course, be celebrated in the cases of "mixed marriages" or "re-marriages."  In those cases, the joint partaking of the Eucharist being excluded, the Sacrament of Matrimony would be celebrated separately from the Divine Liturgy.[16]

---

[16] Ibid.

## E.  FUNERAL DIVINE LITURGY

In some dioceses and parishes, the restoration of the Funeral with the Divine Liturgy is taking place, especially if the newly-departed Orthodox Christian was a seriously active member of the Church (although this is **not** done in the Greek practice). While the order and specifics for such a service need to be according to the instructions of the local bishop, the following seems to be the widely-practiced order for such a service.[17]

This service is similar to a Vesperal Liturgy, where the first half of the service is a Great Vespers that then transitions into the second half of the Divine Liturgy.  Here, the first half of the service is the Funeral service, which then transitions into the second half of the Divine Liturgy.

If the body of the newly-departed in his or her casket has not yet been brought into the church, the singers stand vigilantly on the sidewalk in the front of the church.  When the hearse drives up and the body of the departed is wheeled into the church, the singers lead the procession, singing the *slow*

---

[17] For the Funeral served separately from the Divine Liturgy, cf. below, *Volume 2*, chapter 6, "Funeral, Interment, and Memorial," pp. 431-499.

*The Divine Liturgy*

Processional "Holy God!" ("Holy God! Holy Mighty! Holy Immortal! Have mercy on us!") ***repeatedly*** until the casket of the departed is in the center of the church.

The service begins with the eucharistic doxology, "Blessed is the Kingdom!" The *people* respond by ***singing***, "Amen.", then sing the Trisagion ("Holy God! Holy Mighty! Holy Immortal! Have mercy on us!") ***three*** times. A ***reader*** then reads the Trisagion Prayers ("O Most Holy Trinity, have mercy on us!"; a ***triple*** "Lord, have mercy."; and a full "Glory,… now and ever…!"), followed by the Lord's Prayer. After the exclamation, "For, Yours are the Kingdom, and the power, and the glory,…!", the reader chants, "Amen.", then "Come, let us worship God, our King! Come, let us worship and fall down before Christ, our King and our God! Come, let us worship and fall down before Christ Himself (or, "the very Christ"), our King and our God!", then chants Psalm 90 ("He who dwells in the shelter of the Most High…!"), followed by a full "Glory,… now and ever…!", and then, ***three*** times, "Alleluia! Alleluia! Alleluia! Glory to You, O God!"

The celebrant then chants the verses of the First Stasis from Psalm 118. In between each verse, the people respond with ***one*** "Alleluia!" The celebrant then chants a full "Glory,… now and ever...!", and the people respond one more time with a single "Alleluia!"

The celebrant then chants the verses of the Second Stasis from Psalm 118. In between each verse, the people respond with, "Have mercy upon Your servant!" The celebrant then chants a full "Glory,... now and ever...!", and the people respond one more time with, "Have mercy upon Your servant!"

The celebrant then chants the verses of the Third Stasis from Psalm 118. In between each verse, the people respond with **one** "Alleluia!" The celebrant then chants a full "Glory,... now and ever...!", and the people respond one more time with a single "Alleluia!"

The people then sing, "Blessed are You, O Lord! Teach me Your statutes!" (which is the refrain of this hymn) in tone 5, with its interspersed verses. This hymn ends with the triple singing of, "Alleluia! Alleluia! Alleluia! Glory to You, O God!"

There then follows a Little Litany: two petitions calling for "Lord, have mercy." as the response; one petition calling for "Grant it, O Lord." as the response; one more petition calling for "Lord, have mercy." as the response; and an exclamation, to which the people respond by singing, "Amen." (This is the standard format for **all** Little Litanies at a

Funeral, Funeral Divine Liturgy, and Memorial service.)

Then, the people sing Kathisma Hymns in tone 5, the first one beginning, "Give rest with the just, O our Savior, unto Your servants."

This is followed by the Funeral Kanon, in tone 6. Here, in popular practice, **only** odes 1, 3, 6, and 9 are celebrated. Ode 1 begins, "When Israel passed on foot over the sea,...." Ode 3 starts, "There is none so holy as You, O Lord my God,...." Ode 6 leads off with, "When Israel passed on foot over the sea,...." Ode 9 begins, "It is not possible for men to see God,...." After **each** and **every** ode, the celebrant intones, "Give rest, O Lord, to the soul of Your servant who has fallen asleep!" The people then sing this very same, "Give rest, O Lord,...!" The celebrant then chants, for odes 1, 3, and 6, "Glory to the Father, and to the Son, and to the Holy Spirit!" For ode 9, the celebrant chants, "Let us bless the Father, and the Son, and the Holy Spirit, the Lord!" In **all** of these instances, the people respond by singing, "Now and ever and unto ages of ages! Amen."

In some parishes, there is an effort to restore the troparia of the Kanon chanted by a reader. In that case, the ode is sung, the reader chants the troparia, and **then** the celebrant begins intoning, "Give rest, O Lord,…!"

After ode 6, the Kontakion ("With the saints, give rest,…."), in tone 6, and the Oikos ("You, only, are Immortal,…"), in tone 8.  These are then followed by **either** the chanting of "Give rest, O Lord,…!" **or** by the chanted troparia and **then**, "Give rest, O Lord,…!"

After the Kanon, the Beatitudes are celebrated.  The main celebrant intones the first four verses of the Beatitudes, then the people respond by singing, "Remember us, O Lord, when You come in Your Kingdom!", and after each set of verses.  The celebrant then chants "Glory to the Father, and to the Son, and to the Holy Spirit.", followed by a verse.  The people again sing, "Remember us, O Lord, when You come in Your Kingdom!"  The celebrant chants, "Now and ever and unto ages of ages.  Amen.", followed by a verse.  The people sing "Remember us, O Lord, when You come in Your Kingdom!" a final time.

At this point, the service transitions into the Divine Liturgy through the celebration of the Prokeimenon.  For the Funeral, this is in tone 6, and states, "Blessed is the way in which you shall walk today, O soul!  For, a place of rest is prepared for you!"  The reader chants this, then the people sing it. The reader then chants a response verse ("To You, O Lord, will I call! O my God, be not silent to me!"), and the people sing the Prokeimenon verse ("Blessed is the way…!") again. The reader then chants the first half of the Prokeimenon verse ("Blessed is the way in which you shall walk today, O soul!"), after which the people sing the second half of the verse ("For, a place of rest is prepared for you!").

The reader then chants the Funeral Epistle (1 Thessalonians 4:13-17). This is followed by the "Alleluia!" verses: the reader chants, "And with your spirit! Alleluia! Alleluia! Alleluia!" The people sing a triple "Alleluia!" The reader chants the first verse, "Blessed are they whom You have chosen and taken, O Lord!" The people sing a triple "Alleluia!" The reader chants the second verse, "Their memory is from generation to generation!" The people sing a final triple "Alleluia!"

The Gospel is then proclaimed (John 5:24-30). This is followed by the sermon, and the rest of the Divine Liturgy.

After the triple singing of "Blessed Be the Name of the Lord!", the people sing the Troparia for the Departed, in tone 4, beginning, "With the souls of the righteous departed,…."

This is followed by an Augmented Litany. Just like at Daily Vespers, the Augmented Litany here begins with the petition, "Have mercy on us, O God,....", and the people responding with a **triple** "Lord, have mercy." **right from this first petition**. There are three petitions that call for this triple "Lord, have mercy." as the response. Then comes a petition whereby the people respond with, "Grant it, O Lord." Then, another petition that calls for, as a response, a **single** "Lord, have mercy." This is followed by a long prayer and an exclamation, to which the people respond by singing, "Amen."

After this, the celebrant reads the Final Prayer of Absolution over the body of the departed. The usual sung responses of "Lord, have mercy." and "Amen." occur where appropriate.

The Dismissal then follows, with its exclamations and sung responses: "Wisdom! Most Holy Theotokos, save us!" ("More honorable than the Cherubim,...."), and "Glory to You, O Christ, our God and our Hope, glory to You!" (a full "Glory,... now and ever...!", a triple "Lord, have mercy.", and "Father [or, "Master"; or, "Most Blessed Master"], bless!"). The dismissal prayer is intoned, concluding with an exclamation, to which the people *usually* respond with a **double** "Amen." (or, it **could** be a **single** "Amen.")

The celebrant then takes the censer and, standing on the solea and facing the Altar, intones "Memory Eternal!" for the newly-departed person. The people then sing, "Memory Eternal!" ***three*** times, followed by "[His, Her] soul will dwell with the blessed!"

As the people come forward to pay their respects to the departed person, recessional hymns are sung. These usually consist of "Come, Let Us Give the Last Kiss" (in tone 2) and "The Lord is My Shepherd" (in tone 8). If it is during the Pascha season, "Let God Arise!" may also be added here.

As the pallbearers wheel the body of the deceased back out to the hearse, the singers again lead the procession, singing the ***slow*** Processional "Holy God!" ("Holy God! Holy Mighty! Holy Immortal! Have mercy on us!") ***repeatedly*** until the casket is placed in the hearse.[18]

---

[18] For the rubrics for the Interment at the cemetery, cf. below, *Volume 2*, chapter 6, "Funeral, Interment, and Memorial," pp. 499-502.

## F.  CONSECRATION OF A CHURCH

The consecration of a church takes place immediately preceding the celebration of the Hours and the Divine Liturgy.[19] For that reason, its enumeration is presented here.

For the consecration, the bishop and the priests, along with their other vestments, are vested in a special white garment called, in Russian, "***stratchitza***". The one for the bishop is made out of silk, and the one for the priests is made out of cotton cloth.[20] Before the consecration itself, there ***may*** be a blessing of the holy water.[21]

Since the church building, as a temple, has been superceded by the human being as being the temple and dwelling place of God, and since, furthermore, the church building is fashioned after the image of our bodies, the rite for consecrating a church is analogous to the Sacraments of Baptism and Chrismation for people. In other words, when a church is consecrated, it is "baptized" and "chrismated."[22]

---

[19] Hapgood, pp. 493-511.
[20] Ibid, pp. 494 and 613.
[21] Ibid, p. 614.
[22] Ibid.

After the vesting of the bishop and the celebrants, they enter the sanctuary and bless the new Altar with holy water and consecrated wax. Then, the deacon intones, "Let us pray to the Lord.", and the people respond, singing, "Lord, have mercy." The bishop then recites a prayer that begins, "O Lord God our Savior, Who create all things and make the race of mankind for salvation,…!" After the exclamation that begins, "For, unto You are due all glory,…!", the **_priests_** respond with "Amen."

Then, the people sing Psalm 94, which begins, "I will magnify You, O God, my King,…!"[23] After this, the bishop chants the doxology, "Blessed is our God,…!", and, again, the **_priests_** respond with "Amen." The **_clergy_** then chant Psalm 23 ("The Lord is my Shepherd!…!"). Again, the bishop chants the doxology, "Blessed is our God,…!", and, again, the **_priests_** respond with "Amen."

Following this, the nails for closing the Altar are blessed and then inserted into place. The bishop then comes out of the sanctuary, and the deacon intones, "Again, and again, on bended knees, let us pray to the Lord." The people respond, singing, "Amen." The bishop then chants the prayer that begins, "O God, without beginning and eternal, Who

---

[23] Again, the numbering of the Psalms is according to the Septuagint.

call all things into being out of nothingness,...!". Since there is **no** exclamation at the end of this prayer, the people do **not** respond with an "Amen."

Then, there is a litany that begins with the petition, "Help us, save us, have mercy upon us, and keep us, O God, by Your grace." *Again*, it is **the priests** who sing the "Lord, have mercy." responses to these petitions. **However, the people *do* sing**, in response to the petition, "Commemorating our most holy, most pure,...!", the "To You, O Lord!" **Then, the priests again** sing the "Amen." in response to the exclamation, "For, You are holy, O our God,...!" The deacon then intones, "Let us pray to the Lord!", and **the people sing** the "Lord, have mercy.", as well as the "Amen." at the end of the prayer that begins, "O Lord, Who sanctified the streams of Jordan...!".

Once the clergy have washed the Altar with the red-wine-and-rose-water mixture, a **reader** chants Psalm 83 ("How lovely is Your dwelling place, O Lord of hosts!"). The bishop then intones, "Glory to our God, unto ages of ages!" The **priests** respond, "Amen." The mixture is then poured liberally and cross-wise on the Altar and sprinkled on the various holy items. During this time, the bishop chants, "Purge me with hyssop, and I will be clean! Wash me, and I will be whiter than snow!" After the sprinkling, the **reader** chants Psalm 50, starting with

*The Divine Liturgy*

verse 8 ("Fill me with joy and gladness! Let the bones that You have broken rejoice!") to the end.

After the wiping of the Altar with sponges, the bishop intones, "Blessed is our God,…!" Again, the **_priests_** respond, "Amen." The Altar is then anointed with Holy Chrism. When this is completed, the **_reader_** chants Psalm 132 ("Behold! How good and pleasant it is…!"). The bishop then intones, "Glory to You, O Holy Trinity our God, unto ages of ages!" The **_priests_** respond, "Amen." After the Altar is robed with its first covering, When this is completed, the **_reader_** chants Psalm 131 ("Remember, O Lord, in David's favor,…!"). The bishop intones, "Glory to our God, unto ages of ages!" There is **_no_** response to this. After the Altar is robed with its second covering, the Gospel Book and the Cross are placed upon the Altar, and all is sprinkled with the wine-and-water mixture, the **_reader_** chants Psalm 92 ("The Lord is King! He is robed in majesty!"). The bishop intones, "Blessed is our God,…!", and, again, the **_priests_** respond, "Amen."

The Table of Oblation is then sprinkled, arrayed with a holy cloth, and the sacred vessels are placed on it. As the bishop then censes the Altar, the Table of Oblation, and the sanctuary with the censer, the **_deacon_** chants Psalm 25 ("Vindicate me, O Lord, for I have walked in my integrity!") **_repeatedly_**, until the entire church is censed. The four sides of the church (east, west, south, and north) are anointed with the Holy Chrism. The bishop then enters the sanctuary and chants **both** a full "Glory,... now and ever...!" **and** the "Amen."

The deacon then chants the Little Litany, and **<u>the people sing</u>** the responses. After the "To You, O Lord.", the deacon intones, "Let us pray to the Lord!", to which the people respond with "Lord, have mercy." The bishop then chants a prayer that begins, "O Lord of Heaven and Earth, Who, with ineffable wisdom, have founded the Holy Church,...!" At the exclamation of this prayer, the **<u>priests</u>** respond, "Amen." They **(<u>the priests</u>)** also sing the other responses here ("And with your spirit!" and "To You, O Lord!"), as well as the "Amen." that follows the prayer chanted by the bishop that begins, "We thank You, O Lord God of hosts,...!"

A procession **may** now take place to bring the holy relics of a saint (or saints) into the new church from another church, to be placed in the Altar. The bishop exclaims, "Let us go forth in peace!" There is **no** response sung to this. If there is **no** procession to and from another church (which is the more common practice), the holy relics are placed on a lectern in front of the icon of Christ to the right of the Royal Doors of the iconostasis. In either case, the people sing the following hymn, in tone 4: "Your Church that, in all the world, You have adorned with the blood of Your martyrs, as it were of purple and fine linen, cries aloud through them to You, O Christ our God!  Send down Your bounties upon Your people, giving grace to Your Church, and great mercy to our souls!"  They then sing a full "Glory,... now and ever...!", and then the following hymn, in tone 8: "The universe offers You, O Lord, the God-bearing martyrs, the first-fruits of nature, as to the Founder of Creation!  Through their prayers and those of the Theotokos, O merciful One, establish Your Church in peace!"  Everyone enters the church and the bishop enters the sanctuary.  The deacon chants the Little Litany, and **the priests** outside the sanctuary sing the responses.  **However**, when the bishop intones the exclamation ("For, You are holy, O our God,...!"), it is **the people who sing** the "Amen.", followed by the Trisagion ("Holy God!  Holy Mighty!  Holy Immortal!  Have mercy on us!") **three** times.  The deacon then intones, "Let us pray to the Lord!", and the people respond, "Lord, have mercy."  The bishop then chants a prayer that begins, "O Lord our God, faithful in Your words,...!"  After the exclamation ("Through the mercy and love toward mankind...!"), the people sing, "Amen."  The bishop intones, "Peace be with you all!"  The people respond, "And with your spirit!"  The deacon intones, "Bow your heads unto the Lord!"  The people respond, "To You, O Lord!"  The bishop chants a prayer that begins, "O Lord our God,...!"  After the exclamation ("Blessed and glorified be the majesty of Your Kingdom,...!"), the people sing, "Amen."

The clergy leave the sanctuary to process back with the holy relics. In this procession is first the Holy Cross, then the church banners, **then the singers**, then the priests, then the Altar servers, then the icon of the church being consecrated, then the rest of the faithful. Two deacons cense the holy relics, while other deacons bear sacramental fans over the relics.

The people then chant the following hymn, in tone 3: "O Good One, Who founded Your Church on the rock of faith, direct our petitions and accept Your people who, in faith, cry to You: 'Save us, O our God, save us!'" In *some* parishes, if time allows, the following Kanon odes *may* be sung: in tone 3, "O Lord, the Confirmation of those who set their hope in You,...!"; in tone 8, "O Master and Creator of the vault of Heaven,...!"; in tone 5, "You Who, upon nothing, by Your commanded, erected the Earth,...!"

Everyone processes around the church once (counter-clockwise). When all are in front of the entrance doors to the church building, the people sing the following hymns of ordination for the new church: "O holy martyrs, who fought the good fight and have received your crowns, entreat the Lord that He may have mercy upon us!" and "Glory to

You, O Christ God, the Apostles' Boast, the martyrs' Joy, whose preaching was the consubstantial Trinity!"

There is then a censing of the holy relics, the Gospel Book, the Holy Cross, and the icons. After the censing, the bishop intones, "Blessed are You always, O Christ our God, now and ever and unto ages of ages!" The people sing, "Amen." The bishop chants, "Lift up your heads, gates, and be lifted up, ancient doors, that the King of glory may come in!" The people sing, "Who is the King of glory?" **Again**, the bishop chants, "Lift up your heads, gates, and be lifted up, ancient doors, that the King of glory may come in!", and, **again**, the people sing, "Who is the King of glory?" The deacon intones, "Let us pray to the Lord!" The people sing, "Lord, have mercy." The bishop chants a prayer that begins, "Blessed are You forever, O God and Father of our Lord, Jesus Christ,…!" After the exclamation, "For You are holy, O our God, Who rest in the saints,…!", the people sing, "Amen." The bishop intones, "Peace be with you all!" The people respond, "And with your spirit!" The deacon intones, "Bow your heads unto the Lord!" The people respond, "To You, O Lord!" The bishop chants a prayer that begins, "O Master, Lord our God, Who have appointed in Heaven,…!" After the exclamation, "For unto You are due all glory, honor, and worship,…!", the people sing,

"Amen." As the bishop blesses the doors of the church in the form of the Cross, he intones, "The Lord of hosts, He is the King of glory!" The people then sing, "The Lord of hosts, He is the King of glory!"

Everyone then enters the church, while the people sing the following, in tone 4: "Forasmuch as You have shown forth the splendor of the firmament on high, and the beauty of the holy habitation of Your glory here below, O Lord: Establish the same forever, and accept continually our prayers offered to You, through the Theotokos, O You Who are the Life and the Resurrection of all mankind!"

The relics are then taken into the sanctuary, placed on the Altar, and censed three times. Then, the concelebrating clergy are censed and, finally, the bishop himself is censed. The relics are then placed within the Altar and sealed inside with the blessed wax. The deacon intones, "Let us pray to the Lord!" The people sing, "Lord, have mercy." The bishop chants a prayer that begins, "O Lord our God, Who have bestowed upon the holy martyrs who suffered for Your sake,…!" After the exclamation, "For Yours are the Kingdom, and the power, and the glory,…!", **the priests** sing, "Amen."

The deacon intones, "Again, and again, on bended knees, let us pray to the Lord." **The people** then sing a **triple** "Lord, have mercy."  The bishop then chants a prayer that begins, "O Lord our God, Who, by Your Word alone,…!"  **The bishop** then ends this prayer with an "Amen."  As the bishop and everyone else stands up, the deacon continues the Little Litany, from, "Help us, save us, have mercy on us, and keep us, O God, by Your grace."  The people sing the responses to this Little Litany.  After the bishop intones the exclamation, "For You are holy, O our God,…!", the people sing, "Amen."

Following this is an Augmented Litany that begins, "Have mercy on us, O God,…!", and to which, **from the first petition**, the people respond with a **triple** "Lord, have mercy."  After the exclamation, "For, You are a merciful God,…!", the people sing, "Amen."

The bishop then blesses the church, in all four directions (east, west, south, and north) with the Holy Cross.  The deacon intones, "Let us all say, 'Lord, have mercy.  Lord, have mercy.  Lord, have mercy.'"  The people then sing a **triple** "Lord, have mercy."

Following this is the Dismissal, beginning with the petition, "Wisdom!  Most Holy Theotokos, save us!"  The people then sing, "More honorable than the Cherubim,…!"  The bishop intones, "Glory to You, O Christ our God and our Hope, glory to You!"

The people sing a full "Glory,… now and ever…!", a *triple* "Lord, have mercy.", and, then, "Master, bless!" (or, if the main celebrant is the Metropolitan, "Most Blessed Master, bless!"). After the exclamation, the people sing a double "Amen.", and, then, as the bishop blesses the people with the dikiri and trikiri, the people sing a single "Eis Polla Eti Dhespota!"

At this point, there *may* be a petition of "Many Years!", to which the people respond by singing, "Many Years!"

Having completed the consecration of the church, the Hours and the Divine Liturgy immediately follow.

# 4

# SACRAMENTAL SERVICES

## A. HOLY BAPTISM

The *ordo* for the office of Holy Baptism, when celebrated separately from the Divine Liturgy, is as follows.[24]

***Prayers at the Reception of the Catechumens***

The first part of the baptismal rite is known in the service books as the "Prayers at the Reception of the Catechumens." This section includes the Exorcisms, the Renunciation of Satan, the Conversion to Christ, and the Confession of Faith (the Creed). This section is celebrated in the narthex at the back of the church. During all of these liturgical elements, the various prayers and exclamations are responded to with the appropriate singing of "Lord, have mercy." and "Amen." where

---

[24] Hapgood, pp. 271-280. For the celebration of a Baptismal Divine Liturgy, cf. above, pp. 253-259.

called for. The chanting of "Let us pray to the Lord!" should be **omitted** for the ***first two*** exorcisms, since they both address the devil and **not** the Lord.

When this initial section has been completed, the clergy, servers, initiate(s)-to-be-baptized, his or her sponsors (godparents), and his or her family members proceed from the narthex into the middle of the nave of the church.

### Doxology and The Great Litany

At this point, **even though there is no Divine Liturgy being celebrated**, the celebrant **still** chants the doxology, "Blessed is the Kingdom…!" This manifests the eschatological (Kingdom-centered) dimension of the Sacrament of Holy Baptism. The people sing "Amen." in response, and this is followed by the Great Litany, with petitions appropriate to Baptism being added in.

## The Blessing and Anointing of Water and the Anointing of the Initiate

After the Great Litany, the baptismal rites are celebrated: the Blessing of Water, the Anointing of Water, and the Anointing of the Initiate (both anointings done with "the oil of gladness"). Again, during all of these liturgical elements, the various prayers and exclamations are responded to with the appropriate singing of "Lord, have mercy.", "To You, O Lord.", and "Amen." where called for.

The priest starts by chanting the prayer that begins, "Great are You, O Lord, and marvelous are Your works, and there is no word that suffices to hymn Your wonders!" He chants this exclamation *three* times. In the Byzantine tradition, after *each* of the *three* times, the people respond by singing, "Glory to You, O Lord, glory to You!". The prayer then continues. After stating that, "You hallowed the streams of Jordan, sending down upon them from Heaven Your Holy Spirit, and crushed the heads of the dragons who lurked there!", he chants the exclamation, "Wherefore, O King, Who love mankind, come now and sanctify this water, by the indwelling of Your Holy Spirit!" *This* exclamation, also, is chanted *three* times. In the Byzantine tradition, after each of these times, the people respond by singing, "Amen.". The prayer continues through the phrase, "For, we have called upon Your Name, O Lord, and it is wonderful, and glorious, and terrible to adversaries!"

After this, he chants the exclamation, "Let all adverse powers be crushed beneath the sign of the image of Your Cross!" In the Byzantine tradition, after each of these times, the people respond by singing, "Amen.". After intoning this, he dips his hand into the water, making the sign of the Cross in it, and **then** breathing upon the water, **also** in the form of the Cross. This exclamation ("Let all adverse powers...!"), blessing of the water, and breathing upon the water, **all** of this is done by the priest **three** times. The prayer then continues. After the exclamation that begins, "For, unto You are due all glory, honor, and worship,...!", the people sing, "Amen." Then, the priest, facing the people, blesses them, as he chants, "Peace be with you all!" The people sing, "And with your spirit!" The deacon intones, "Bow your heads to the Lord." The people sing, "To You, O Lord." The priest then silently blesses the vessel containing the holy oil, **three** times. The deacon then intones, "Let us pray to the Lord." The people sing, "Lord, have mercy." The priest chants a prayer that begins, "O Lord and Master, the God of our fathers,...!" At the conclusion of the exclamation (which ends,"...now and ever and unto ages of ages!"), the people sing, "Amen."

The deacon then intones, "Let us be attentive!" At this point, the people do **_not_** sing anything, but wait for the priest to anoint the water with the holy oil. During the anointing of the water, the celebrant makes the sign of the Cross as he pours the oil over the water three times. **Each** of the **three** times, he intones, "Alleluia! Alleluia! Alleluia!" The people then respond, **each** of the **three** times, by singing, "Alleluia! Alleluia! Alleluia!" (except in the Byzantine tradition). During the anointing of the initiate, as the celebrant anoints the various parts of the body, he intones a phrase appropriate to that portion of the body ("Unto the hearing of faith!", "Your hands have made and fashioned me!.", "That he may walk in the way of Your commandments!"). As each phrase is intoned, the people respond with "Amen."

## The Baptism by Triple Immersion and the Chanting of Psalm 31

The Baptism proper (the triple immersion in water) now takes place. The people respond with an "Amen." at the three distinct sections of the baptismal exclamation: "The servant of God, [name], is Baptized, in the Name of the Father," ("Amen!"), "and of the Son," ("Amen!"), and of the Holy Spirit!" ("Amen!"). The reader then ***immediately*** chants Psalm 31 ("Blessed is he whose transgression is forgiven, whose sin is covered!"). This is **not** done in the Byzantine tradition.

### *"Grant Unto Me the Robe of Light"*

Following this, the white baptismal garment is placed on the newly-baptized, as the celebrant chants, "The servant of God, [name], is clothed with the robe of gladness, in the Name of the Father, and of the Son, and of the Holy Spirit!" In the Byzantine tradition, the placing of the baptismal garment is done ***after*** Chrismation. The people respond with "Amen!", and then ***immediately*** sing the following hymn, in tone 8:

> Grant unto me the robe of light, O most merciful Christ our God, Who clothe Yourself with light as with a garment!

## B. HOLY CHRISMATION

In the Orthodox Church, when both the Sacraments of Holy Baptism and Holy Chrismation are celebrated separately from the Divine Liturgy, the Sacrament of Holy Chrismation ***immediately*** follows the Sacrament of Holy Baptism![25]

*Prayer Before Holy Chrismation*

After the placement of the white baptismal garment on the newly-baptized, the priest chants a prayer that begins, "Blessed are You, O Lord God Almighty, the Source of all good things, the Sun of Righteousness,…!" After the exclamation that begins, "For, You are our God,…!", the people sing, "Amen."

---

[25] Hapgood, pp. 281-285. Again, for the celebration of a Baptismal Divine Liturgy (which includes the Sacrament of Holy Chrismation), cf. above, pp. 253-259.

### The Anointing With the Holy Chrism

The newly-baptized is then anointed with the Holy Chrism.  Similar to the anointing with the oil of gladness, the person is anointed over their entire body.  At each point of anointing, the celebrant intones, "The seal of the gift of the Holy Spirit!", to which the people respond, each time, with "Amen." (in the Byzantine tradition, instead of "Amen.", the people respond with, "Seal.").  A final prayer is said, to which the people, again, respond by singing "Amen."  Also, in the Byzantine tradition, **immediately** after Chrismation, the Holy Chrism is washed off and the child is tonsured and dressed.  During this time, depending on the season, the Katavasiae of either the Cross or Pascha is chanted.

### "As Many as Have Been Baptized"

Following this, a special version of the Trisagion is sung.  In place of "Holy God!", the people sing "As Many As Have Been Baptized!"  The text is as follows:  "As many as have been Baptized into Christ have put on Christ!  Alleluia!"  This is sung **three** times.  At **each** of the **three** times, the celebrant leads the newly-chrismated, with his or her sponsors and his or her family members, around the baptismal font and the center icon analoi. After the third encircling and singing, the people continue by singing a full "Glory,... now and ever...!" During the singing of the "Glory!", the celebrant enters the sanctuary and the reader, carrying the Epistle book or Holy Bible, goes to receive a blessing. The people then sing an abbreviation of the hymn ("Have put on Christ! Alleluia!"), followed by a final full "As Many As Have Been Baptized!"

*The Prokeimenon*

The reader, now standing in the center of the church, but **behind** the baptismal font, the newly-baptized, and his or her sponsors and family, is in place for the celebration of the Prokeimenon. The chanting of the Prokeimenon is as follows:

> **Deacon:** Wisdom! Let us be attentive!
> **Priest:** Peace be with you all!
> **Reader:** And with your spirit!
> **Deacon:** Wisdom!

| | |
|---|---|
| *Reader:* | The prokeimenon is in the 3rd tone: The Lord is my Light and my Salvation! Whom should I fear? |
| *People:* | The Lord is my Light and my Salvation! Whom should I fear? |
| *Reader:* | The Lord is the Upholder of my life! Of whom, then, should I be afraid? |
| *People:* | The Lord is my Light and my Salvation! Whom should I fear? |
| *Reader:* | The Lord is my Light and my Salvation! |
| **People:** | Whom should I fear? |

This is **not** done in the Byzantine tradition. What is done there is that the reader chants the Prokeimenon and the accompanying verse **once** before going on to the Epistle.

***The Epistle and "Alleluia!"***

The Epistle reading is Romans 6:3-11. It is intoned as follows:

**Priest:** Wisdom!
**Reader:** The Reading is from the Epistle of the Holy Apostle Paul to the Romans!
**Deacon:** Let us be attentive!

The reader then begins the chanting of the Epistle with, "Brethren!"

After the conclusion of the Epistle reading, the priest blesses the reader, saying, "Peace be with you, Reader!" The reader chants, in response, "And with your spirit! Alleluia! Alleluia! Alleluia!" The people then sing a *triple* "Alleluia!" **<u>Note:</u>** Since there are *no* special "Alleluia!" verses called for in the Sacraments of Holy Baptism and Holy Chrismation, the people *only* sing this triple "Alleluia!" *once!*

## *The Gospel*

The Gospel reading is Matthew 28:16-20. In many parishes, the priest will intone aloud the prayer before the Gospel reading, which begins "Illumine our hearts, O Master, Who love mankind, with the pure light of Your knowledge!" In some of these parishes, the people, after the priest concludes with "...now and ever and unto ages of ages!", will sing an "Amen."

In all cases, at this point, the priest will come out from the sanctuary and bless the people with the sign of the Cross as he says, "Wisdom! Let us be attentive! Let us listen to the Holy Gospel! Peace be with you all!" The people then sing "And with your spirit!" The priest then chants "The reading is from the Holy Gospel according to Saint Matthew!" The people then sing "Glory to You, O Lord! Glory to You!" The deacon then intones "Let us be attentive!", and the priest then chants the Gospel reading.

At the conclusion of the Gospel reading, the people again sing "Glory to You, O Lord! Glory to You!"

## [Communion of the Newly – Baptized]

In the Byzantine tradition, after the Gospel, the godparents bring the newly-baptized child forward, and he or she is given Holy Communion, either from the Divine Liturgy earlier that morning (if it is a Sunday), or from the Reserved Sacrament (if it is any other day of the week).

## [Augmented Litany]

At this point, the service books call for the celebration of the Augmented Litany. **However**, these **same** service books have a parenthetical indication that says, "**Usually omitted**!"

**If** the Augmented Litany is to be celebrated, it begins with the petition, "Have mercy on us, O Lord,…," which is responded to by the **triple** "Lord, have mercy." This **triple** "Lord, have mercy." is then sung after each subsequent petition. After the exclamation that begins, "For, You are a merciful God, Who love mankind,…!", the people sing, "Amen."

## The Washing Off of the Holy Chrism

Even though the service books call for washing off the Holy Chrism and tonsuring the newly baptized eight days later, in **most** cases, nowadays, it is done at the conclusion of this service (**except** in the Byzantine tradition, as stated earlier).

The deacon intones, "Let us pray to the Lord.", and the people sing, "Amen." The priest then chants a prayer that begins, "O You Who, through Baptism, have given to Your servant remission of sins,…!" This is concluded with the exclamation that begins, "For, blessed and glorified is Your all-honorable and majestic Name,…!", and the people respond by singing, "Amen."

A second time, the deacon intones, "Let us pray to the Lord.", and the people sing, "Amen." The priest then chants a second prayer, beginning, "O Master, Lord our God, Who, through the Font, bestow heavenly Illumination on them who are Baptized,…!" This is concluded with the exclamation that begins, "For, You are our Sanctification,…!", and the people respond by singing, "Amen." **Note:** There is **no** second prayer in the Byzantine tradition. **Only** the **first** one is celebrated.

Then, the priest, facing the people, blesses them, saying, "Peace be with you all!" (In the Byzantine tradition, since this was done earlier, this section is omitted.) The people sing, "And with your spirit!" The deacon intones, "Bow your heads to the Lord." The people sing, "To You, O Lord." The priest then chants a prayer that begins, "[He, She], who have put on You, O Christ our God,…!" At the end of the exclamation ("…now and ever and unto ages of ages!"), the people sing, "Amen."

The priest, having dipped the sponge in water, then proceeds to wash the Holy Chrism off the newly-baptized, saying, as he goes, "You are Baptized! You are Illumined! You have received Anointment with the Holy Chrism! You are sanctified! You are washed! In the Name of the Father, and of the Son, and of the Holy Spirit!" The people sing, "Amen."

Then, the priest, facing the people, blesses them, saying, "Peace be with you all!" The people sing, "And with your spirit!" The deacon intones, "Bow your heads to the Lord." The people sing, "To You, O Lord." The priest then chants a prayer that begins, "O Lord our God, Who, through the fulfilling of the baptismal font,…!" After the exclamation that begins, "For, unto You are due all glory, honor, and worship,…!", the people sing, "Amen."

The priest then cuts hair from the head of the newly-baptized, in the form of the Cross, saying, "The servant of God, [name],is tonsured, in the Name of the Father, and of the Son, and of the Holy Spirit!" The people sing, "Amen."

**The Dismissal**

The Dismissal is then celebrated, with the priest intoning, "Glory to You, O Christ, our God and our Hope, glory to You!" The people then sing a full "Glory,… now and ever…!", a *triple* "Lord, have mercy.", and, then, "Father, bless!" The priest chants the dismissal prayer, and then the people sing a *double* "Amen." ("Amen. Amen.").

**"Many Years"**

The deacon will intone the formula for the "Many Years!", commemorating the newly-baptized and his or her sponsors and family, concluding with, "…and grant them many years!" The people then sing, "God grant you many years!" as the celebrant blesses the people with the Holy Cross. The singing of "Many Years" is *not* done in the Greek tradition for anyone except the diocesan bishop or the parish priest.

## C. HOLY MATRIMONY

When the Sacrament of Holy Matrimony is celebrated separately from the Divine Liturgy, the order of the service is as follows.[26]

### The Betrothal

The betrothal takes place at the entrance from the narthex into the nave of the church. However, in the Antiochian and Serbian traditions, it is the practice to have the betrothal take place on the solea, in front of the Royal Doors. This betrothal may take place the evening before, at the end of Vespers.[27] (In *some* Antiochian parishes, this *may* take place as much as a month before the wedding.

---

[26] Hapgood, pp. 291-301. For the celebration of a Matrimonial Divine Liturgy, cf. above, pp. 259-263.
[27] Cf. Meyendorff, John, *Marriage: An Orthodox Perspective*, SVS Press, Crestwood, NY, 1984, Chapter VIII, "A Liturgical Suggestion," pp. 42-43.

In the Greek tradition, the betrothal takes place the *same day* as the wedding itself.)

At this point, in the Byzantine tradition, the questions asked of the prospective couple ("Do you, [name], having a good, free, and unconstrained will and a firm intention,…?" [see below, pages 302-303]) are celebrated at this point, **before** the doxology. The priest intones the doxology, "Blessed is our God, always now and ever and unto ages of ages!" The people sing, "Amen." The deacon then chants a litany whose petitions are specific to the Sacrament of Matrimony. Following each petition, the people sing, "Lord, have mercy." After the petition that begins, "Commemorating out most holy, most pure,…!", the people sing, "To You, O Lord." The priest intones the exclamation, "For, to You are due all glory, honor, and worship,…!", and the people sing, "Amen."

The priest then chants a prayer that begins, "O eternal God, Who have brought into unity…!" After the exclamation, "For, You are a merciful God…!", the people sing, "Amen." Then, the priest, facing the people, blesses them, saying, "Peace be with you all!" The people sing, "And with your spirit!" The deacon intones, "Bow your heads to the Lord." The people sing, "To You, O Lord." The priest then chants a prayer that begins, "O Lord our God, Who have espoused the Church as a pure Virgin…!".

Again, after the exclamation, "For, You are a merciful God...!", the people sing, "Amen."

The priest then takes the wedding rings and blesses each person of the bridal couple with them. To the groom, he chants, "The servant of God, [name], is betrothed to the handmaiden of God, [name], in the Name of the Father, and of the Son, and of the Holy Spirit!" In some parishes, the priest chants the "Amen.", and, in other places, the people sing it. As always, the main celebrant makes the decision as to which practice is followed. Then, to the bride, the priest chants, "The handmaiden of God, [name], is betrothed to the servant of God, [name], in the Name of the Father, and of the Son, and of the Holy Spirit!" Again, depending on the local practice, either the priest chants the "Amen.", or the people sing it.

The deacon then intones, "Let us pray to the Lord." The people sing, "Lord, have mercy." The priest then chants a prayer that begins, "O Lord our God, Who accompanied the servant of the patriarch, Abraham, into Mesopotamia,...!" Following the exclamation, "For, You are He Who bless and sanctify all things,...!", the people sing, "Amen."

## Holy Matrimony

Now, the Sacrament of Holy Matrimony proper begins. Again, if the betrothal immediately precedes the Sacrament, then, at this point, the priest leads the bridal couple into the middle of the church (the nave). If the betrothal took place the evening before, then, when the Sacrament takes place on the following day, it begins in the middle of the church (the nave).

The priest then intones, "Glory to You, our God, glory to You!" (In the Byzantine tradition, the priest first chants, "Blessed are all they who fear the Lord, who walk in His ways!.) The people then sing this same doxology, "Glory to You, our God, glory to You!" The priest then chants verses from Psalm 127 ("Blessed are they who fear the Lord!", "Who walk in His ways!", etc.). After each verse is chanted by the priest, the people again sing the doxology, "Glory to You, our God, glory to You!"

In distinction from the churches in the West, in the Orthodox Church, there are *no* vows exchanged between the two people of the bridal couple! This is in obedience to our Lord's command in the Gospel: "But, I say to you: Do not swear at all, either by Heaven, for it is the throne of God, or by the Earth, for it is His footstool, or by Jerusalem, for it is the city of the great King! And do not swear by your head, for you cannot make one hair white or black! Let what you say be simply 'Yes!' or 'No!' Anything more than this comes from the evil one!" (Matthew 5:34-37). **Instead**, as the liturgical "Yes!" in response to the Lord's commandment, the priest first asks the groom, "Do you, [name], having a good, free, and unconstrained will and a firm intention, take to yourself as a wife this woman, [name], whom you see here before you?" The groom answers, "I have, reverend Father!" The priest then asks him, "Have you promised yourself to any other woman?" The groom answers, "I have not, reverend Father!" Then, turning to the bride, the priest asks her, ""Do you, [name], having a good, free, and unconstrained will and a firm intention, take to yourself as a husband this man, [name], whom you see here before you?" The bride answers, "I have, reverend Father!" The priest then asks him, "Have you promised yourself to any other man?" The bride answers, "I have not, reverend Father!"

**The Doxology and the Great Litany**

It is **only** after this liturgical "Yes!" from **both** members of the bridal couple that the deacon intones, "Bless, Father! (or, "Master!)" The priest then chants the doxology, "Blessed is the Kingdom of the Father, and of the Son, and of the Holy Spirit, now and ever and unto ages of ages!" The people sing, "Amen."

The deacon then chants the petitions of the Great Litany, which includes specific petitions for the bridal couple and their life that they will live together in Christ. Following each petition, the people sing, "Lord, have mercy." After the petition that begins, "Commemorating out most holy, most pure,...!", the people sing, "To You, O Lord." The priest intones the exclamation, "For, to You are due all glory, honor, and worship,...!", and the people sing, "Amen."

The deacon then intones, "Let us pray to the Lord." The people sing, "Lord, have mercy." The priest then chants a prayer that begins, "O God most pure, the Creator of every living thing...!" After the exclamation, "For, You are the God of mercies, and bounties, and love towards mankind,...!", the people sing, "Amen." The deacon then again intones, "Let us pray to the Lord." The people again sing, "Lord, have mercy." The priest then chants a prayer that begins, "Blessed are You, O Lord our God, the Priest of mystical and pure marriage,...!" After the exclamation, "For, to You are due all glory, honor, and worship,...!", the people sing, "Amen." A third time, the deacon intones, "Let us pray to the Lord."

The people sing, "Lord, have mercy." The priest then chants a prayer that begins, "O holy God, Who created man out of the dust,...!" After the exclamation, "For, Yours is the majesty,...!", the people sing, "Amen."

**The Crowning**

The priest then crowns the bridal couple. He first takes the crown for the groom, and chants, "The servant of God, [name], is crowned to the handmaiden of God, [name], in the Name of the Father, and of the Son, and of the Holy Spirit!" The people sing, "Amen." He then takes the crown for the bride, and chants, "The handmaiden of God, [name], is crowned to the servant of God, [name], in the Name of the Father, and of the Son, and of the Holy Spirit!" The people sing, "Amen." The priest then blesses the bridal couple, intoning, "O Lord our God, crown them with glory and honor!" He does this **three** times.

## The Prokeimenon

Then, the Prokeimenon is celebrated. The reader comes out to the middle of the church and receives a blessing from the priest. The reader then stands behind the priest and the bridal couple in the middle of the church for the chanting of the Prokeimenon. The order for this chanting is as follows:

| | |
|---|---|
| ***Deacon:*** | Wisdom! Let us be attentive! |
| ***Priest:*** | Peace be with you all! |
| ***Reader:*** | And with your spirit! |
| ***Deacon:*** | Wisdom! |
| ***Reader:*** | The prokeimenon is in the 8$^{th}$ tone: You have set upon their heads crowns of precious stones! They asked life of You, and You gave it to them! |
| ***People:*** | You have set upon their heads crowns of precious stones! They asked life of You, and You gave it to them! |

| | |
|---|---|
| ***Reader:*** | For, You will bless them forever and ever! You will make them glad with the light of Your countenance! |
| ***People:*** | You have set upon their heads crowns of precious stones! They asked life of You, and You gave it to them! |
| ***Reader:*** | You have set upon their heads crowns of precious stones! |
| ***People:*** | They asked life of You, and You gave it to them! |

This is *not* done in the Byzantine tradition. What is done there is that the reader chants the Prokeimenon and the accompanying verse *once* before going on to the Epistle.

## The Epistle and "Alleluia!"

The Epistle reading is Ephesians 5:20-33. It is intoned as follows:

**Priest:** Wisdom!

**Reader:** The Reading is from the Epistle of the Holy Apostle Paul to the Ephesians!

**Deacon:** Let us be attentive!

The reader then begins the chanting of the Epistle with, "Brethren!"

After the conclusion of the Epistle reading, the priest blesses the reader, saying, "Peace be with you, Reader!" The reader chants, in response, "And with your spirit! Alleluia! Alleluia! Alleluia!" The people then sing a *triple* "Alleluia!" **Note:** Since there are *no* special "Alleluia!" verses called for in the Sacraments of Holy Matrimony, the people *only* sing this triple "Alleluia!" *once!*

## *The Gospel*

The Gospel reading is John 2:1-12. In *many* parishes, the priest will intone aloud the prayer before the Gospel reading, which begins "Illumine our hearts, O Master, Who love mankind, with the pure light of Your knowledge!" In some of these parishes, the people, after the priest concludes with "…now and ever and unto ages of ages!", will sing an "Amen."

In **all** cases, at this point, the priest will come out from the sanctuary and bless the people with the sign of the Cross as he says, "Wisdom! Let us be attentive! Let us listen to the Holy Gospel! Peace be with you all!" The people then sing "And with your spirit!" The priest then chants "The reading is from the Holy Gospel according to Saint John the Theologian!" The people then sing "Glory to You, O Lord! Glory to You!" The deacon then intones "Let us be attentive!", and the priest then chants the Gospel reading.

At the conclusion of the Gospel reading, the people again sing "Glory to You, O Lord! Glory to You!"

In the practice in most parishes, there is **no** sermon given at this point. Rather, the priest waits until the end of the Sacrament, when the bridal couple is standing at the foot of the ambo, to give words of exhortation and encouragement. Instead, the service proceeds **immediately** to the celebration of the Augmented Litany.

## Augmented Litany

The form of the Augmented Litany at this Sacrament is to begin with **two** petitions that are responded by "**single** 'Lord, have mercy's", the first of which is "Let us say with all our soul and with all our mind, let us say." Then comes the petition beginning, "Have mercy on us, O Lord,…," which is responded to by a **triple** "Lord, have mercy," that is, "Lord, have mercy" sung **three** times. Each subsequent petition is responded to by singing a **triple** "Lord, have mercy." When the deacon chants the petition that begins, "Commemorating our most holy…," the people respond with, "To You, O Lord." After the exclamation, "For, You are a merciful God,…!" is chanted by the priest, the people respond with, "Amen."

The deacon then intones, "Let us pray to the Lord." The people sing, "Lord, have mercy." The priest then chants a prayer that begins, "O Lord our God, Who, in Your saving providence,…!" After the exclamation, "For You are our God, the God of mercy and salvation,…!", the people sing, "Amen."

## Litany of Supplication

Then, an abbreviated form of the Litany of Supplication is celebrated (***except*** in the Byzantine tradition, which goes ***immediately*** to the Lord's Prayer). The deacon intones the petition that begins, "Help us! Save us! Have mercy on us,…!", and the people sing, "Lord, have mercy." Then, the deacon chants the petition, "That the whole day may be perfect, holy, peaceful, and sinless, let us ask of the Lord." The people sing, "Grant it, O Lord." following this and the subsequent petitions. After the petition that begins, "Having asked for the unity of the Faith,…!", the people sing, "To You, O Lord."

## The Lord's Prayer

The priest then chants, "And make us worthy, O Master, that, with boldness and without condemnation, we may dare to call on You, the supra-heavenly God, as Father, and to say:" Everyone stands and the people sing the Lord's Prayer. In some parishes that have a kleros rather than a choir loft, to encourage more congregational singing, the choir director turns and faces the people in the nave, directing them in the singing of the

Lord's Prayer being led by the choir.  The celebrant chants the exclamation, "For, Yours are the Kingdom and the power and the glory,…!", to which the people respond by singing, "Amen."

The celebrant then comes out, stands on the ambo, and blesses the people, while intoning, "Peace be with you all!"  The people sing, "And with your spirit!"  The deacon then says, "Bow your heads unto the Lord."  The people sing, "To You, O Lord."

## *The Common Cup*

When the Sacrament of Matrimony is celebrated separately from the Divine Liturgy, the bridal couple share drinking from the Common Cup.  The deacon intones, "Let us pray to the Lord."  The people sing, "Lord, have mercy."  The priest then chants a prayer that begins, "O God, Who have created all things by Your might,…!"  After the exclamation that begins, "For, blessed is Your Name,…!", the people sing, "Amen."  The priest first gives the Common Cup to the groom to drink, and then to the bride.  This double giving of the Cup is done **three** times, **except** in the Byzantine tradition, whereby the groom first takes three sips from the Cup, and then the bride does likewise.

Sacramental Services

## The Triple Procession

A ***triple*** procession then occurs, with the main celebrant leading the bridal couple ***three*** times around the analoi holding the icon in the middle of the church. During the first encircling, the people sing, "Rejoice, O Isaiah! A Virgin is with Child, and will bear a Son, Emmanuel, both God and Man! And 'Orient' is His Name, Whom, magnifying, we called the Virgin 'Blessed!'" During the second encircling, the people sing, "O holy martyrs, who fought the good fight and have received your crowns, entreat the Lord that He may have mercy upon us!" During the third encircling, the people sing, "Glory to You, O Christ God, the Apostles' Boast, the martyrs' Joy, whose preaching was the consubstantial Trinity!"

## The Removal of the Crowns

The removal of the crowns by the main celebrant then takes place. As he removes the crown from the head of the groom, the priest chants, "Be exalted, O bridegroom, like unto Abraham, and be blessed, like unto Isaac, and multiply, like unto Jacob, walking in peace, and keeping the commandments of God in righteousness!" As he removes the crown from the head of the bride, the priest chants, "Be exalted, like unto Sarah, and exult, like unto Rebecca, and multiply, like unto Rachel, and rejoice in your husband, fulfilling the conditions of the Law, for so it is well-pleasing to God!" **_Note:_** At both of these prayers, there are **_no_** responses sung, **_except_** in the Byzantine tradition, whereby each prayer is responded to by the people singing, "Amen"!

**Prayers and Blessing**

The deacon intones, "Let us pray to the Lord." The people sing, "Lord, have mercy." The priest then chants a prayer that begins, "O God, our God, Who came to Cana of Galilee, and there blessed the marriage feast,...!" After the conclusion of the exclamation, "...unto ages of ages!", the people sing, "Amen."

The priest then stands on the ambo and blesses the people, while intoning, "Peace be with you all!" The people sing, "And with your spirit!" The deacon then says, "Bow your heads unto the Lord." The people sing, "To You, O Lord." He then chants the prayer that begins, "May the Father, and the Son, and the Holy Spirit, the All-Holy, consubstantial, and life-creating Trinity,…!" After the conclusion of the exclamation, "…through the prayers of the holy Theotokos and of all the saints!", the people sing, "Amen."

**The Dismissal**

The Dismissal begins with the priest chanting, "Wisdom! Most Holy Theotokos, save us!" The people respond with, "More honorable than the Cherubim and more glorious beyond compare than the Seraphim! Without defilement, you gave Birth to God the Word! True Theotokos, we magnify you!"

The priest then ***usually*** chants, "Glory to You, O Christ our God and our Hope, glory to You!" When that occurs, the people sing a full "Glory,… now and ever…!", then a ***triple*** "Lord, have mercy.", then, "Father, bless!" If it is during the time between Pascha and Bright Saturday, the celebrant sings the Paschal troparion ("Christ is Risen from the dead, trampling down death by death, and, upon those in the tombs, bestowing life!") ***three*** times, followed by the people singing this same Paschal troparion ***three*** times. If it is during the time from Thomas Sunday until the leavetaking of Pascha, the celebrant then chants the Paschal troparion **two-and-a-half times**, with **the people singing the final half**. In other words, the celebrant chants the full Paschal troparion **twice**; for the third time, he **only** chants, "Christ is Risen from the dead, trampling down death by death!" The people **then** respond *with the final half* of the third time, "And, upon those in the tombs, bestowing life!"

The priest then chants the dismissal prayer that begins, "May He Who, by His presence at the marriage feast in Cana of Galilee,…!". At the conclusion of the exclamation, "…for, He is good and loves mankind!", the people sing a **double** "Amen." ("Amen. Amen.").

Then, as mentioned, with the bridal couple standing at the foot of the ambo, the priest gives words of exhortation and encouragement to the bridal couple.

### "Many Years"

Then, the deacon intones the formula for the commemorations, concluding with, "…and grant them many years!" The people then sing, "God grant you many years!" as the celebrant blesses the people with the Holy Cross. The people come forward to venerate the Holy Cross and icons, and to congratulate the bridal couple.

The order of a second marriage differs from that of a first marriage, and contains prayers of repentance and contrition for the bridal couple.[28] This does ***not*** directly change anything for the choir director and the singers. As with the regular wedding service, the prayers, petitions, and exclamations are answered with the appropriately sung responses.

## D. HOLY UNCTION

The Sacrament of Holy Unction is celebrated whenever an Orthodox Christian is severely ill. Also, in many places, it is celebrated at the end of Great Lent. It may be celebrated on the Sunday evening of the 5th Sunday of Great Lent. In some traditions, it also may be celebrated on Wednesday evening during Holy Week, in place of the Matins for Holy Thursday. In order not to omit the celebration of the Matins of Holy Thursday, it is probably best to celebrate the Sacrament of Holy Unction on the

---

[28] Hapgood, pp. 302-305.

evening of the 5th Sunday of Great Lent. The order for the service is as follows.[29]

## The Doxology, the Trisagion Prayers, and the Lord's Prayer

The service is celebrated either with a bishop and many priests presiding, or with at least seven priests presiding.[30]

The service begins with the bishop intoning, "Blessed is our God, always now and ever and unto ages of ages!" A reader then chants the response, "Amen. Glory to You, our God, glory to You!"[31] (In the Byzantine tradition, the priest would chant the "Glory to You, our God, glory to You!".) Then, the reader continues with the Trisagion Prayers, followed by the Lord's Prayer. After the exclamation, "For, Yours are the Kingdom, and the power, and the glory,…!", the reader chants,

---

[29] Ibid, pp. 332-359.
[30] For the sake of clarity, and to avoid endless references labeled "either/or," we will present the service here as though a bishop with many priests were presiding.
[31] Since the service involves much chanting of prayers and Psalms throughout, it is customary to have many readers sharing these duties.

"Amen.", followed by "Lord, have mercy." **twelve** times, a full "Glory,... now and ever,...!", and a full, "Come, let us worship God, our King!".

## Psalm 142 [and the Little Litany]

The reader then chants Psalm 142, which begins, "Hear my prayer, O Lord!  Give ear to my supplications!"  This is followed by a full "Glory,... now and ever...!", and then, "Alleluia!  Alleluia!  Alleluia!  Glory to You, O Lord!" chanted **three** times.

Even though the service books call for the Little Litany to be celebrated at this point, in many places it is **omitted**.

## "Alleluia!" and Penitential Hymns

Then, the deacon intones a **triple** Alleluia!" The people then sing a **triple** "Alleluia!"  The deacon then chants, "O Lord, rebuke me not in Your anger, nor chasten me in Your wrath!"  The people sing another **triple** "Alleluia!"  The deacon then chants, "Have mercy on me, O Lord, for I am weak!  Heal me,

O Lord, for my bones are troubled!" Again, the people sing another *triple* "Alleluia!"

The people then sing a series of penitential hymns: "Have mercy on us, O Lord, have mercy on us! For, laying aside all excuse, we sinners offer to You, as to our Master, this supplication: 'Have mercy on us!' Glory to the Father, and to the Son, and to the Holy Spirit! O Lord, have mercy on us, for in You have we put our trust! Do not be angry with us, nor remember our iniquities! But, look down on us even now, since You are compassionate, and deliver us from our enemies! For, You are our God, and we are Your people! We are all the work of Your hands, and we call on Your Name! Now and ever and unto ages of ages. Amen. O blessed Theotokos, open the doors of compassion to us, whose hope is in you, that we may not perish but be delivered from adversity through you, who are the salvation of the Christian people!"

### Psalm 50

A reader then chants Psalm 50 ("Have mercy on me, O God, according to Your steadfast love!"). This is *immediately* followed by the people singing the Kanon, in tone 4.

## The Kanon

The first ode begins with the people singing, "Israel of old crossed the depths of the Red Sea with dry steps,…!"  Then, a **deacon** responds with the refrains (such as, "Christ, Master, have mercy on Your servants!") and a **priest** chanting the troparia (such as, "The whole Earth, Master, is full of Your mercy!").  <u>Note:</u>  This pattern of celebrating the Kanon, with **the people** singing the odes, **a deacon** chanting the refrains, and **a priest** chanting the troparia, will continue throughout the **entire** Sacrament of Holy Unction, **except** in the Antiochian tradition, whereby the people usually sing the entire Kanon,  and also **except** in the Greek tradition, where the entire Kanon is chanted by various readers!

After the troparion following the "Now and ever…!" refrain, the people sing ode 3, which begins, "The Church rejoices in You, O Christ!"  Following the refrains and troparia, the people then sing the Kathisma Hymns in tone 4, the first one beginning, "You, Who are like a river of divine mercy,…!" and the second one beginning, "Physician and Helper of those in illness,…!"  (In the Byzantine tradition, the first Kathisma Hymn is in tone 8 and the second one is in tone 4.)

The Kanon resumes with ode 4, beginning, "Seeing You, the Sun of Righteousness,...!"; then, ode 5, beginning, "You, my Lord, came into the world as a Light,...!"; then, ode 6, beginning, "Having been cleansed from the blood of demons,...!" Again, throughout these odes, a deacon chants the refrains and a priest chants the troparia. After the conclusion of ode 6, it is the practice in **some** parishes to have a reader chant a **triple** "Lord, have mercy."

Ode 6 is followed by the singing of the Kontakion in tone 2, which begins, "Most good One, the Fountain of mercy,...!" After this is ode 7, beginning, "The children of Abraham in the Persian furnace,...!"; then, ode 8, beginning, "Daniel stretched out his hands...!"; then, ode 9, beginning, "From you, the unhewn mountain, O Virgin,...!" Once again, throughout these odes, a deacon chants the refrains and a priest chants the troparia. After the conclusion of ode 9, it is the practice in **some** parishes to repeat ode 9 ("From you, the unhewn mountain, O Virgin,...!") as the **Katavasia**. In the Byzantine tradition, after the conclusion of ode 9, the people sing, "It is Truly Meet!".

## The Exapostilarion

After the Kanon, it is the ***bishop*** (or, a ***priest***) who chants the Exapostilarion (except in the Byzantine tradition, where the people sing it): "O Good One, mercifully look down on our supplications with Your eyes! For, we have gathered in Your holy temple to anoint Your suffering servants with divine oil!"

## The Praises

The people then sing the Praises, in tone 4. The first two sets begin, "Let every breath praise the Lord!" and, "Praise Him, all you angels of His!" A reader then chants the refrain, "Praise Him with timbrel and dance! Praise Him with strings and pipe!" The people then sing the stikheron beginning, "You have given Your grace,…!" The reader then chants the refrain, "Praise with sounding cymbals!…". The people then sing the stikheron beginning, "Having sealed our senses…!". The reader then chants the refrain, "Let every breath praise the Lord!…". The people then sing the stikheron beginning, "By the anointing of Your oil…!". The reader then chants a full "Glory,… now and ever...Amen." The people then sing the stikheron beginning, "We entreat you, O most pure pavilion of our King,...!"

## The Trisagion Prayers, the Lord's Prayer, and a Hymn

A reader then chants the Trisagion Prayers (***usually omitted*** in the Byzantine tradition) and the Lord's Prayer. After the exclamation beginning, "For, Yours are the Kingdom, and the power, and the glory,...!", the reader chants, "Amen." The people then sing a hymn, in tone 4, beginning, "You, Who, alone, are a speedy Help, O Christ...!"

## The Great Litany and Prayer for Blessing the Oil

At this point, in the Byzantine tradition, the doxology "Blessed is the Kingdom...!" and the responding "Amen." are celebrated. The deacon now chants the petitions to the Great Litany, which includes petitions for those who are ill and suffering. The people respond by singing, "Lord, have mercy." following each petition. After the petition that begins, "Commemorating our most holy, most pure,…!", the people sing, "To You, O Lord." The bishop then chants the prayer for blessing the oil: "Lord, Who, through Your mercy and compassion, heal the crushing of our souls and bodies, sanctify this oil Yourself, Master, that it may be for the healing and the assuaging of all passions, all defilement of flesh and spirit, and of every evil, to those anointed with it, that, through it, may be glorified Your all honorable and majestic Name: of the Father, and of the Son, and of the Holy Spirit, now and ever and unto ages of ages!" The people sing, "Amen."

## *Troparia*

The people then sing a series of troparia. In most parishes, not all of the troparia are sung, so the choir director must check with the bishop or presiding priest (whomever is the main celebrant) for the specifics. The first troparion, in tone 4, begins, "You alone, O Christ, are quick to defend us!" (In the Byzantine tradition, the first troparion begins, "Blind of my spiritual eyes, I come to You, O Christ!".) The next one, in tone 3, starts, "By Your divine intercession, O Lord!" Then, a troparion in tone 2 begins, "As a disciple of the Lord, O righteous one!" This is followed by one in tone 4, beginning,

"The only-begotten Word of God the Father!" Then, in tone 3, "To them of Mary, O Saint Nicholas!". Another one in tone 3 begins, "The world has found in you a champion!", and the next one, also in tone 3, states, "O endurer of pain, and healer, Panteleimon!" The next one, "O unmercenaries and wonderworkers!", is in tone 8. The final one, in tone 2, begins, "Who will declare your grandeur?"

### Prokeimenon # 1, Epistle # 1, and "Alleluia" Verses

Prokeimenon # 1 is now celebrated. The order for it is as follows.

| | |
|---|---|
| ***Deacon:*** | Wisdom! Let us be attentive! |
| ***+ Bishop:*** | Peace be with you all! |
| ***Deacon:*** | And with your spirit! |
| ***+ Bishop:*** | Wisdom! |
| ***Deacon:*** | The Prokeimenon is in the 1$^{st}$ tone: Let Your mercy be upon us, O Lord, even as we have set our hope in You! |

*Sacramental Services*

| | |
|---|---|
| ***People:*** | Let Your mercy be upon us, O Lord, even as we have set our hope in You! |
| ***Deacon:*** | Rejoice in the Lord, O you righteous! Praise befits the just! |
| ***People:*** | Let Your mercy be upon us, O Lord, even as we have set our hope in You! |
| ***Deacon:*** | Let Your mercy, O Lord, be upon us! |
| ***People:*** | As we have set our hope in You! |

This is **not** done in the Byzantine tradition. What is done there is that the reader chants the Prokeimenon and the accompanying verse once before going on to the Epistle. This will continue throughout the **entire** Sacrament of Holy Unction.

The deacon then chants the Epistle reading, James 5:10-16. At the conclusion of the Epistle reading, the bishop blesses the deacon, chanting, "Peace be with you, Reader!" The deacon chants, "And with your spirit! Alleluia! Alleluia! Alleluia!" The people then sing a **triple** "Alleluia!", in tone 8. Then, the deacon chants the verse, "O Lord, I will sing to You of mercy and justice!"  The people then sing another **triple** "Alleluia!", in tone 8.

## Gospel # 1

Gospel # 1, from Luke 10:25-37, is then celebrated, as follows:

| | |
|---|---|
| ***Deacon:*** | Wisdom!  Let us be attentive!  Let us listen to the Holy Gospel! |
| ***+ Bishop:*** | Peace be with you all! |
| ***People:*** | And with your spirit! |
| ***+ Bishop:*** | The Reading is from the Holy Gospel according to Saint Luke! |
| ***People:*** | Glory to You, O Lord, glory to You! |
| ***Deacon:*** | Let us be attentive! |

The **bishop** then chants the Gospel lesson.  At its conclusion, the people once more sing, "Glory to You, O Lord, glory to You!"

This is the pattern that will be used for the remaining Gospel lessons.


### [Augmented Litany]

An abbreviated form of the Augmented Litany *may* now be celebrated, though it is often omitted. The deacon chants, "Have mercy on us, O God,…!", to which the people sing a *triple* "Lord, have mercy." The deacon chants the next petition, beginning, "Furthermore, we pray…!", to which the people sing another *triple* "Lord, have mercy." The next petition has the deacon chanting, "That [he, she] may be pardoned all [his, her] sins,…!", and, again, the people sing a *triple* "Lord, have mercy." The bishop then intones the exclamation that begins, "For, You are a merciful God,…!", and the people sing, "Amen."


### Post – Gospel Prayer # 1

The deacon intones, "Let us pray to the Lord.", and the people sing, "Lord, have mercy." The bishop then chants a prayer that begins, "For, You, Lord, are great and wonderful, keeping Your covenant and

Your mercy towards those who love You!" (In the Byzantine tradition, this prayer begins, "You Who are Unoriginate, eternal, the Holy of Holies, Who sent down Your only-begotten Son,…!".) After the exclamation that begins, "For, Yours it is to be merciful and to save us,…!", the people sing, "Amen."

If this is a Sacrament of Holy Unction for just one or a few sick person(s), the presiding priest will then anoint that person at this point, and then chant the prayer that begins, "O holy Father, Physician of souls and bodies,…!" After the exclamation, "For, You are the Fountain of healing,…!", the people sing, "Amen." This is done for each of the seven units of the service, that is, after each Post-Gospel Prayer. If it is the Sacrament of Holy Unction at the end of Great Lent, whereby a multitude of people are present, the service goes immediately to Prokeimenon # 2 and the anointing is done at the end of the service.

## Prokeimenon # 2, Epistle # 2, and "Alleluia" Verses

Prokeimenon # 2, chanted by the deacon, is in tone 2: "The Lord is my Strength and my Song! He has become my Salvation!"  The people then sing this entire Prokeimenon.  The deacon then chants the verse, "The Lord has chastened me sorely, but He has not given me over to death!"  The people then again sing the entire Prokeimenon.  The deacon then chants the **_first_ _half_** of the Prokeimenon, "The Lord is my Strength and my Song!", and the people sing the **_second_ _half_** of the Prokeimenon, "He has become my Salvation!"

The deacon then chants Epistle # 2, from Romans 15:1-7.  After the deacon chants, "And with your spirit!  Alleluia!  Alleluia!  Alleluia!", the people sing a **_triple_** "Alleluia!", in tone 5.  The deacon then chants the verse, "I will sing to You of mercies, O Lord, forever!"  The people then again sing a **_triple_** "Alleluia!", in tone 5.

### Gospel # 2

Gospel # 2, from Luke 19:1-10, is then chanted, with the usual sung responses from the people.

## [Augmented Litany]

Again, the abbreviated form of the Augmented Litany **may** now be celebrated, though it is often **omitted**.

## Post – Gospel Prayer # 2

The deacon intones, "Let us pray to the Lord.", and the people sing, "Lord, have mercy." The bishop then chants a prayer that begins, "Great and Most High God, worshipped by all creation, Fountain of wisdom,…!" After the exclamation that begins, "For, Yours it is to be merciful and to save us, Christ our God,…!", the people sing, "Amen."

## Prokeimenon # 3, Epistle # 3, and "Alleluia" Verses

Prokeimenon # 3, chanted by the deacon, is in tone 3: "The Lord is my Light and my Salvation! Whom should I fear?" The people then sing this entire Prokeimenon. The deacon then chants the verse, "The Lord is the Defender of my life! Of whom shall I be afraid?"  The people then again sing the entire Prokeimenon.  The deacon then chants the **_first half_** of the Prokeimenon, "The Lord is my Light and my Salvation!", and the people sing the **_second half_** of the Prokeimenon, "Whom should I fear?"

The deacon then chants Epistle # 3, from 1 Corinthians 12:27-13:8a .  After the deacon chants, "And with your spirit!  Alleluia!  Alleluia!  Alleluia!", the people sing a **_triple_** "Alleluia!", in tone 2.  The deacon then chants the verse, "In You, O Lord, have I hoped!  Let me never be put to shame!"  The people then again sing a **_triple_** "Alleluia!", in tone 2.

## Gospel # 3

Gospel # 3, from Matthew 10:1-8, is then chanted, with the usual sung responses from the people.

## [Augmented Litany]

Again, the abbreviated form of the Augmented Litany **may** now be celebrated, though it is often **omitted**.

## Post – Gospel Prayer # 3

The deacon intones, "Let us pray to the Lord.", and the people sing, "Lord, have mercy." The bishop then chants a prayer that begins, "Almighty Master, Holy King, Who chasten but do not kill,…!" After the exclamation that begins, "For, Yours it is to be merciful and to save us, Christ our God,…!", the people sing, "Amen."

## Prokeimenon # 4, Epistle # 4, and "Alleluia" Verses

Prokeimenon # 4, chanted by the deacon, is in tone 4: "Answer me speedily in the day when I call!" The people then sing this entire Prokeimenon. The deacon then chants the verse, "Hear my prayer, O Lord, and let my cry come to You!" The people then again sing the entire Prokeimenon.  The deacon then chants the **_first half_** of the Prokeimenon, "Answer me speedily!", and the people sing the **_second half_** of the Prokeimenon, "In the day when I call!"

The deacon then chants Epistle # 4, from 2 Corinthians 6:16-7:1 .  After the deacon chants, "And with your spirit!  Alleluia!  Alleluia!  Alleluia!", the people sing a **_triple_** "Alleluia!", in tone 2.  The deacon then chants the verse, "I waited patiently for the Lord!  He inclined to me and heard my cry!"  The people then again sing a **_triple_** "Alleluia!", in tone 2.

## Gospel # 4

Gospel # 4, from Matthew 8:14-23, is then chanted, with the usual sung responses from the people.

## [Augmented Litany]

Again, the abbreviated form of the Augmented Litany **_may_** now be celebrated, though it is often **_omitted_**.

## Post – Gospel Prayer # 4

The deacon intones, "Let us pray to the Lord.", and the people sing, "Lord, have mercy." The bishop then chants a prayer that begins, "Good and compassionate Lord of many mercies,…!" After the exclamation that begins, "For, Yours it is to be merciful and to save us, Christ our God,…!", the people sing, "Amen."

## Prokeimenon # 5, Epistle # 5, and "Alleluia" Verses

Prokeimenon # 5, chanted by the deacon, is in tone 5: "You, O Lord, will protect us and preserve us from this generation forever!" The people then sing this entire Prokeimenon. The deacon then chants the verse, "Save me, O Lord! For, there are no longer any who are godly!" The people then again sing the entire Prokeimenon. The deacon then chants the **_first_ half** of the Prokeimenon, "You, O Lord, will protect us!", and the people sing the **_second_ half** of the Prokeimenon, "And preserve us from this generation forever!"

Sacramental Services

The deacon then chants Epistle # 5, from 2 Corinthians 1:8-11 .  After the deacon chants, "And with your spirit!  Alleluia!  Alleluia!  Alleluia!", the people sing a *triple* "Alleluia!", in tone 5.  The deacon then chants the verse, "I will sing to You of mercies, O Lord, forever!"  The people then again sing a *triple* "Alleluia!", in tone 5.

**Gospel # 5**

Gospel # 5, from Matthew 25:1-13, is then chanted, with the usual sung responses from the people.

**[Augmented Litany]**

Again, the abbreviated form of the Augmented Litany **may** now be celebrated, though it is often **omitted**.

## Post – Gospel Prayer # 5

The deacon intones, "Let us pray to the Lord.", and the people sing, "Lord, have mercy." The bishop then chants a prayer that begins, "Lord our God, Who chasten and again heal,…!" After the exclamation that begins, "For, You are the Hope of the hopeless,…!", the people sing, "Amen."

## Prokeimenon # 6, Epistle # 6, and "Alleluia" Verses

Prokeimenon # 6, chanted by the deacon, is in tone 6: "Have mercy on me, O God, according to Your steadfast love!" The people then sing this entire Prokeimenon. The deacon then chants the verse, "Create in me a clean heart, God, and put a new and right Spirit within me!" The people then again sing the entire Prokeimenon. The deacon then chants the ***first half*** of the Prokeimenon, "Have mercy on me, O God!", and the people sing the ***second half*** of the Prokeimenon, "According to Your steadfast love!"

The deacon then chants Epistle # 6, from Galatians 5:22-6:2 .  After the deacon chants, "And with your spirit!  Alleluia!  Alleluia!  Alleluia!", the people sing a *triple* "Alleluia!", in tone 5.  The deacon then chants the verse, "Blessed is the man who fears the Lord, who greatly delights in His commandments!"  The people then again sing a *triple* "Alleluia!", in tone 5.

## Gospel # 6

Gospel # 6, from Matthew 15:21-28, is then chanted, with the usual sung responses from the people.

## [Augmented Litany]

Again, the abbreviated form of the Augmented Litany *may* now be celebrated, though it is often *omitted*.

## Post – Gospel Prayer # 6

The deacon intones, "Let us pray to the Lord.", and the people sing, "Lord, have mercy." The bishop then chants a prayer that begins, "We thank You, Lord our God, Who are good and love mankind,….!" After the exclamation that begins, "For, Your mercy is as Your greatness,….!", the people sing, "Amen."

## Prokeimenon # 7, Epistle # 7, and "Alleluia" Verses

Prokeimenon # 7, chanted by the deacon, is in tone 7: "O Lord, rebuke me not in Your anger, nor chasten me in Your wrath!" The people then sing this entire Prokeimenon. The deacon then chants the verse, "Have mercy on me, O Lord, for I am weak! Heal me, O Lord, for my bones are troubled!" The people then again sing the entire Prokeimenon. The deacon then chants the ***first half*** of the Prokeimenon, "O Lord, rebuke me not in Your anger!", and the people sing the ***second half*** of the Prokeimenon, "Nor chasten me in Your wrath!"

The deacon then chants Epistle # 7, from 1 Thessalonians 5:14-23 . After the deacon chants, "And with your spirit! Alleluia! Alleluia! Alleluia!", the people sing a **triple** "Alleluia!", in tone 7. The deacon then chants the verse, "The Lord hear you in the day of trouble! The Name of the God of Jacob protect you!" The people then again sing a **triple** "Alleluia!", in tone 7.

## Gospel # 7

Gospel # 7, from Matthew 9:9-13, is then chanted, with the usual sung responses from the people.

## [Augmented Litany]

Again, the abbreviated form of the Augmented Litany **may** now be celebrated, though it is often **omitted**.

## Post – Gospel Prayer # 7

The deacon intones, "Let us pray to the Lord.", and the people sing, "Lord, have mercy." The bishop then chants a prayer that begins, "Master and Lord, our God, Physician of souls and bodies,...!" After the exclamation that begins, "For, You have not fashioned man for him to perish,...!", the people sing, "Amen."

## Prayer at the Elevated Gospel

If this is a Sacrament of Holy Unction for just one or a few sick person(s), the presiding priest will then anoint that person at this point, and then chant the prayer that begins, "Holy King, compassionate and of many mercies, Lord Jesus Christ, Son and Word of the Living God,...!" After the exclamation, "For, Your mercy is as Your greatness,...!", the people sing, "Amen." If it is the Sacrament of Holy Unction at the end of Great Lent, whereby a multitude of people are present, the gathered clergy hold up the Gospel Book over the heads of those who are to receive anointment (this is the common practice, even though the service books call for the elevated Gospel to be held above the head of the bishop), while the bishop chants the prayer that begins, "Holy King, compassionate and of many mercies, Lord Jesus Christ, Son and Word of the Living God…!"  After the exclamation, "For, Your mercy is as Your greatness,…!", the people sing, "Amen."

## The Dismissal

The Dismissal begins with the bishop chanting, "Wisdom!  Most Holy Theotokos, save us!"  The people respond with, "More honorable than the Cherubim and more glorious beyond compare than the Seraphim!  Without defilement, you gave Birth to God the Word!  True Theotokos, we magnify you!"

The bishop then chants, "Glory to You, O Christ, our God and our Hope, glory to You!"  The people sing a full "Glory,… now and ever…!", a **triple** "Lord, have mercy.", and "Master, bless!" (or, if it is the Metropolitan, "Most blessed Master, bless!").  The bishop then chants the dismissal prayer that begins, "May Christ our God, through the prayers of His most pure Mother,…!".  At the exclamation, "Have mercy on us and save us, for as much as He is good and loves mankind!", the people sing a **double**

"Amen." ("Amen. Amen."), and, then, "Eis Polla Eti Dhespota!"

In the Byzantine tradition, the Dismissal is celebrated *after* the Anointing with Holy Unction.

### Prayer Before the Anointing with Holy Unction

The deacon intones, "Let us pray to the Lord." The people sing, "Lord, have mercy." The bishop then chants a prayer that begins, "Holy Father, Physician and Healer of souls and bodies,…!" After the exclamation, "For, You are the Fountain of healings, O our God,…!", the people sing, "Amen."

### The Anointing with Holy Unction

The people come forward to be anointed. The practice is for the deacons and/or junior priests to hold the Gospel Book up while the people pass beneath It to come up for anointing (this is not done in the Greek tradition). Anointing is done on the forehead, cheeks, breast, and the palm and back of each hand.

The people sing the appointed troparia while everyone comes forward to be anointed by the bishop or a priest: In tone 4, "I come to You, O Christ, with my spiritual eyes blinded,…!"; in tone 3, "As you raised the paralytic of old,…!"; in tone 2, "As the Lord's disciple, you received the Gospel, O righteous James!…!"; in tone 4, "God, the only-begotten Word of the Father,…!"; in tone 3, "You revealed yourself to be a true priest in Myra,…!"; in tone 3, "In times of need, the universe found in you, O martyr, a champion,…!"; in tone 3, "O holy martyr and healer, Panteleimon,…!"; in tone 8, "O holy wonderworkers and unmercenaries, Cosmos and Damian,…!"; in tone 2, "Who will proclaim your greatness, O virginal John?…!"; and, finally, the Theotokion, in tone 2, "We fervently beseech you, O Lady Theotokos,…!" **Note: All** or **only some** of these troparia may be sung, depending on the directives by the presiding bishop.

# 5

# NON – SACRAMENTAL SERVICES

## A.  THE HOURS

The Hours are part of the Liturgy of Time (as are Vespers and Matins).  They are comprised of the 1st Hour (corresponding to 7 o'clock in the morning), the 3rd Hour (corresponding to 9 o'clock in the morning), the 6th Hour (corresponding to 12 noon), and the 9th Hour (corresponding to 3 o'clock in the afternoon).  Each of the Hours has its corresponding theme:  thankfulness for the new day at the 1st Hour, the descent of the Holy Spirit upon the Apostles on the Day of Pentecost at the 3rd Hour, the Crucifixion of Christ at the 6th Hour, and the Death of Christ at the 9th Hour.  Because the Hours are all basically the same with some minor variations (the Psalms that are chanted, etc.), they will be treated here as one unit, with discussions on the differences as we go along.  Since the Lenten Hours and Royal Hours of Christmas, Theophany, and Holy Friday differ radically from these "*regular*" Hours, they will be dealt with in the following sections.

### Doxology, "O Heavenly King," Trisagion Prayers

The 3rd, 6th, and 9th Hours all begin at this point (because the 1st Hour can immediately follow Matins, it bypasses these liturgical elements and only begins with the chanting of "Come, Let Us Worship God, Our King!").[32] The main celebrant intones the doxology, "Blessed is our God, always now and ever and unto ages of ages!" The reader responds with "Amen. Glory to You, our God! Glory to You!" (except in the Byzantine tradition, whereby the priest chants this). The reader then proceeds with "O Heavenly King!", followed by the Trisagion Prayers (a *triple* "Holy God!", a full "Glory,... now and ever...!", "Most Holy Trinity, have mercy on us!...", a *triple* "Lord, have mercy.", and another full "Glory,... now and ever...!"), and the Lord's Prayer. After the exclamation ("For, Yours is the

---

[32] Hapgood, Isabel Florence, *Service Book of the Holy Orthodox-Catholic Apostolic Church*, 4th Edition, Syrian Antiochian Orthodox Archdiocese, Brooklyn, NY, 1965 (hereafter referred to as "Hapgood"), pp. 38-57.

Kingdom,….!"), the reader responds with an "Amen.", followed by "Lord, have mercy." **twelve** times, then a full "Glory, …now and ever…!"

## "Come, Let Us Worship"

Again, it is at **this** point, with the chanting of "Come, Let Us Worship!", that the 1st Hour begins when it follows Matins.

In each of the four Hours (1st, 3rd, 6th, and 9th), the reader chants, "Come, let us worship God our King! Come, let us worship and fall down before Christ, our King and our God! Come, let us worship and fall down before Christ Himself (or, "the very Christ"), our King and our God!"

## 3 Psalms

After the "Come, Let Us Worship!", the reader chants 3 Psalms. These are different in each of the Hours: At the 1st Hour, they are Psalms 5, 89, and 100; at the 3rd Hour, they are Psalms 16, 24, and 50;

at the 6th Hour, they are Psalms 53, 54, and 90; and, at the 9th Hour, they are Psalms 83, 84, and 85.[33]

### "Glory,… Now and Ever…!", "Alleluia!"

The 3 Psalms are followed by the intoning of a full "Glory,… now and ever…!", then "Alleluia! Alleluia! Alleluia! Glory to You, O God!" *three* times, and a *triple* "Lord, have mercy.".

### Troparion

There then follows the first half of a "split 'Glory!'" ("Glory to the Father, and to the Son, and to the Holy Spirit!"), and then the troparion (or troparia) of the day, *still* chanted by the reader.

---

[33] Here, as elsewhere in this book, the Psalms are numbered according to the Septuagint rendering, which is the official numbering of the Orthodox Church. Hapgood, pp. 38-39, 43-45, 48-49, and 53-55.

## *Theotokion*

The reader then chants the second half of the "split 'Glory!'" ("Now and ever and unto ages of ages! Amen."), and then the theotokion of the Hour, *still* chanted by the reader.

## *Trisagion Prayers and Lord's Prayer*

In the *regular* Hours, the reader, at this point, chants the Trisagion Prayers and the Lord's Prayer, just as at the beginning of the Hour.

## *Kontakion*

After the Lord's Prayer, its exclamation, and the "Amen." by the reader, the reader then chants the Kontakion (or kontakia) of the day. In the Byzantine tradition, if it is the 1st Hour for Sunday, the Hypakoe in the tone of the week is sung instead.

## Prayer to Christ

The reader then chants "Lord, have mercy." *twelve* times (in some parishes, it is chanted *forty* times). He then chants the Prayer to Christ, "You, Who at every season and every hour, in Heaven and on Earth, are worshiped and glorified, O Christ our God;...!"

## Hymn to the Theotokos

This is followed by a *triple* "Lord, have mercy." and a full "Glory,... now and ever...." Then, the reader immediately chants the second half of the Hymn to the Theotokos, beginning, "More honorable than the Cherubim....", followed by, "In the Name of the Lord, give the blessing, Father" (or, if it be a bishop, "Master"; or, if it be the Metropolitan, "Most Blessed Master").

If it is the 3$^{rd}$ or the 6$^{th}$ Hour, the celebrant intones the exclamation, "Through the prayers of our holy fathers,...!", to which the reader responds, "Amen." If it is the 1$^{st}$ or 9$^{th}$ Hour, the celebrant intones the exclamation, "God be bountiful to us,...!", to which the reader responds, "Amen." In the Byzantine tradition, the celebrant intones the exclamation, "God be bountiful to us,…!" for **all** of the Hours.

## 1ˢᵗ Hour Conclusion

If it is the 1ˢᵗ Hour, the following is what concludes it.

The reader chants a full "Glory,… now and ever…!", followed by "Lord, have mercy." **twelve** times (except in the Byzantine tradition).

Then, the reader intones the prayer that begins, "O Christ, the true Light, Who enlighten and sanctify everyone who comes into the world,…!" This is followed by a full "Glory,… now and ever…!", a **triple** "Lord, have mercy.", and then, "In the Name of the Lord, give the blessing, Father" (or, if it be a bishop, "Master"; or, if it be the Metropolitan, "Most Blessed Master"). The celebrant then chants the exclamation, "Through the prayers of our holy fathers,…!", to which the reader responds, "Amen." (except in the Byzantine tradition).

Then, the reader chants a prayer to the Theotokos that begins, "We, your servants, in that we have been delivered from calamities,…!"

The celebrant then intones, "Glory to You, O Christ our God and our Hope, glory to You!" The **people** then **sing** a full "Glory,... now and ever...!", a **triple** "Lord, have mercy.", and, finally, "In the Name of the Lord, give the blessing, Father" (or, if it be a bishop, "Master"; or, if it be the Metropolitan, "Most Blessed Master"). The priest then pronounces the Dismissal, followed by the people singing, "Amen.", and then a **triple** "Lord, have mercy."

### 9th Hour Conclusion

If it is the 9th Hour, the following is what concludes it.

The reader intones a prayer to Christ that begins, "O Master, Lord Jesus Christ our God, Who are long-suffering toward our sins, and Who have led us even to the present hour,...!"

If the Typika do **not** to follow the 9th Hour, then the reader chants a full "Glory,... now and ever...!", a **triple** "Lord, have mercy.", and then "In the Name of the Lord, give the blessing, Father" (or, if it be a bishop, "Master"; or, if it be the Metropolitan, "Most Blessed Master"). The priest then pronounces the Dismissal, followed by the people singing, "Amen.", and then a **triple** "Lord, have mercy." (except in the Byzantine tradition, which just ends with the "Amen").

## The Typika

If the Typika **do** follow the 9th Hour, the beginning is the chanting by a reader of Psalms 102 and 145, followed by the Beatitudes, **except** during Great Lent, when they are omitted.[34] The order for singing them is: Psalm 102, "Glory...Spirit!", Psalm 145, "Now and ever...!" In the Byzantine tradition, the Typika are celebrated **only** during Great Lent.

Whether or not it is Great Lent, after the "Now and ever...!", the people sing "Only-Begotten Son."

The people sing, "The heavenly choir hymns You, and cries: 'Holy! Holy! Holy! Lord God of Hosts! Heaven and Earth are full of Your glory!" The reader then chants, "Come unto Him and be enlightened, and your faces will not be put to shame!" The people then **repeat** the singing of "The heavenly choir hymns You and cries:...!" The reader then chants the first half of a "split 'Glory!'" ("Glory...Spirit!"). The people then sing, "The choir

---

[34] Hapgood, pp. 58-63.

of holy angels and archangels, with all the powers of Heaven, sing Your praises and cry: 'Holy! Holy! Holy! Lord God of Hosts! Heaven and Earth are full of Your glory!" The reader then chants the second half of the "split 'Glory!'" ("Now and ever...Amen.").

The people then sing the Creed.

The reader then chants a prayer that begins, "Loose, remit, and pardon, O God, our transgressions,...!"

The people then sing the Lord's Prayer. At its conclusion, the celebrant chants the exclamation, and the people respond with, "Amen."

If it is a Saturday, the people sing the hymn that begins, "Unto You, O Lord, the Author of Creation,...!"

Then, the people sing the Kontakion of Transfiguration.

After this, the Kontakion for the day is sung, with its corresponding theme: the angels (Monday), St John the Baptist (Tuesday), the Cross (Wednesday and Friday), the Holy Apostles and St Nicholas (Thursday).

Then, a "Glory,...Spirit!" is sung, followed by the singing of, "Give rest, O Lord, to the souls of Your servants…!", followed by "Now and ever…!", and then, "Steadfast Protectress."

Then, the reader intones "Lord, have mercy." **twelve** times, followed by the prayer that begins, "O All-Holy Trinity, mighty and one in essence, Kingdom undivided, Origin of all good things,…!"

The people then sing the first half of the Hymn to the Theotokos ("It is truly meet to bless you, O Theotokos, ever-blessed and most pure and the Mother of our God!"). The celebrant then intones, "Wisdom! Most Holy Theotokos, save us!" The people continue singing the rest of the Hymn to the Theotokos, starting with "More honorable than the Cherubim,…!"

The celebrant then chants, "Glory to You, O Christ, our God and our Hope, glory to You!" The people sing a full "Glory,… now and ever…!", a **triple** "Lord, have mercy.", and then "In the Name of the Lord, Father, (or, if it be a bishop, "Master"; or, if it be the Metropolitan, "Most Blessed Master"), bless!" The celebrant pronounces the exclamation, and the people sing either a single or a double "Amen."

## B. THE LENTEN HOURS

During Great Lent, there are liturgical elements inserted into the 6th Hour on Monday through Friday during the first week of Great Lent,[35] and on Monday through Wednesday during Holy Week, and at the 1st Hour on Holy Thursday.[36]

On the first Monday, the Troparion of the Prophecy, in tone 5, begins, "Lord, O Lord, at the presence of Your power,…!" A full "Glory,…now and ever…!" follows, with "Lord, O Lord!" then **repeated**. The First Prokeimenon (tone 4), is, "The Lord knows the way of the righteous, / and the way of the wicked will perish!", with the verse, "Blessed is the man who walks not in the counsel of the wicked or stands in the way of sinners!" The Old Testament reading is Isaiah 1:1-20. The Second Prokeimenon (tone 7), is, "Serve the Lord with fear, / and rejoice in Him with trembling!", with the verse, "Why have the heathen raged and the people meditated on empty things?"

---

[35] *Triodion*, pp. 196, 216, 234-235, 253, and 272-273.
[36] Ibid, pp. 517, 529, 541, and 557-558.

On the first Tuesday, the Troparion of the Prophecy, in tone 1, begins, "We are strangers on the Earth, as all our fathers were!"  A full "Glory,…now and ever…!" follows, with "We are strangers on the Earth!" then **repeated**.  The First Prokeimenon (tone 4), is, "Hearken to the voice of my prayer, / my King and my God!", with the verse, "Give ear to my words, O Lord!  Attend to my cry!"  The Old Testament reading is Isaiah 1:19-2:3.  The Second Prokeimenon (tone 4), is, "O Lord, rebuke me not in Your anger, / nor chasten me in Your wrath!", with the verse, "Have mercy on me, O Lord, for I am weak!"

On the first Wednesday, the Troparion of the Prophecy, in tone 4, begins, "O Lord, Who love mankind, You know our created nature,…!"  A full "Glory,…now and ever…!" follows, with "O Lord, Who love mankind!" then **repeated**.  The First Prokeimenon (tone 4), is, "I will praise You, O Lord, / with my whole heart!", with the verse, "I will be glad and rejoice in You."  The Old Testament reading is Isaiah 2:3-11.  The Second Prokeimenon (tone 6), is, "The Lord is righteous and loves righteousness! / His countenance looks upon justice!", with the verse, "In the Lord, I have put my trust!  How can you say to my soul, 'Flee as a bird to the mountains'?"

On the first Thursday, the Troparion of the Prophecy, in tone 1, begins, "Deliver us, O Lord, from enemies visible and invisible,...!" A full "Glory,...now and ever...!" follows, with "Deliver us, O Lord!" then **repeated**. The First Prokeimenon (tone 1 [in some editions, tone 4]), is, "When the Lord has turned back the captivity of His people, / Jacob will rejoice and Israel will be glad!", with the verse, "The fool says in his heart, 'There is no God!'" The Old Testament reading is Isaiah 2:11-21. The Second Prokeimenon (tone 4), is, "O Lord, who will abide in Your tabernacle? / And who will dwell in Your holy mountain?", with the verse, "He who walks blamelessly, and works righteousness!"

On the first Friday, the Troparion of the Prophecy, in tone 5 (in some editions, tone 8), begins, "Our lives are full of sin and empty of repentance,...!" A full "Glory,...now and ever...!" follows, with "Our lives are full of sin!" then **repeated**. The First Prokeimenon (tone 7 [in some editions, tone 4]), is, "I will love You, O Lord, my Strength! / The Lord is my Foundation and my Refuge!", with the verse, "My God and my Helper, and I will hope in Him!" The Old Testament reading is Isaiah 3:1-14. The Second Prokeimenon (tone 6), is, "O Lord, my Helper / and my Redeemer!", with the verse, "The Heavens are telling the glory of God, and the firmament proclaims His handiwork!"

On Holy Monday, the Troparion of the Prophecy, in tone 6, begins, "With a contrite soul, we fall before You,…!"  A full "Glory,…now and ever…!" follows, with "With a contrite soul!" then *repeated*.  The First Prokeimenon (tone 4), is, "When the Lord turned again / the captivity of Zion!", with the verse, "Then, our mouth was filled with joy."  The Old Testament reading is Ezekiel 1:1-20.  The Second Prokeimenon (tone 6), is, "Except the Lord build the house, / those who build it labor in vain!", with the verse, "Except the Lord keep the city, the watchman stays awake in vain!"

On Holy Tuesday, the Troparion of the Prophecy, in tone 1, begins, "To those who sin beyond measure,…!"  A full "Glory,…now and ever…!" follows, with "To those who sin!" then *repeated*.  The First Prokeimenon (tone 6), is, "For, with the Lord, there is mercy, / and, with Him, is plenteous redemption!", with the verse, "Out of the depths have I cried to You, O Lord!"  The Old Testament reading is Ezekiel 1:21-28.  The Second Prokeimenon (tone 4), is, "Let Israel hope in the Lord, / from this time forth and forevermore!", with the verse, "Lord, my heart is not lifted up! My eyes are not raised too high!"

On Holy Wednesday, the Troparion of the Prophecy, in tone 2, begins, "Today, the evil Sanhedrin has gathered together,...!" A full "Glory,...now and ever...!" follows, with "Today, the evil Sanhedrin!" then *repeated*. The First Prokeimenon (tone 8), is, "The Lord, Who made Heaven and Earth, / bless you out of Zion!", with the verse, "Behold! Now, bless the Lord, all you servants of the Lord!" The Old Testament reading is Ezekiel 2:3-3:3. The Second Prokeimenon (tone 2), is, "You, who fear the Lord, / bless the Lord!", with the verse, "Praise the Name of the Lord! O you servants, praise the Lord!"

At the 1st Hour on Holy Thursday, the Troparion of the Prophecy, in tone 3, begins, "You were struck on the face for the sake of mankind,...!" A full "Glory,...now and ever...!" follows, with "You were struck on the face!" then *repeated*. The First Prokeimenon (tone 1), is, "Let the nations understand / that 'The Lord' is Your Name!", with the verse, "O God, Who is like unto You?" The Old Testament reading is Jeremiah 11:18-12:15. The Second Prokeimenon (tone 6 [in some editions, tone 8]), is, "Make a vow unto the Lord our God, / and keep it!", with the verse, "In Judah, God is known! His Name is great in Israel!" After this, the prayer, "Order my steps in Your Word...!" is chanted by the reader. The Kontakion of Holy Thursday (tone 2) is, "With his hands, the betrayer receives the bread!...!"

At the Typika after the 9th Hours, the Beatitudes are **chanted by a reader** instead of sung.

## C.  THE ROYAL HOURS

There are three times in the year when the Royal Hours are celebrated: on the feasts of Christmas,[37] Theophany,[38] and on Holy Friday.[39] Here, we will present the Royal Hours of Christmas and Theophany. The Royal Hours of Holy Friday will be presented in Chapter 8, "Holy Week and Pascha."

---

[37] Nassar, pp. 372-396.
[38] Ibid, pp. 436-456.
[39] *Triodion*, pp. 600-611.

## The 1ˢᵗ Hour

The 1ˢᵗ Hour begins with the exclamation, "Blessed is our God,…!" The reader responds with, "Amen. Glory to You, our God, glory to You!" (except in the Byzantine tradition, where a priest chants this), then the reader follows with O Heavenly King!", and then the Trisagion Prayers: a **triple** "Holy God!", a full "Glory,… now and ever…!", the Trinitarian Prayer ("O Most Holy Trinity, have mercy on us!…!"), a **triple** "Lord, have mercy.", **another** full "Glory,… now and ever…!", and the Lord's Prayer. After the exclamation, "For, Yours are the Kingdom, and the power, and the glory,…!", the reader continues with an "Amen.", "Lord, have mercy." **twelve** times, **another** full "Glory,… now and ever…!", and then, "Come, let us worship God, our King! Come, let us worship and fall down before Christ, our King and our God! Come, let us worship and fall down before Christ Himself (or, "the very Christ"), our King and our God!"

At this point, the reader chants three Psalms. For Christmas, the three are Psalms 5, 44, and 45.[40] For Theophany, the three are Psalms 5, 22, and 26.

---

[40] Again, the numbering of the Psalms is according to the Septuagint.

For both feasts, this is followed by a full "Glory,... now and ever...!", a *triple* "Alleluia! Alleluia! Alleluia! Glory to You, O God!", a *triple* "Lord, have mercy.", and **then** the *first half* of a "*split* 'Glory!'" ("Glory...Spirit!"), followed by the people singing the troparion of the prefeast (for Christmas, "Mary was of David's seed,...!"; for Theophany, "The River Jordan was turned back...!"), both, by the way, in tone 4.  If, however, the feast falls on a Sunday or Monday and the Royal Hours are transferred to Friday, then the prefeast troparion for Christmas is, "Make ready, O Bethlehem!  Eden has been opened to all", and for Theophany it is, "Make ready, O Zebulon!  Prepare yourself, O Naphthali!", both in tone 4.  After this, the reader chants the *secon*d half of the "*split* 'Glory!'" ("Now and ever...Amen!"), followed by the people singing the Theotokion of the prefeast (for **both** Christmas **and** Theophany, "What should we call you, O full of grace?...!"), again, in tone 4.

Stikhera for each feast then follow.  For Christmas, the first stikheron sung, in tone 8, begins, "Make ready, O Bethlehem!".  The reader then chants the verse beginning, "God will come from Teman,...!"  The next sung stikheron, in tone 3, begins, "Now the prophecy approaches its fulfillment!"  The reader then chants a full "Glory,... now and ever...!", and the people sing in tone 8, beginning, "Joseph said to the Virgin!" (*except* in the Byzantine tradition, whereby a "split 'Glory'" is done because "Joseph said to the Virgin!" is *repeated*).

For Theophany, the first stikheron sung, in tone 8, begins, "Today, the nature of the waters is sanctified!". The reader then chants the verse beginning, "Therefore, I remember You,…!" The next sung stikheron, still in tone 8, begins, "You have come to the river as a Man,…!" The reader then chants a full "Glory,… now and ever…!", and the people sing, still in tone 8, beginning, "To the voice of one crying in the wilderness!" (*except* in the Byzantine tradition, whereby a "split 'Glory'" is done because "To the voice of one crying in the wilderness!" is *repeated*).

In each case, this is followed by the Prokeimenon of the Prophecy, in the 4$^{th}$ tone. For Christmas, the Prokeimenon is "The Lord said to Me, 'You are My Son! Today, I have begotten You!'" After the reader chants this, the people sing it, followed by the reader chanting, "'Ask of Me, and I will give You the nations for Your inheritance, and the Ends of the Earth as Your possession!'" The people then again sing the full Prokeimenon. The reader then chants the ***first* half** ("The Lord said to Me, 'You are My Son!'"), and the people finish by singing the ***second* half**, "'Today, I have begotten You!'"

On Theophany, the Prokeimenon is "The Lord thundered in the Heavens! The Most High gave forth His voice!" After the reader chants this, the people sing it, followed by the reader chanting, "I will love You, O Lord, my Strength! The Lord is my Support!" The people then again sing the full Prokeimenon. The reader then chants the ***first*** ***half*** ("The Lord thundered in the Heavens!"), and the people finish by singing the ***second half***, "The Most High gave forth His voice!"

After this, the reader chants the Old Testament reading: for Christmas, it is Micah 5:2-4; for Theophany, it is Isaiah 35:1-10. This is followed by the Epistle: for Christmas, it is Hebrews 1:1-12; for Theophany, it is Acts 13:25-33. For **both** feasts, there are **no** "Alleluia!" verses. Instead, the Gospel is *immediately* chanted: for Christmas, it is Matthew 1:18-25; for Theophany, it is Matthew 3:1-11.

For **both** feasts, the reader then chants the prayer beginning, "Order my steps in Your Word, and so will no wickedness have dominion over me!", followed *immediately* by the Trisagion Prayers, the Lord's Prayer, the exclamation by the celebrant, and an "Amen." by the reader. The people then sing the Kontakion for the prefeast: for Christmas, "Today, the Virgin comes to the cave!", in tone 3; for Theophany, "Today, the Lord enters the Jordan...!", in tone 4.

Again, for **both** feasts, the reader then chants "Lord, have mercy." **twelve** times (in **some** parishes, it is **forty** times), followed by the prayer that begins, "You, Who at every season and every hour,…!", then a **triple** "Lord, have mercy.", a full "Glory,… now and ever…!", the prayer to the Theotokos beginning, "More honorable than the Cherubim,…!", and, finally, "In the Name of the Lord, Father (or, with the bishop, "Master"; or, with the Metropolitan, "Most Blessed Master"), bless!" The celebrant pronounces the exclamation beginning, "God be bountiful to us,…!". The reader intones an "Amen.", and then the prayer that begins, "O Christ, the true Light, Who enlighten and sanctify everyone who comes into the world!" This concludes the 1st Hour.

## 3rd Hour

The 3rd, 6th, and 9th Hours do **not** begin, as did the 1st Hour, with "O Heavenly King!", the Trisagion Prayers, the Lord's Prayer, and the exclamation. Rather, they **all** begin with the prayer beginning, "Come, let us worship God, our King!" In each case, the reader then proceeds to the three Psalms for the particular Hour.[41] In the 3rd Hour, the three at

---

[41] Nassar, pp. 378, 383, 391, 440, 444, and 450.

Christmas are Psalms 66, 86, and 50; the three at Theophany are Psalms 28, 41, and 50.

For both feasts, this is followed by a full "Glory,... now and ever...!", a *triple* "Alleluia! Alleluia! Alleluia! Glory to You, O God!", a *triple* "Lord, have mercy.", and **then** the **first half** of a "*split* 'Glory!'" ("Glory...Spirit!"), followed by the people singing the troparion of the prefeast (for Christmas, "Mary was of David's seed,...!"; for Theophany, "The River Jordan was turned back...!"), both, by the way, in tone 4.  If, however, the feast falls on a Sunday or Monday and the Royal Hours are transferred to Friday, then the prefeast troparion for Christmas is, "Make ready, O Bethlehem! Eden has been opened to all", and for Theophany it is, "Make ready, O Zebulon! Prepare yourself, O Naphthali!", both in tone 4.  After this, the reader chants the *secon*d half of the "*split* 'Glory!'" ("Now and ever...Amen!"), followed by the people singing the Theotokion of the prefeast (for **both** Christmas **and** Theophany, "O Theotokos, you are the true vine,...!"), again, in tone 4.

Stikhera for each feast then follow.  For Christmas, the first stikheron sung, in tone 6, begins, "He is our God!".  The reader then chants the verse beginning, "God will come from Teman,...!" The next sung stikheron, in tone 8, begins, "Before Your Birth, O Lord,...!" The reader then chants a full "Glory,...

now and ever...!", and the people sing in tone 3, beginning, "Tell us, O Joseph,...!"

For Theophany, the first stikheron sung, in tone 8, begins, "The prophet, above all prophets in honor,...!". The reader then chants the verse beginning, "Therefore, I remember You,...!" The next sung stikheron, in tone 4, begins, "Today, our God, the Trinity,...!" The reader then chants a full "Glory,... now and ever...!", and the people sing, in tone 5, beginning, "The Father bore witness to You,...!"

In each case, this is followed by the Prokeimenon of the Prophecy. For Christmas, the Prokeimenon, in tone 4, is "For, unto us a Child is Born! Unto us a Son is given!" After the reader chants this, the people sing it, followed by the reader chanting, "And the government will be upon His shoulder!" The people then again sing the full Prokeimenon. The reader then chants the ***first half*** ("For, unto us a Child is Born!"), and the people finish by singing the ***second half***, "Unto us a Son is given!"

On Theophany, the Prokeimenon, in tone 6, is "The waters saw You, O God! The waters saw You and were afraid!" After the reader chants this, the people sing it, followed by the reader chanting, "I cried to the Lord with my voice, even to God with my voice, and He heard me!" The people then again sing the full Prokeimenon. The reader then chants the **_first half_** ("The waters saw You, O God!"), and the people finish by singing the **_second half_**, "The waters saw You and were afraid!"

After this, the reader chants the Old Testament reading: for Christmas, it is Baruch 3:35-4:4; for Theophany, it is Isaiah 1:16-20. This is followed by the Epistle: for Christmas, it is Galatians 3:23-29; for Theophany, it is Acts 19:1-8. For **both** feasts, there are **no** "Alleluia!" verses. **Instead**, the Gospel is **_immediately_** chanted: for Christmas, it is Luke 2:1-20; for Theophany, it is Mark 1:1-8.

After the Gospel, the reader then chants the prayer beginning, "Blessed be the Lord God! Blessed be the Lord from day to day,…!", followed **_immediately_** by the Trisagion Prayers, the Lord's Prayer, the exclamation by the celebrant, and an "Amen." by the reader. The people then sing the Kontakion for the prefeast: for Christmas, "Today, the Virgin comes to the cave!", in tone 3; for Theophany, "Today, the Lord enters the Jordan…!", in tone 4.

Again, for **both** feasts, the reader then chants "Lord, have mercy." **twelve** times (in **some** parishes, **_forty_** times), followed by the prayer that begins, "You, Who at every season and every hour,…!", then a ***triple*** "Lord, have mercy.", a full "Glory,... now and ever...!", the prayer to the Theotokos beginning, "More honorable than the Cherubim,...!", and, finally, "In the Name of the Lord, Father (or, with the bishop, "Master"; or, with the Metropolitan, "Most Blessed Master"), bless!" The celebrant pronounces the exclamation beginning, "God be bountiful to us,...!". The reader intones an "Amen.", and then a prayer, "O God, the Master, Father Almighty,...!". This concludes the 3$^{rd}$ Hour.

## 6$^{th}$ *Hour*

The reader chants the prayer beginning, "Come, let us worship God, our King!...". For both feasts, the reader then proceeds to the three Psalms for the particular Hour. In the 6$^{th}$ Hour, the three at Christmas are Psalms 71, 131, and 90; the three at Theophany are Psalms 73, 76, and 90.

For both feasts, this is followed by a full "Glory,... now and ever...!", a ***triple*** "Alleluia! Alleluia! Alleluia! Glory to You, O God!", a ***triple*** "Lord, have mercy.", and ***then*** the ***first half*** of a "***split*** 'Glory!'" ("Glory...Spirit!"), followed by the people singing the troparion of the prefeast (for Christmas, "Mary was of David's seed,...!"; for

Theophany, "The River Jordan was turned back...!"), both, by the way, in tone 4. If, however, the feast falls on a Sunday or Monday and the Royal Hours are transferred to Friday, then the prefeast troparion for Christmas is, "Make ready, O Bethlehem! Eden has been opened to all", and for Theophany it is, "Make ready, O Zebulon! Prepare yourself, O Naphthali!", both in tone 4. After this, the reader chants the **secon**d half of the "**split** 'Glory!'" ("Now and ever...Amen!"), followed by the people singing the Theotokion of the prefeast (for **both** Christmas **and** Theophany, "We have no boldness because of the multitude of our sins,...!"), again, in tone 4.

Stikhera for each feast then follow. For Christmas, the first stikheron sung, in tone 1, begins, "Come, O God-inspired people!". The reader then chants the verse beginning, "God will come from Teman,...!", **and then**, the verse, "O Lord, I have heard what You have done, and am filled with awe!" The next sung stikheron, in tone 4, begins, "Listen, O Heaven! Give ear, O Earth!...". The reader then chants a full "Glory,... now and ever...!", and the people sing in tone 5, beginning, "Come, O Christ-bearing people!...".

For Theophany, the first stikheron sung, in tone 8, begins, "'O prophet!', the Lord now says to John,...!". The reader then chants the verse beginning, "Therefore, I remember You,...!" The next sung stikheron, in tone 6, begins, "Today, the prophecy of the Psalm...!" The reader then chants a full "Glory,... now and ever...!", and the people sing, in tone 5, beginning, "Why do you stop the flow of your waters, O Jordan?...!"

In each case, this is followed by the Prokeimenon of the Prophecy, **both** in tone 4. For Christmas, the Prokeimenon is "Out of the womb, before the morning star, have I begotten You! The Lord has sworn and will not change His mind!" After the reader chants this, the people sing it, followed by the reader chanting, "The Lord said to my Lord: 'Sit at My right hand, until I make Your enemies Your footstool!'" The people then again sing the full Prokeimenon. The reader then chants the ***first half*** ("Out of the womb, before the morning star, have I begotten You!"), and the people finish by singing the ***second half***, "The Lord has sworn and will not change His mind!"

On Theophany, the Prokeimenon is "Your way was through the sea, and Your paths through the great waters!" After the reader chants this, the people sing it, followed by the reader chanting, "The crash of Your thunder was in the whirlwind!" The people then again sing the full Prokeimenon. The reader then chants the ***first half*** ("Your way was through the sea!"), and the people finish by singing the **_second half_**, "And Your paths through the great waters!"

After this, the reader chants the Old Testament reading: for Christmas, it is Isaiah 7:10-16; 8:1-4,9-10; for Theophany, it is Isaiah 12:3-6. This is followed by the Epistle: for Christmas, it is Hebrews 1:10-2:4; for Theophany, it is Romans 6:3-11. For **both** feasts, there are **no** "Alleluia!" verses. Instead, the Gospel is **_immediately_** chanted: for Christmas, it is Matthew 2:1-12; for Theophany, it is Mark 1:9-11.

After the Gospel, the reader then chants the prayer beginning, "Let Your tender mercies, O Lord, speedily go before us!...", followed **_immediately_** by the Trisagion Prayers, the Lord's Prayer, the exclamation by the celebrant, and an "Amen." by the reader. The people then sing the Kontakion for the prefeast: for Christmas, "Today, the Virgin comes to the cave!", in tone 3; for Theophany, "Today, the Lord enters the Jordan...!", in tone 4.

Again, for **both** feasts, the reader then chants "Lord, have mercy." **_twelve_** times (in **_some_** parishes, **_forty_** times), followed by the prayer that begins, "You, Who at every season and every hour,...!", then a **_triple_** "Lord, have mercy.", a full "Glory,... now and ever...!", the prayer to the Theotokos beginning, "More honorable than the Cherubim,...!", and, finally, "In the Name of the Lord, Father (or, with the bishop, "Master"; or, with the Metropolitan, "Most Blessed Master"), bless!" The celebrant pronounces the exclamation beginning, "God be bountiful to us,…!". The reader intones an "Amen.", and then a prayer, "O God, the Lord of hosts, and Author of all creation,…!". This concludes the 6th Hour.

## 9th Hour

The reader chants the prayer beginning, "Come, let us worship God, our King!…". For both feasts, the reader then proceeds to the three Psalms for the particular Hour. In the 9th Hour, the three at Christmas are Psalms 109, 110, and 85; the three at Theophany are Psalms 92, 113, and 85.

For both feasts, this is followed by a full "Glory,… now and ever…!", a **triple** "Alleluia! Alleluia! Alleluia! Glory to You, O God!", a **triple** "Lord, have mercy.", and **then** the **first half** of a "**split** 'Glory!'" ("Glory…Spirit!"), followed by the people singing the troparion of the prefeast (for Christmas, "Mary was of David's seed,…!"; for Theophany, "The River Jordan was turned back…!"), both, by the way, in tone 4. If, however, the feast falls on a Sunday or Monday and the Royal Hours are transferred to Friday, then the prefeast troparion for Christmas is, "Make ready, O Bethlehem!  Eden has been opened to all", and for Theophany it is, "Make ready, O Zebulon!  Prepare yourself, O Naphthali!", both in tone 4.  After this, the reader chants the **second** half of the "***split*** 'Glory!'" ("Now and ever…Amen!"), followed by the people singing the Theotokion of the prefeast (for **both** Christmas **and** Theophany, "O loving Lord, Who, for our sakes, was Born of a Virgin,…!"), again, in tone 4.

Stikhera for each feast then follow.  For Christmas, the first stikheron sung, in tone 7, begins, "Herod was filled with alarm…!".  The reader then chants the verse beginning, "God will come from Teman,…!", then, in tone 2, the stikheron, "When Joseph went up to Bethlehem,…!", then the verse, "O Lord, I have heard what You have done, and am filled with awe!"  The next sung stikheron, in tone 2, begins, "When Joseph went up to Bethlehem…!".  The reader then chants a full "Glory,… now and ever…!", and the people sing in tone 6, beginning, "Today, He Who holds the whole creation in His hand…!".

For Theophany, the first stikheron sung, in tone 7, begins, "What wonder, to look down in the River…!".  The reader then chants the verse beginning, "Therefore, I remember You,…!"  The next sung stikheron, in tone 2, begins, "When he saw the Lord of glory draw near,...!" The reader then chants a full "Glory,... now and ever...!", and the people sing, in tone 5, beginning, "With your hand, O Baptist,...!"

In each case, this is followed by the Prokeimenon of the Prophecy. For Christmas, the Prokeimenon, in tone 4, is "'Zion is my mother,' a man will say, 'and such a man was born in her!'" After the reader chants this, the people sing it, followed by the reader chanting, "His foundations are on the holy mountains! The Lord loves the gates of Zion more than all the dwelling places of Jacob!" The people then again sing the full Prokeimenon. The reader then chants the ***first* half** ("'Zion is my mother,' a man will say!"), and the people finish by singing the ***second* half**, "'And such a man was born in her!'"

On Theophany, the Prokeimenon, in tone 3, is "The Lord is my Light and my Salvation! Whom should I fear?" After the reader chants this, the people sing it, followed by the reader chanting, "The Lord is the Defender of my life! Of whom should I be afraid?" The people then again sing the full Prokeimenon. The reader then chants the ***first* half** ("The Lord is my Light and my Salvation!"), and the people finish by singing the ***second* half**, "Whom should I fear?"

After this, the reader chants the Old Testament reading: for Christmas, it is Isaiah 9:6-7; for Theophany, it is Isaiah 49:8-15. This is followed by the Epistle: for Christmas, it is Hebrews 2:11-18; for Theophany, it is Titus 2:11-3:7. For **both** feasts, there are **no** "Alleluia!" verses. Instead, the Gospel is **immediately** chanted: for Christmas, it is Matthew 2:13-23; for Theophany, it is Matthew 3:1-18.

After the Gospel, the reader then chants the prayer beginning, "For Your holy Name's sake, do not abandon us forever!...", followed **immediately** by the Trisagion Prayers, the Lord's Prayer, the exclamation by the celebrant, and an "Amen." by the reader. The people then sing the Kontakion for the prefeast: for Christmas, "Today, the Virgin comes to the cave!", in tone 3; for Theophany, "Today, the Lord enters the Jordan...!", in tone 4.

Again, for **both** feasts, the reader then chants "Lord, have mercy." **twelve** times (in **some** parishes, **forty** times), followed by the prayer that begins, "You, Who at every season and every hour,...!", then a **triple** "Lord, have mercy.", a full "Glory,... now and ever...!", the prayer to the Theotokos beginning, "More honorable than the Cherubim,...!", and, finally, "In the Name of the Lord, Father (or, with the bishop, "Master"; or, with the Metropolitan, "Most Blessed Master"), bless!" The celebrant pronounces the exclamation beginning, "God be bountiful to us,...!". The reader intones an "Amen.", and then a prayer, "O Master, Jesus Christ, our God,...!". This concludes the 9$^{th}$ Hour.

**The Typika**

For both feasts, the Typika begin *immediately*, with *no* exclamation or intonation of any kind. (If, however, the feast falls on a Sunday or Monday and the Royal Hours are transferred to Friday, then, in the Byzantine tradition, the Typika are *not* celebrated, but the 9$^{th}$ Hour ends only with the Dismissal.) The reader chants Psalm 102 ("Bless the Lord, O my soul! Blessed are You, O Lord!"), then the ***first half*** of a "split 'Glory'" ("Glory...Spirit!"), followed by Psalm 145 ("Praise the Lord, O my soul! I will praise the Lord as long as I live!"), followed by the ***second half*** of a "split 'Glory'" ("Now and ever...Amen."), followed by "Only-Begotten Son." *All* of this is chanted by the reader, rather than sung by the people. The reader then chants the Beatitudes.

At this point, *two* readers usually respond in chanting, back-and-forth, between them. The first reader chants, "The heavenly choir sings Your praises, saying, Holy! Holy! Holy! Lord of Sabaoth!

Heaven and Earth are full of Your glory!'" The second reader then responds with, "Draw near to Him, and be enlightened, and, so, your faces will never be ashamed!" The first reader then repeats, "The heavenly choir sings Your praises, saying, Holy! Holy! Holy! Lord of Sabaoth! Heaven and Earth are full of Your glory!'" The second reader then responds with, "Glory to the Father, and to the Son, and to the Holy Spirit!" The first reader then chants, "The choir of the holy angels and archangels, with all the powers of Heaven, sings Your praises, saying, 'Holy! Holy! Holy! Lord of Sabaoth! Heaven and Earth are full of Your glory!'" " The second reader then responds with, "Now and ever and unto ages of ages! Amen."

    A reader then chants the Creed, and, following this, another reader (usually) chants this prayer, "Forgive, remit, and pardon, God, our sins, both voluntary and involuntary, in word, deed, or thought, committed in knowledge or in ignorance, by night or by day! Forgive us all of them! For, You are good and love mankind!" A reader then chants the Lord's Prayer and, after the exclamation, "For Yours are the Kingdom, and the power, and the glory,…!", the "Amen."

    The people then sing the Kontakion for the prefeast: for Christmas, "Today, the Virgin comes to the cave!", in tone 3; for Theophany, "Today, the Lord enters the Jordan...!", in tone 4.

For both feasts, a reader then chants, "Most Holy Trinity, consubstantial Power, undivided Kingship, the Cause of all good: Be gracious to us sinners! Confirm and instruct our hearts, and take away from us every defilement! Enlighten our minds, that we may ever glorify, praise, and worship You, saying: "One is Holy! One is Lord, Jesus Christ, to the glory of God the Father! Amen!"

The people then sing, "Blessed be the Name of the Lord, henceforth and forevermore!" **three** times! A reader then chants Psalm 33 ("I will bless the Lord at all times! His praise will continually be in my mouth!"). Another reader (usually) chants the Hymn to the Theotokos ("It is truly meet to bless you, O Theotokos,...!").

Following this is the Dismissal, according to the usual formula: the main celebrant chants, "Most Holy Theotokos, save us!". The people then sing, "More honorable than the Cherubim,...!". The celebrant then chants, "Glory to You, O Christ our God and our Hope, glory to You!" The people then sing a full "Glory,... now and ever...!", a **triple** "Lord, have mercy.", and "Father (or, with the bishop, "Master"; or, with the Metropolitan, "Most Blessed Master"), bless!" The celebrant then pronounces the Dismissal Prayer appropriate to the prefeast, and the people usually sing a **double** "Amen." ("Amen. Amen.").

## D. GRAND COMPLINE

Grand Compline (also called, "Great Compline") is usually served in parishes as the first part of the Vigils for both Christmas and Theophany (followed, in both cases, by Matins), and, celebrated with the Kanon of St Andrew of Crete, during the first four days (Monday through Thursday) of the first week of Great Lent as well as the fifth Thursday of Great Lent. The pairing of Grand Compline with the Kanon of St Andrew will be presented in chapter 7, "Lenten Services." The order for the service as prescribed in the service book is as follows.[42] **However**, **_most_** parishes celebrate a **_very abbreviated_** form of this Grand Compline on Christmas and Theophany, keeping the order of the Matins that follows more intact.

---

[42] Hapgood, pp. 147-163.

## The Trisagion Prayers and Psalm Reading

The service begins with the exclamation, "Blessed is our God, always now and ever and unto ages of ages!" The reader chants, "Amen.", then "Glory to You, our God, glory to You!" (*except* in the Byzantine tradition, where the *priest* chants this), then the reader chants, "O Heavenly King!", the Trisagion Prayers, and the Lord's Prayer. At the exclamation, "For, Yours are the Kingdom, and the power, and the glory,…!", the reader chants, "Amen."

Then, the reader goes on with, "Lord, have mercy." *twelve* times, followed by a full "Glory,… now and ever…!", and then the full prayer beginning, "Come, let us worship God, our King!" Then the reader chants three Psalms: Psalm 4 (beginning, "Answer me when I call, O God of my right!"), Psalm 6 (beginning, "O Lord, rebuke me not in Your anger, nor chasten me in Your wrath!"), and Psalm 12 (beginning, "Help, Lord! For, there are no longer any who are godly!").[43] The reader then chants a full "Glory,… now and ever…!", then "Alleluia! Alleluia! Alleluia! Glory to You, O God!" *three* times, a *triple*

---

[43] Again, the numbering of the Psalms is according to the Septuagint.

"Lord, have mercy.", and another full "Glory,… now and ever…!"

The reader (or, another reader, perhaps) then chants another three Psalms: Psalm 24 (beginning, "To You, O Lord, I lift up my soul! O my God, in You I trust!"), Psalm 30 (beginning, "I will extol You, O Lord, for You have drawn me up!"), and Psalm 90 (beginning, "He who dwells in the shelter of the Most High!"). Again, the reader then chants a full "Glory,… now and ever…!", then "Alleluia! Alleluia! Alleluia! Glory to You, O God!" **three** times, a **triple** "Lord, have mercy.", and another full "Glory,… now and ever…!"

**"God is With Us"**

Following this, "God is With Us!" is celebrated. The deacon chants the full exclamation: "God is with us! Understand, all you nations, and submit yourselves! For, God is with us!" The people then sing this entire exclamation, in tone 4, in full voice. The deacon then chants the prayer that begins, "Hear this, all you ends of the Earth! Submit yourselves, you mighty ones! Even if your strength returns, you will be overthrown once more!…" The people then repeatedly sing an abbreviated ending of the exclamation: "For, God is with us!"  In *some* parishes, this is done *very* quietly during the entire chanting of the prayer by the deacon, which, in effect, ends up *covering over* the prayer itself.  For this reason, in *other* parishes, after the deacon chants each paragraph of the prayer, the people then sing the abbreviated ending, with the deacon *waiting* until the singing is concluded before going on with the prayer.  That way, everyone in church gets to hear and meditate on the entire prayer.  Obviously, this second method of celebrating the prayer is the preferred one.  However, as always, the decision remains with the main celebrant of the service.  After completing the prayer with a full "Glory,… now and ever…!", the deacon full proclaims the entire exclamation again:  "God is with us! Understand, all you nations, and submit yourselves!  For, God is with us!"  The people then sing this entire exclamation fully, one last time.

In the Antiochian tradition, the reader chants the "God is with us!", with the two choirs (right and left) alternating with the prayer while everyone sings the refrain.  Then, everyone sings the final, "God is with us!".  In the Greek tradition, the priest and/or chanters sing the "God is with us!" at the beginning and at the end, and then a reader chants the prayer with the congregation singing the refrain.

## Prayers and the Creed

After this, the reader chants some prayers: "The day is past! I thank You, O Lord! Grant me to pass this evening and this night without sin, and save me, O my Savior! Glory to the Father, and to the Son, and to the Holy Spirit! The day is past! I glorify You, O Master! Grant me to pass this evening and this night without giving offense, and save me, O my Savior! Now and ever and unto ages of ages! Amen. The day is past! I sing to You, O Holy One! Grant me to pass this evening and this night free from temptation, and save me, O my Savior!" (In the Byzantine tradition, there are ten other prayers chanted, the first one beginning, "With never-silent hymns, the bodiless powers of the Cherubim glorify You!", and all of them ending with, "Holy! Holy! Holy! Thrice-Holy Lord: Have mercy on us and save us! Amen!".) This is followed by the reader (or, another reader) chanting the Creed.

## Verses of Supplication

The main celebrant then exits the sanctuary and stands on the solea before the Royal Doors, chanting a series of petitions. After *each* petition, the people sing this *same* petition. The petitions are as follows:

- All-holy sovereign Lady Theotokos, pray for us sinners! (In the Byzantine tradition, this petition *only* is done *three* times.)
- All you heavenly hosts of angels and archangels, pray for us sinners!
- Holy John, the prophet and Forerunner and Baptist of our Lord Jesus Christ, pray for us sinners!
- Holy glorious Apostles, prophets, martyrs, and all the saints, pray for us sinners!
- Our reverent and God-bearing fathers, pastors, and ecumenical teachers, pray for us sinners!
- Saint(s) [name of the saint(s) of the parish church], pray for us sinners!
- Invincible, ineffable, and divine power of the honorable and life-giving Cross, forsake not us sinners!
- God, cleanse us sinners!

- God, cleanse us sinners!
- God, cleanse us sinners, and have mercy on us!

With this last petition, the people sing it in a musical manner (final musical chord, etc.) to show that this is the end of this liturgical element.

## The Trisagion Prayers and the Lord's Prayer

Then, the reader chants the Trisagion Prayers and the Lord's Prayer. After the exclamation and the "Amen.", the reader chants, "Lord, have mercy." **twelve times**, then a full "Glory,… now and ever…!"

## The Troparion of the Feast

After this, the troparion of the feast is sung: for Christmas, it is, "Your Nativity, O Christ our God,…!", in tone 4; for Theophany, it is, "When You, O Lord, were Baptized in the Jordan,…!", in tone 1.

## Petition and Exclamation

This is followed by the reader chanting, "Lord, have mercy." **forty** times (in **some** parishes, the practice is to chant it **twelve** times). Then, the reader chants the prayer to the Theotokos that begins, "More honorable than the Cherubim!", and then, "In the Name of the Lord, Father (or, with the bishop, "Master"; or, with the Metropolitan, "Most Blessed Master"), bless!" The celebrant intones the exclamation that begins, "Through the prayers of our holy fathers,…!", and the reader responds with, "Amen."

## Prayer, Psalms 50 and 101, and the Prayer of Manasseh

Then, a reader chants a prayer that begins, "O Lord, Lord, Who deliver us from all the arrows that fly by day,…!" (**except** in the Byzantine tradition, where the **priest** chants this prayer). After this prayer, the reader intones the prayer, "Come, let us worship God, our King!…" This is followed by the reader chanting Psalm 50 (beginning, "Have mercy on me, O God,…!") and Psalm 101 (beginning, "Hear my prayer, O Lord! Let my cry come unto You!").

The reader (or, another reader) then chants the Prayer of Manasseh (beginning, "O Lord Almighty, God of our fathers, of Abraham and Isaac and Jacob and of their posterity,...!"). (In the Byzantine tradition, the **priest** chants the Prayer of Manasseh.)

### The Trisagion Prayers and the Lord's Prayer

Then, the reader chants the Trisagion Prayers and the Lord's Prayer. After the exclamation and the "Amen.", the reader chants, "Lord, have mercy." **twelve times**, then a full "Glory,... now and ever...!"

### The Kontakion of the Feast

The people then sing the Kontakion of the feast: for Christmas, it is, "Today, the Virgin gives Birth to the Transcendent One,...!", in tone 3; for Theophany, it is, "Today, You have appeared to the universe,...!", in tone 4.

## Petition and Exclamation

This is followed by the reader chanting, "Lord, have mercy." ***forty*** times (in some parishes, the practice is to chant it ***twelve*** times). Then, the reader chants the prayer to the Theotokos that begins, "More honorable than the Cherubim!", and then, "In the Name of the Lord, Father (or, with the bishop, "Master"; or, with the Metropolitan, "Most Blessed Master"), bless!" The celebrant intones the exclamation that begins, "Through the prayers of our holy fathers,…!", and the reader responds with, "Amen." This is followed by the priest chanting the prayer, "O God, the Master, Father Almighty,…!".

## Psalms 69 and 142

After this prayer, the reader intones the prayer, "Come, let us worship God, our King!…" This is followed by the reader chanting Psalm 69 (beginning, "Be pleased, O God, to deliver me! O Lord, make haste to help me!") and Psalm 142 (beginning, "Hear my prayer, O Lord! Give ear to my supplications!").

## The Great Doxology [The Lesser Doxology]

The celebrant intones, "Glory to You, Who have shone us the Light!" The people then sing the Great Doxology ("Glory to God in the highest,…!") [**Note:** The service book calls for the Lesser Doxology, to be chanted by a reader (which is **still** celebrated that way in the Byzantine tradition).[44] However, most parishes have the people sing this as a Great Doxology.]

## Litya Stikhera

After this, Litya stikhera are sung. For Christmas, each begins as follows: "Today, let Heaven and Earth make glad prophetically!" (tone 1); "Heaven and Earth are united today!" (tone 1); "'Glory to God in the Highest!' I hear today in Bethlehem!" (tone 1); "Beholding him who was in God's image and likeness!" (tone 1); "Glory,…Spirit!"; "The Magi, kings of Persia!" (tone 5); "Now and ever…Amen."; "All the angels in Heaven!" (tone 6).

---

[44] Mother Mary and Ware, Archimandrite Kallistos, *The Festal Menaion*, Faber and Faber, London, 1977 (hereafter referred to as "*Menaion*"), p. 262.

For Theophany, the Litya stikhera each begins as follows: "He Who covers Himself with light as with a garment!" (tone 4); "John the Baptist saw You draw near!" (tone 4); "Come, let us do as the wise virgins!" (tone 4); "Christ is Baptized! He comes up out of the waters!" (tone 4); "The hand of the Baptist trembled!" (tone 4); "Glory,...Spirit!"; "O Lord, wishing to fulfill!" (tone 8); "Now and ever...Amen."; "Today, the creation is enlightened!" (tone 8).

[**Note:** In **most** parishes, the practice is to take **only one or two** of these stikhera, to give the clergy time to process to the back of the church.]

## Litya Petitions

When the clergy are at the back of the nave and the singing of the Litya verses is concluded, the priest or deacon chants five special petitions. After the first **three** petitions, the people respond with "Lord, have mercy" sung **twelve** times. After the next **two** petitions, the people respond with "Lord, have mercy" sung **three** times. (In the Byzantine tradition, all five petitions are responded to with the singing of "Lord, have mercy" **only three** times.) Then, there is the conclusion of these petitions, which is similar to the conclusion of the Litany of Supplication:  After an exclamation by the priest and the "Amen" by the people, the priest faces the people and, blessing them, says, "Peace be with you all!"  The people then respond by singing, "And with your spirit!"  The priest or deacon then says, "Bow your heads unto the Lord."  The people sing, "To You, O Lord."  The priest reads a prayer, ending with an exclamation, to which the people respond with, "Amen."

## The Apostikha

There now follows the Apostikha.  For Christmas, the people sing, "A great and marvelous wonder!" in tone 2.  The reader chants the verse, "The Lord said to my Lord, 'Sit at My right hand, until I make Your enemies Your footstool!'"  The people then sing, "Today, the Virgin gives Birth to the Maker of all!" in tone 3.  The reader chants the verse, "From the womb, before the morning star, have I begotten you!"  The people sing, "When the Lord Jesus was Born!" in tone 3.  The reader chants, "Glory,...Spirit!"  The people sing, "Make glad, O Jerusalem!" in tone 4.  The reader chants, "Now and ever...Amen."  The people sing, "You have come to dwell in a cave!" in tone 4.

For Theophany, the people sing, "Seeing You, O Christ our God!" in tone 2. The reader chants the verse, "The sea saw it and fled! Jordan turned back!'" The people then sing, "The waters saw You, O God!" in tone 2. The reader chants the verse, "What ails you, O sea, that you flee? O Jordan, that you turn back?" The people sing, "Today, the Maker of Heaven and Earth!" in tone 2. The reader chants a full "Glory,...now and ever...!" The people sing, "Seeing the Sun, Who came from a Virgin!" in tone 6.

**The Troparion of the Feast**

The people then sing the troparion for the feast: for Christmas, it is, "Your Nativity, O Christ our God,...!", in tone 4; for Theophany, it is, "When You, O Lord, were Baptized in the Jordan,...!", in tone 1.

**["Blessed Be the Name of the Lord"]**

Although it is not called for in the service books, in *many* parishes the people sing, "Blessed be the Name of the Lord, henceforth and forevermore!" *three* times.

## The Dismissal

The celebrant comes out of the sanctuary, stands on the ambo, and blesses the people, as he intones, "The blessing of the Lord be upon you, through His grace and love for mankind, always now and ever and unto ages of ages!" The people sing, in response, "Amen."

The celebration of Matins then begins *immediately*, with the people singing, "Glory to God in the highest!" *three* times, and "O Lord, open my lips!" *two* times.

## E. THANKSGIVING

The service of Thanksgiving (called, in Russian, "*Molieben*", from the word meaning "prayer"), can be celebrated on any occasion, and its order is prescribed as follows (this service is usually *not* celebrated in the Byzantine tradition).[45]

---

[45] Hapgood, pp. 559-563.

## The Trisagion Prayers and the Lord's Prayer

The service begins with the doxology, "Blessed is our God, always now and ever and unto ages of ages!" The **_people_ then _sing_**, "Amen." and "O Heavenly King!" The **_reader_ then _chants_** the Trisagion Prayers and the Lord's Prayer, with the usual exclamation and the "Amen.", and then, a full "Come, let us worship God, our King…".

## Psalms 117 and 29

The reader then chants Psalm 117 ("O give thanks to the Lord, for He is good,…!") in full. This is followed by a full "Glory,… now and ever…!", and then, "Alleluia! Alleluia! Alleluia! Glory to You, O God!" **three** times. If the Thanksgiving is being offered for someone recovering from illness, Psalm 29 ("I will extol You, O Lord,…!") is then chanted, concluded, as the previous Psalm, with the full "Glory,… now and ever…!", and then, "Alleluia! Alleluia! Alleluia! Glory to You, O God!" **three** times.

## The Great Litany

The Great Litany is chanted by the clergy, with responses sung by the people. There are eleven petitions, with the people singing, "Lord, have mercy" after each one. When the priest or deacon chants the petition that begins, "Commemorating our most holy, most pure, most blessed and glorious Lady,…," the people respond to that petition with, "To You, O Lord!" The priest (or bishop) then chants the exclamation, to which the people respond by singing, "Amen."

## "God is the Lord" and Troparia

The deacon then intones "God is the Lord!" The singing of "God is the Lord!" is interspersed with verses Psalm 117, chanted by the deacon (or priest, if there is no deacon serving). The chanting between the deacon and the people is as follows:

**Deacon:** God is the Lord, and has revealed Himself to us. Blessed is He Who comes in the Name of the Lord! O give thanks to the Lord, for He is good! For, His steadfast love endures forever!

**People:** God is the Lord, and has revealed Himself to us. Blessed is He Who comes in the Name of the Lord!

**Deacon:** All nations surrounded me! But, in the Name of the Lord, I destroyed them!

**People:** God is the Lord, and has revealed Himself to us. Blessed is He Who comes in the Name of the Lord!

**Deacon:** I will not die, but live, and recount the deeds of the Lord!

**People:** God is the Lord, and has revealed Himself to us. Blessed is He Who comes in the Name of the Lord!

**Deacon:** The stone that the builders has become the head of the corner! This is the Lord's doing, and it is marvelous in our eyes!

**People:** God is the Lord, and has revealed Himself to us. Blessed is He Who comes in the Name of the Lord!

The people then sing the following: the first troparion ("We, Your unworthy servants, O Lord,…!") in tone 4; "Glory,…Spirit!"; the second troparion ("Freely, You grant us rich blessings, O Master,…!"); "Now and ever…Amen."; and, finally, the theotokion, "O Mother of God, help of Christians". **If** this Thanksgiving is being petitioned to a particular saint, **then** the order of singing would be the first troparion ("We, Your unworthy servants, O Lord,…!"), in tone 4; "Glory…Spirit!"; the second troparion, for the saint; "Now and ever…Amen."; and, finally, the theotokion in the **_same tone_** as the troparion for the saint.

## The Little Litany

After this, a Little Litany is celebrated. This consists of the following:

**Deacon:** Again and again, in peace, let us pray to the Lord.

**People:** Lord, have mercy.

**Deacon:** Help us, save us, have mercy on us, and keep us, O God, by Your grace.

**People:** Lord, have mercy.

**Deacon:** Commemorating our most holy, most pure, most blest and glorious Lady, the Theotokos and ever-Virgin Mary, with all the saints, let us commend ourselves and each other and all our life unto Christ our God.

**People:** To You, O Lord.

There follows then a prayer chanted by the priest or bishop, concluding with the exclamation,

"For, to You are due all glory, honor, and worship: to the Father, and to the Son, and to the Holy Spirit, now and ever and unto ages of ages." The people then respond with "Amen."

## Prokeimenon

This is followed by the Prokeimenon. There are special prokeimena for special occasions, such as a Thanksgiving to our Savior ("Lord, we will walk in the light of Your countenance,…!") or to the Theotokos ("I will call on your name…!"). For a regular Thanksgiving, the Prokeimenon is as follows:

| | |
|---|---|
| **Deacon:** | Wisdom! Let us be attentive! |
| **Priest:** | Peace be with you all! |
| **Reader:** | And with your spirit! |
| **Deacon:** | Wisdom! |
| **Reader:** | The prokeimenon is in the 4$^{th}$ tone: I will sing to the Lord, for He has dealt lovingly with me. |
| **People:** | I will sing to the Lord, for He has dealt lovingly with me. |

| | |
|---|---|
| **Reader:** | I have trusted in Your mercy. My heart will rejoice in Your salvation. |
| **People:** | I will sing to the Lord, for He has dealt lovingly with me. |
| **Reader:** | I will sing to the Lord. |
| **People:** | For, He has dealt lovingly with me. |

### The Epistle and the "Alleluia!"

The Epistle is then chanted by the reader. If it is a regular Thanksgiving, the Epistle reading is Ephesians 5:8-21. If the service is for a civil holiday, the Epistle reading is Romans 13:1-8.

At the conclusion of the Epistle reading, the priest or bishop will bless the reader with the sign of the Cross, saying, "Peace be with you, Reader!" The reader then responds with, "And with your spirit! Alleluia! Alleluia! Alleluia! The people then sing a triple "Alleluia!" Since there are *no* "Alleluia!" verses assigned to the Thanksgiving, the service *immediately* proceeds to the Gospel reading.

## *The Gospel*

For a regular Thanksgiving, the Gospel reading is Luke 17:12-19.  If the service is for a civil holiday, the Gospel reading is Matthew 22:15-22.

In many parishes, the priest or bishop will intone aloud the prayer before the Gospel reading, which begins "Illumine our hearts, O Master, Who love mankind, with the pure light of Your knowledge!"  In some of these parishes, the people, after the priest concludes with "…now and ever and unto ages of ages!", will sing an "Amen."

In all cases, at this point, the priest or bishop will come out from the sanctuary and bless the people with the sign of the Cross as he says, "Wisdom!  Let us be attentive!  Let us listen to the Holy Gospel!  Peace be with you all!"  The people then sing "And with your spirit!"  The priest or bishop then chants "The reading is from the Holy Gospel according to Saint [Luke; Matthew]!"  The people then sing "Glory to You, O Lord!  Glory to You!"  The deacon then intones "Let us be attentive!", and the priest or bishop then chants the Gospel reading.

At the conclusion of the Gospel reading, the people again sing "Glory to You, O Lord! Glory to You!"

**The Augmented Litany**

The Augmented Litany is then celebrated, with the first petition being chanted, "Have mercy on us, O God,...!" The people respond with a *triple* "Lord, have mercy." Each subsequent petition is responded to by singing a *triple* "Lord, have mercy." After the exclamation chanted by the celebrant, the people respond with, "Amen." The deacon then intones, "Let us pray to the Lord." The people sing, "Lord, have mercy." The celebrant then chants a prayer that begins, "O Lord Jesus Christ our God, the God of all mercies and bounties,...!" At the conclusion of the exclamation, the people sing, "Amen."

**[Hymn of Saint Ambrose]**

Even though the service books do not call for it, at this point *many* parishes have the people singing the Hymn of Saint Ambrose, which begins, "We praise You, O God! We acknowledge You to be the Lord! All the Earth worships You, the Father Everlasting!...". The decision as to whether or not to celebrate this liturgical element at this point rests with the main celebrant, whom the choir director should consult with beforehand.

### *The Dismissal*

Then, the Dismissal is celebrated. The celebrant chants, "Most Holy Theotokos, save us!" The people respond with, "More honorable than the Cherubim and more glorious beyond compare than the Seraphim! Without defilement, you gave Birth to God the Word! True Theotokos, we magnify you!"

During most of the year, the priest then chants, "Glory to You, Christ our God and our Hope, glory to You!" The people then respond with "Glory...now and ever...Amen. Lord, have mercy (three times). Father, bless!" (or, if a bishop is present, "Master, bless!" If the Metropolitan is present, the people will sing, "Most blessed Master, bless!") If it is Pascha or Bright Week, the priest will sing "Christ is Risen!" *three* times, and the people will respond also by singing "Christ is Risen!" *three* times. If it is between Bright Week and Ascension, the priest will chant the usual, "Glory to You, Christ our God and our Hope, glory to You!", and the people respond by singing, "Christ is Risen!" **three** times. (Though it is not called for, in some parishes, the practice for the period between Bright Week and Ascension is for the priest to chant "Christ is Risen!" ***two-and-a-half*** times, with the people responding with the ***final half***, "and, upon those in the tombs, bestowing life!" Again, this is purely a local practice in some places, and is **not** called for in the rubrics of the Typikon.)

In any case, the priest will then chant the Dismissal. The people respond with "Amen," sung either once or twice, according to the parish practice. If it is during the time between Pascha and Ascension, the people then sing, "And, unto us, He has given eternal life! Let us worship His Resurrection on the third day!"

### ["Many Years"]

After the Dismissal, some parishes will celebrate the singing of "Many Years" for people being commemorated. The deacon will intone the formula for the commemorations, concluding with, "...and grant them many years!" The people then sing, "God grant you many years!" as the celebrant blesses the people with the Holy Cross.

As the people come forward to venerate the Holy Cross and the icons, the troparia and kontakia of the day may be sung.

## F. CHURCHING OF WOMEN

The churching of a woman is called for in the service books on the fortieth day after giving birth to a child. Most of the time, however, it is done whenever both the mother and the child are first able to come to church. In many instances, it is done after Vespers the evening preceding the celebration of the Divine Liturgy, although it could also be done before the Divine Liturgy itself. (In the Byzantine tradition, this **may** be done at Resurrection Matins after the Great Doxology, at the Divine Liturgy after "Blessed be the Name of the Lord!", or after the Divine Liturgy itself.) The order of the service is as follows.[46]

---

[46] Hapgood, pp. 268-270.

## The Trisagion Prayers and the Lord's Prayer

The service begins with the mother and child at the back of the church, in the entrance to the nave from the narthex. The celebrant intones the doxology, "Blessed is our God, always now and ever and unto ages of ages!" The reader chants, "Amen.", "O Heavenly King!" (done by the priest in the Byzantine tradition), and then the Trisagion Prayers and the Lord's Prayer, with the usual exclamation and the "Amen."

## Prayers

The deacon intones, "Let us pray to the Lord." The people sing, "Lord, have mercy." The priest chants the prayer that begins, "O Lord God Almighty, the Father of our Lord, Jesus Christ, Who, by Your Word, created all things,…!" If the child was stillborn or did not survive, after ending with, "and make her worthy to partake, uncondemned, of Your Holy Mysteries!", he would intone the exclamation that begins, "For, You are a good God Who love mankind,…!", to which the people would sing, "Amen!" If, God-willing, the child is alive and with the mother at church, after ending with, "and make her worthy to partake, uncondemned, of Your Holy Mysteries!", the priest would continue the prayer with, "And bless the child who has been born of her….!" After the exclamation, the people would sing, "Amen." The priest, then facing the people and blessing them, intones, "Peace be with you all!" The people sing, "And with your spirit!" The deacon intones, "Bow your heads to the Lord." The people sing, "To You, O Lord." The priest then reads another prayer that begins, "O Lord our God, Who came for the redemption of the human race,…!" After the exclamation that begins, "For, blessed and glorified is Your all-honorable and majestic Name,…!", the people sing, "Amen."

Once again, the deacon intones, "Let us pray to the Lord." The people sing, "Lord, have mercy." The priest chants the prayer that begins, "O Lord our God, Who was brought, on the fortieth day, as an Infant into the Temple, according to the Law,…!" After the exclamation that begins, "For, unto You are due all glory, honor, and worship,…!", the people sing, "Amen." Again, the priest, then facing the people and blessing them, intones, "Peace be with you all!" The people sing, "And with your spirit!" The deacon intones, "Bow your heads to the Lord." The people sing, "To You, O Lord." The priest then reads another prayer that begins, "O God the Father Almighty, Who, by Your trumpet-voiced prophet,

Isaiah, foretold to us the Incarnation...!" After the exclamation that begins, "For, You are He Who dwell on high,...!", the people sing, "Amen." (***All*** of the prayers in this paragraph are ***not*** done in the Antiochian tradition.)

The churching of the child is then done at the proper time.

## G.  NEW HOUSE BLESSING

When an Orthodox Christian and/or his or her family moves into a new house, apartment, or condominium, there is a special rite for a new house blessing that is more expanded than the annual house blessing that takes place each year after Theophany. The order for a new house blessing is as follows.[47]

---

[47] *The Great Book of Needs, Expanded and Supplemented: Volume IV: Services of Supplication (Moliebens)*, St Tikhon's Seminary Press, South Canaan, PA, 1999, pp. 361-367.

## The Trisagion Prayers and the Lord's Prayer

The service begins with the doxology, "Blessed is our God, always now and ever and unto ages of ages!" The **_people then sing_**, "Amen." and "O Heavenly King!" (in the Byzantine tradition, the **_priest_** chants "O Heavenly King!"; in the Greek tradition, the people sing [in tone 8] a hymn, "All-holy Virgin Theotokos, guide the works of our hands...!"). The **_reader then chants_** the Trisagion Prayers and the Lord's Prayer, with the usual exclamation and the "Amen.", and then, a **_triple_** "Lord, have mercy.", a full "Glory,... now and ever...!", and then a full "Come, let us worship God, our King...". (At this point, in the Greek tradition, the service **_immediately_** goes to the Prokeimenon, "In the beginning, You laid the foundation of the Earth!")

## Psalm 90

This is followed by the reader chanting Psalm 90 ("He who dwells in the shelter of the Most

High,…!").⁴⁸ At the conclusion of the Psalm, the reader chants a full "Glory,… now and ever…!", and then, "Alleluia! Alleluia! Alleluia! Glory to You, O God!" ***three*** times.

### *Troparion*

The people then sing, in tone 8, a troparion that begins, "As salvation came to the house of Zacchaeus at Your entrance, O Christ,…!"

### *Prayers*

At this point, a table is prepared, covered with a fine cloth, and on it are placed the Gospel Book, the Holy Cross, lighted candles, and the vessels containing holy water and oil. In the room where this is being celebrated, the priest faces the east. The deacon then intones, "Let us pray to the Lord." The people sing, "Lord, have mercy." The priest then chants a prayer that begins, "O Lord Jesus Christ our God, Who were pleased to enter under the roof of

---

[48] As mentioned elsewhere, the numbering of the Psalms is according to the Septuagint.

Zacchaeus the publican,…!" At the exclamation, "For, unto You are due all glory, honor, and worship,…!", the people sing, "Amen." The priest turns and, blessing the people, intones, "Peace be with you all!" The people sing, "And with your spirit!" The deacon chants, "Bow your heads to the Lord." The people sing, "To You, O Lord."

The priest then chants a second prayer, beginning, "O Master, Lord our God, Who live on high and look down on the humble of heart,…!" After the exclamation, "For, Yours it is to be merciful and to save us, O our God,…!", the people sing, "Amen." Then, the priest, having made the sign of the Holy Cross over the oil three times, chants, "In the Name of the Father, and of the Son, and of the Holy Spirit! Amen." He then chants a third prayer, beginning, "O Lord our God, look down now with mercy on the prayer of me, Your humble and unworthy servant,…!" After the exclamation,"For, You are He Who bless and sanctify all things,…"!, the people sing, "Amen."

## The Blessing of the Home with Holy Water and the Anointing with Oil

Then, the priest goes through the whole house, sprinkling the walls, in crosswise form, with holy water, all the while repeating the exclamation, "In the Name of the Father, and of the Son, and of the Holy Spirit! By the sprinkling of this holy water, let every evil and demonic activity be put to flight! Amen." He then takes the oil and anoints each room, beginning with the eastern wall of the home, then the western wall, then the northern wall, and ending with the southern wall. At each place, he chants the exclamation, "This house is blessed through the anointing of this holy oil, in the Name of the Father, and of the Son, and of the Holy Spirit! Amen."

During **both** the sprinkling with holy water **and** the anointing with holy oil, it is customary in **many** parishes, at this time, for the people to continuously sing the troparion, in tone 1, of Theophany: "When You, O Lord, were Baptized in the Jordan,…!" Again, this is at the discretion of the celebrating priest.

## Stikheron

After the anointing with holy oil is completed, the people sing a stikheron in tone 5, beginning, "Bless this house, O Lord, and fill it with Your earthly good things…..!".

## [Prokeimenon, Epistle, and "Alleluia!"]

At this point, in the Greek tradition, the Prokeimenon, "In the beginning, O Lord, You laid the foundation of the Earth!", with its accompanying verse, "The Lord will bless this house and all who live in it!", is celebrated. This is *immediately* followed by the Epistle reading, Hebrews 3:1-6, and the *triple* singing of "Alleluia!".

## The Gospel

This is *immediately* followed by the Gospel reading. The Gospel reading is Luke 19:1-10. The deacon intones, "And, that we may be accounted worthy of listening to the Holy Gospel, let us pray to the Lord God!" The people then sing a *triple* "Lord, have mercy."  The priest then blesses the people with the sign of the Cross as he says, "Wisdom!  Let us be attentive!  Let us listen to the Holy Gospel!  Peace be with you all!"  The people then sing "And with your spirit!"  The priest or bishop then chants "The reading is from the Holy Gospel according to Saint Luke!"  The people then sing "Glory to You, O Lord!  Glory to You!"  The deacon then intones "Let us be attentive!", and the priest then chants the Gospel reading.  At the conclusion of the Gospel reading, the people again sing "Glory to You, O Lord!  Glory to You!"

**[Great Litany and the Blessing of Water]**

At this point, in the Greek tradition, there is a version of the Great Litany with interspersed petitions for the blessing of a new house.  This is followed by a prayer to bless the water that begins, "Incline Your ear, O Lord, and hear us, You Who accepted to be Baptized in the Jordan!".  After this, the blessing of the home is immediately celebrated, beginning with the priest immersing a cross in the water, and chanting, ***three*** times, "O Lord, save Your people!", and the people sing the hymn, "Make us worthy of your gifts, O Theotokos!"  The Prayer of

Zacchaeus is then celebrated, followed by the Augmented Litany and the Dismissal.

### Psalm 100

At this point, the priest censes the entire house. The service book calls for the priest to say the following Psalm. However, in **many** parishes, a **reader** is given the task of chanting aloud Psalm 100, which begins, "I will sing of loyalty and of justice! To You, O Lord, I will sing!"

### Augmented Litany

There then follows the Augmented Litany, with the deacon intoning the first petition, "Have mercy on us, O God, according to Your steadfast love,…!" To this and each subsequent petition, the people sing a **triple** "Lord, have mercy." After the exclamation that begins, "Hearken to us, O God our Savior,…!", the people sing, "Amen."

## Dismissal

The Dismissal begins with the priest or deacon chanting, "Wisdom!" Then, the people respond with "Father, bless!" The priest says, "Christ, the One Who Is, is blessed always, now and ever and unto ages of ages!" The people respond with "Amen. Preserve, O God, the Holy Orthodox Faith and Orthodox Christians, now and ever and unto ages of ages."

The priest then chants, "Most Holy Theotokos, save us!" The people respond with, "More honorable than the Cherubim and more glorious beyond compare than the Seraphim! Without defilement, you gave Birth to God the Word! True Theotokos, we magnify you!"

During most of the year, the priest then chants, "Glory to You, Christ our God and our Hope, glory to You!" The people then respond with "Glory…now and ever…Amen. Lord, have mercy (*three* times). Father, bless!" (or, if a bishop is present, "Master, bless!" If the Metropolitan is present, the people will sing, "Most blessed Master, bless!") If it is Pascha or Bright Week, the priest will sing "Christ is Risen!" *three* times, and the people will respond also by singing "Christ is Risen!" *three* times. If it is between Bright Week and Ascension, the priest will chant the usual, "Glory to You, Christ our God and our Hope, glory to You!", and the people respond by singing, "Christ is Risen!" **three** times. (Though it is not called for, in some parishes, the practice for the period between Bright Week and Ascension is for the priest to chant "Christ is Risen!" **two-and-a-half** times, with the people responding with the **final half**, "and, upon those in the tombs, bestowing life!" Again, this is purely a local practice in some places, and is **not** called for in the rubrics of the Typikon.)

In any case, the priest will then chant the Dismissal. The people respond with "Amen," sung either once or twice, according to the parish practice. If it is during the time between Pascha and Ascension, the people then sing, "And, unto us, He has given eternal life! Let us worship His Resurrection on the third day!"

**"Many Years"**

The Dismissal is following by the celebration of "Many Years!". The deacon intones the "Many Years!" for the members of the household whose new home is being blessed. As the people then sing the "Many Years!", the priest takes the Holy Cross and blesses the house and the people with the sign of the Cross in the four directions, starting with the east, the west, the south, and then the north.

As the people come up to venerate the Holy Cross, the priest anoints each person with the sprinkling of holy water.

## H.   HOUSE BLESSING

While the various service books do not give a detailed *ordo* for the blessing of a house, apartment, or condominium after Theophany, the following is a standard celebration of this rite.[49]

---

[49] Again, as with all other liturgical rites, the details for the celebration are determined by the main celebrant, in this case, the parish priest.

## Doxology and Troparion

The priest intones the doxology, "Blessed is our God, always, now and ever and unto ages of ages!" The people present sing, "Amen." (In the Byzantine tradition, this is followed by, "Glory to You, our God, glory to You!", "O Heavenly King!", the Trisagion Prayers, the Lord's Prayer, and the singing of the Troparion of Theophany ["When You, O Lord, were Baptized in the Jordan,….!"].)

Then, the priest takes the holy water and, led by the head of the household who is proceeding with a lighted candle, blesses all the rooms in the entire house. (In the Byzantine tradition, the house blessing itself is done at the **end** of the service. At this point, the Byzantines go **directly** to the Augmented Litany.) During this time, the people present **repeatedly** sing the Troparion of Theophany, in tone 1: "When You, O Lord, were Baptized in the Jordan, the worship of the Trinity was made manifest! For, the voice of the Father bore witness to You and called You His beloved Son! And the Spirit, in the form of a dove, confirmed the truthfulness of His word! O Christ our God, Who have revealed Yourself and have enlightened the world: Glory to You!"

## Augmented Litany

When the blessing of the house with holy water is completed, the priest (or, if a deacon is present) chants the Augmented Litany, beginning with the petition, "Have mercy on us, O God, according to Your steadfast love,…!" To this and all subsequent petitions, the people present sing a *triple* "Lord, have mercy." At the exclamation by the priest, "For, You are a merciful God,…!", the people present sing, "Amen." Then, the priest (or, if a deacon is present) chants, "Let us pray to the Lord." The people present sing, "Lord, have mercy." The priest then chants a prayer that begins, "O Lord, Jesus Christ our God, Who were Baptized by John in the Jordan River to renew all by the waters of Baptism,…!" After the exclamation ("For, to You are due all glory, honor, and worship,…!"), the people present sing, "Amen."

## Kontakion

The people present then immediately sing the Kontakion of Theophany, in tone 4: "Today, You have appeared to the universe, and Your Light, O Lord, has shown on us, who, with understanding, praise You!  You have come and revealed Yourself, O Light Unapproachable!"  (The Kontakion is **not** celebrated in the Byzantine tradition.  **Instead**, the house blessing proper takes place at this point.)

## Dismissal

The priest then intones the exclamation, "Glory to You, O Christ, our God and our Hope, glory to You!"  The people present then sing a full "Glory,… now and ever…!", a **triple** "Lord, have mercy.", and, then, "Father, bless!"  The priest intones the dismissal prayer, ending with the exclamation, "For, He is good and loves mankind!"  The people present sing, "Amen."  (In the Byzantine tradition, the priest then chants, "Through the prayers of our holy fathers,…!", which is followed by the singing of "Amen.".)

## "Many Years"

The priest (or, if a deacon is present) intones the "Many Years!" for the members of the household whose home is being blessed.  As the people present then sing the "Many Years!", the priest takes the Holy Cross and blesses the house and the people with the sign of the Cross in the four directions, starting with the east, the west, the south, and then the north.

As the people come up to venerate the Holy Cross, the priest anoints each person with the sprinkling of holy water.

# BIBLIOGRAPHY

*Liturgical Books*

**The Great Book of Needs, Expanded and Supplemented**, St Tikhon's Seminary Press, South Canaan, PA. Very crisp and clear presentation of the texts. In four volumes: **Volume I: The Holy Mysteries** (1998); **Volume II: The Sanctification of the Temple and other Ecclesiastical and Liturgical Blessings** (1998); **Volume III: The Occasional Services** (2002); and **Volume IV: Services of Supplication (Moliebens)** (1999).

Hapgood, Isabel Florence, **Service Book of the Holy Orthodox-Catholic Apostolic Church**, 4th Edition, Syrian Antiochian Orthodox Archdiocese, Brooklyn, New York, 1965. Although the translations are quite archaic, the book does present all the services of the Church.

Mother Mary and Ware, Archimandrite Kallistos, ***The Festal Menaion***, Faber and Faber, London, 1977. A little cumbersome with the heavy use of the "Thee-and-Thou" translations, it still is a very thorough presentation of the liturgical services of the Twelve Great Feasts.

_____, ***The Lenten Triodion***, Faber and Faber, London and Boston, 1978. Again, although still cumbersome with the translations, it presents a complete rendering of the services from the Sunday of the Publican and the Pharisee through Holy Saturday.

Nassar, the late Reverend Seraphim, ***Divine Prayers and Services of the Catholic Orthodox Church of Christ***, Antiochian Orthodox Christian Archdiocese, Englewood, New Jersey, 1979. Also archaic in textual usage, it nevertheless presents the rubrical propers of the liturgical services.

## Books

Bogdanos, Theodore, ***The Byzantine Liturgy: Hymnology and Order***, Greek Orthodox Diocese of Denver Choir Federation, 1993. A basic presentation on the history of the Typikon.

Hopko, Thomas, ***The Lenten Spring***, SVS (St Vladimir's Seminary) Press, Crestwood, NY, 1983. A collection of 40 meditations, one for each day of Great Lent, with much useful information from Scripture, patristic texts, and stikhera from the Lenten services.

Meyendorff, John, ***Marriage: An Orthodox Perspective***, SVS Press, Crestwood, NY, 1984. A solid presentation on the theology of marriage, with an excellent outline on the proposed order for a Matrimonial Liturgy.

Schmemann, **Great Lent: Journey to Pascha**, SVS Press, Crestwood, NY, 1974.  A treasure trove of detail regarding the liturgical services of Great Lent, as well as explanations of Great Lent as preparation for Baptism, the different meanings of fasting and Communion, the liturgical meanings of Saturday (the Sabbath) and Sunday (the Lord's Day), as well as a wonderful Appendix on Confession and Communion.

_____, **Of Water and the Spirit:  A Liturgical Study of Baptism**, SVS Press, Crestwood, NY, 1974.  A great analysis of Baptism and Chrismation, and their meaning in the Orthodox Church.

www.ingramcontent.com/pod-product-compliance
Lightning Source LLC
Chambersburg PA
CBHW052041220426
43663CB00012B/2400